1993

University of St. Francis
G-E 370.78 M167
McMillan, James H.
Educational research :

W9-CJD-378

Educational Research

Educational Research

Fundamentals for the Consumer

JAMES H. McMILLAN
Virginia Commonwealth University

College of St. Francis Library
Joliet, Illinois

HarperCollins*Publishers*

Executive Editor: Christopher Jennison
Project Editor: Brigitte Pelner
Design Supervisor: Heather A. Ziegler
Cover Design: Zina Scarpulla
Production Administrator: Beth Maglione/Kathleen Donnelly
Compositor: Maryland Composition Company, Inc.
Printer and Binder: R. R. Donnelley & Sons Company
Cover Printer: New England Book Components, Inc.

For permission to use copyrighted material, grateful acknowledgment is
made to the copyright holders on pp. 321–322, which are hereby made
part of this copyright page.

Educational Research: *Fundamentals for the Consumer*

Copyright © 1992 by James H. McMillan

All rights reserved. Printed in the United States of America. No part of
this book may be used or reproduced in any manner whatsoever without
written permission, except in the case of brief quotations embodied in
critical articles and reviews. For information address HarperCollins
Publishers Inc., 10 East 53rd Street, New York, NY 10022.

Library of Congress Cataloging-in-Publication Data

McMillan, James H.
   Educational research : fundamentals for the consumer / James H.
McMillan.
      p.   cm.
   Includes bibliographical references (p.   ) and index.
   ISBN 0-673-38449-7
   1. Education—Research.   I. Title.
LB1028.M364   1992
370'.7'8—dc20   91-18491
                                                    CIP

92 93 94 9 8 7 6 5 4 3

G-E
370.78
M167

To Janice, Jon, and Ryann

148, 335

Contents

8. EXPERIMENTAL AND SINGLE-SUBJECT RESEARCH   165

9. ANALYZING STATISTICAL INFERENCES   192

10. HISTORICAL AND QUALITATIVE RESEARCH 208

11. ANALYZING DISCUSSION AND CONCLUSIONS 229

To the Instructor

This book is primarily for consumers, rather than producers, of educational research. Consumers locate, read, understand, critique, and then use the results of research to become more effective professionally and to make sound educational decisions. This book is designed to enable students to become intelligent consumers of educational research and to introduce its basic principles to those who may eventually be involved in research in their work. The book is intended for a one-semester or one-term course in educational research. It is best suited for advanced undergraduate and beginning graduate students in education, and it is ideal for students enrolled in extended teacher preparation programs for initial certification, which include graduate-level coursework, emphasizing research on effective teaching. The examples and excerpts from published studies are drawn largely from research that teachers will find interesting and informative. The book is also appropriate for students in more traditional masters' programs, who will be consumers of educational research, and for students in related social sciences, who need to learn how to read and understand research. Students who intend to conduct research will find that this book provides an excellent introduction to research methods.

The goal is to educate students to be intelligent consumers, first to understand the intent of the researcher, the procedures, and the results and then to analyze and evaluate the research, judging the usefulness of the findings for educational practice. More specifically, the book will help students to

- Apply the principles of scientific inquiry to everyday problem solving and decision making.
- Obtain a healthy skepticism about "studies" that purport to advance our knowledge.
- Understand the process of conceptualizing and conducting educational research.
- Understand strengths and weaknesses of different methodologies used in research.
- Be able to read, understand, critique, and use published reports of research.

- Understand the probabilistic, uncertain nature of knowledge about educational practice generated through research.
- Keep a balanced perspective about the relative contributions of research and professional judgment.

These goals are reached by presenting in a concise manner principles for conducting research and criteria for evaluating its overall credibility. Although the style of the book is informal, the language is nontechnical, and no prerequisite courses in measurement or statistics are needed, the material is not oversimplified. Illustrations and excerpts from actual studies are highlighted as examples to familiarize students with the style and format of published articles. These examples introduce students to the language of research.

The book covers fundamental principles in the sequence found in the research process, beginning with research problems and ending with conclusions. The emphasis is on teaching students that all aspects of conducting and reporting research are important in judging the overall credibility of the findings. The format of research articles is included in the first chapter with the hope that students will read published studies as early as possible in the semester. Suitable articles, in addition to the three examples in the book, are identified as references in the book and in the *Instructor's Manual*. My experience is that students need as much practice in reading and critiquing articles as possible.

Since good consumers know how to find helpful research, the chapter on reviewing literature includes skills in locating primary and secondary sources and in evaluating a review of literature section of an article. The chapters on measurement are fairly extensive because of its important role in educational research. Basic statistical principles are presented first to enhance understanding. For example, students must know about correlation to understand reliability and validity. The emphasis in the discussion of each methodology—descriptive, correlational, survey, experimental, single subject, historical, and qualitative—is on what to look for in evaluating the credibility of the design and procedures. A conceptual introduction to inferential statistics is included to clarify the results sections of quantitative articles. The final chapter provides in outline form important questions to guide an evaluation of a research report or article, with examples from actual studies. These questions can be used in conjunction with the criteria for evaluating different sections of studies.

The chapters include aids to facilitate the learning of essential skills and knowledge. Key research terms are highlighted in the margins to reinforce their importance, chapter summaries in the form of outlines organize the material succinctly, and study questions allow students to check their knowledge. Throughout the book special sections, called Consumer Tips: Criteria for Evaluating Research, emphasize the skills needed to judge studies critically. Examples from 50 published articles are included in the form of direct excerpts or examples from actual research.

Numerous individuals have contributed much to this book. I am most grateful to my editor, Chris Jennison, for his support, encouragement, and needed recommendations. I am also indebted to Judy Singh for her careful reading of the manuscript, and to many students who provided feedback to my approach and materials. The following reviewers contributed constructive suggestions: Judith Kenniston, Ithaca College; Jack Barnett, Pittsburg State University; John Neel, Georgia State University; Larry A. Hudson, University of Central Florida; Bert I. Greene, Eastern Michigan University; and Ayres D'Costa, The Ohio State University. Finally, I am grateful to the staff at Scott, Foresman and HarperCollins, who have been exemplary in their editing and production of the book.

As this is being written, ideas are germinating for possible changes in organization and content. Please write with any suggestions. Your comments will be most helpful.

James H. McMillan

To the Student

It was not too long ago that I sat, somewhat nervously, in a university auditorium waiting for my first class in educational research. Perhaps you have had, or will have, a similar experience. I distinctly remember thinking, given what I had heard about "research," that I needed to learn only enough to pass the course and would not have to worry about it again! It was another hurdle that I was forced to jump to graduate. I was not bad in mathematics but my interest was in working with people, not numbers. It was incomprehensible that I would someday teach and write about educational research. But something happened to me as I grudgingly struggled through the course. What I discovered was that research is a way of thinking, a tool that I could use to improve the work I do with other people. My hope is that this book can instill a similar goal in you, providing knowledge, skills, and attitudes to improve your life and the welfare of others. Although learning the content and skills needed to become an intelligent consumer of research is not easy, my experience in teaching hundreds of students is that you will improve yourself, professionally and otherwise, through your efforts. In the beginning, especially as you read research articles, not everything will make sense. But as your experience in being an informed consumer increases, so will your understanding. Good luck and best wishes, and please write to me if you have suggestions for improving the book.

James H. McMillan

Educational Research

Chapter
1

Introduction to Research in Education

This book is about helping others to lead a richer, more satisfying life. That may seem like a strange beginning for a textbook, but I want to stress that there are good reasons for increasing your knowledge of research. It is clear that research in education has made, and will continue to make, important contributions to our understanding of teaching and learning at all levels. Educators, like other professionals, must be able to read and interpret research to keep abreast of these contributions. There is also great variation in the quality of educational research, and it is essential to be able to make informed judgments about the credibility and usefulness of the studies. Because education is a complex, situation-specific endeavor, these judgments must be made by each of us in our own context. It is this judgmental process that can influence the lives of others positively. A proper, balanced perspective on research will strengthen the judgments we make constantly in educational settings, and in that way touch the lives of others.

SOURCES OF KNOWLEDGE

Judgments are based on knowing. We "know" something when it is accepted as true or valid, when we can be more or less certain of its consequences. For example, good teachers seem to "know" when they are losing the students' interest and need to change the method of instruction, when students need a strong rebuke or a soft reprimand, and how to phrase questions to elicit involvement from most students. How do these teachers obtain such knowledge? There are several ways, identified here as sources of knowledge. Each is important, and by examining them we will be able to put research as a source of knowledge in perspective.

Personal Experience

It has been said that there is no substitute for experience, whether it is your own or someone else's. In education we rightfully depend a great deal on direct experience to know what works. Professionals become effective through practice, and teaching is no exception. But imagine if experience was the only way to obtain knowledge, or if you were confined to your own experiences and those of friends. Not only would it be difficult to know where to begin; it would also be hard to know how to improve and how to handle new demands and situations. When research can be used as the experience of others to stimulate, inform, reinforce, challenge, and question one's own experiences, the intuitive professional judgment that is absolutely essential for effective teaching and leadership is enhanced.

There are other limitations to using our personal experiences as sources of knowledge. We frequently need to know things with which we have not had nor will have experience. Much of our knowledge from experience depends on what we have observed and how we interpreted it. But as humans we can and do make mistakes in our observations. Sometimes we fail to see things that are clearly evident, and we make inaccurate observations and interpretations. We bring our own biases to situations and sometimes selectively observe, seeing what we want to. Finally, because we are personally involved with our own interpretations, we have a natural inclination to protect our self-esteem and ego, and consequently may not be totally objective.

Tradition

There are many things that seem to be done in certain ways simply because they have always been done in that way. Advice, rules, approaches to handling problems, and "right" and "wrong" answers are passed from year to year, from one group to another, as accepted "truths." Tradition eliminates the need to search for knowledge and understanding because we simply accept what has always been done as the best or right way. But reliance on tradition makes it difficult to accept new knowledge and may mitigate our desire to question existing practices. For example, the tradition of a 180-day school year, with a summer vacation, in American public education makes it difficult to change to year-round schooling.

Authority

A major source of knowledge is those we consider to be experts or authorities. An authority has experience or unique expertise in something and is able to provide insights and understandings that we are unable to see. We depend on such authorities, whether they are doctors, lawyers, professors, teachers, or plumbers, particularly in our specialized culture. But like personal experience and tradition, authority can also hinder our knowledge of something. Authorities can be wrong, and there is the tendency to accept as fact what are actually opinions. In fields such as education, where practice is heavily influenced by complex interactions among students, environments, and teachers, there is room for "experts" to disagree about what is "known." Perhaps you have read one author who suggests one approach and another who suggests the opposite approach for the same situation or question. A good example is the research on computer-aided instruction (CAI). Some studies report that CAI is more effective than traditional instructional methods, but just as many studies fail to show that CAI is better or more effective than traditional methods. Thus it is quite easy for experts to disagree about the effect of CAI on student learning. Also, there seem to be so many "authorities" in education that it can be quite confusing. It is best to be able to analyze the suggestions of each authority and to make your own decisions.

The Scientific Approach

The **scientific** approach to research is objective, systematic, and testable and is relatively uninfluenced by personal beliefs, opinions, and feelings. Rather, science seeks to obtain knowledge objectively by relying on verifiable observation and experimentation. The scientific approach uses a methodology that cannot reasonably be questioned, that decision makers can rely on. It is objective in that different individuals, given the same information, would agree in their judgments. It is verifiable because the process is open to public scrutiny and the results are tested by others.

Scientific: Systematic, testable, and objective.

THE NATURE OF SCIENTIFIC INQUIRY

We expect "scientists" to use the scientific approach. It is easy to understand its usefulness in fields such as agriculture, medicine, engineering, biology, and the like, but is education or teaching a science? Without debating this question, the important point is that the scientific approach is a method, a logic of inquiry, and not a body of knowledge. It is not tied to particular fields of study, to laboratory situations, or to men and women in white coats developing complex theories. Consequently, we can study education in a scientific manner, even though in reality it is not a science. What is important is to emphasize the principles that comprise a scientific approach and then to use these principles to the extent possible in analyzing educational problems and making decisions. Further, it is important to understand the nature of scientific inquiry simply because most research in education uses a scientific approach.

The Purpose of Scientific Inquiry

The primary purpose of scientific inquiry is to explain natural phenomena, to understand the relationships that underlie these phenomena, and then to predict and influence behavior as a result. For example, we can use scientific inquiry to explain why some teachers appear to be more effective than others. The explanation leads to a knowledge base that novice teachers can use to become more effective. Explanation in this sense is closely related to developing and testing theories about phenomena, a method discussed in greater detail in a later section of this chapter.

Explanation provides information related to three practical purposes of scientific inquiry: to describe, to predict, and to control. Description provides fundamental knowledge about a phenomenon and is usually necessary before pursuing explanation or prediction. Accurate description is essential to understanding explanations of events or people, and it depends heavily on tests and other instruments and principles of measurement to provide objective, valid information. For example, accurate descriptions of various teaching styles and student achievement are needed before these two phenomena can be related. Once phenomena are adequately described, one may be predicted by knowledge of the other. This predictive power is very important since educators must constantly make predictive-type decisions (e.g., put Johnny in group A because he will do better with those children; admit a select group of students for a special program because they will benefit most; use cooperative teaching techniques because they will keep the students interested longer; advise against a particular occupation because the student will have difficulty passing the certification examination). Finally, control over phenomena provides information about cause-and-effect relationships. By controlling factors in experiments, as will be discussed in detail in Chapter 8, we can determine if one factor influences another, or stated differently, if there is a causal relationship between the phenomena studied. Causal relationships are the most powerful and provide explanations that can be useful in a variety of situations. They are also the most difficult to establish.

Characteristics of Scientific Inquiry

The characteristics of scientific inquiry are summarized in Table 1.1. Each of the characteristics will be evident in varying degrees in each study. The phenomena studied in education involve behaviors that are influenced by a large number of factors in complex social situations; hence the "ideals" of scientific inquiry may only be approximated. Obviously, rigid controls that may be possible with laboratory studies are usually not possible in schools. Measurement in educational research is often indirect and imprecise, and the verification of findings by replicating studies may be difficult. Thus scientific inquiry is a standard against which the adequacy of educational research may be judged, but most studies will not adhere rigidly to the characteristics in Table 1.1.

The Purpose of Theories

Much scientific inquiry is conducted to develop theories about how phenomena are related. A **theory** can be defined as a set of propositions that explain the relationships among observed phenomena. Thus, theories are general explanations of behavior. By providing a more general explanation, the theory can be used in more situ-

Theory: Explains relationships among phenomena.

Table 1.1   CHARACTERISTICS OF SCIENTIFIC INQUIRY

Objectivity: In observation, data collection, and reporting of results there is only one meaning or interpretation.

Control of bias: Personal prejudices, beliefs, and attitudes must not influence the research.

Willingness to alter beliefs: When justified by the evidence, beliefs are changed.

Verification: The findings are replicated by others.

Induction: General conclusions are drawn from specific observations.

Precision: Definitions of terms and instruments, such as tests, contain sufficient detail to convey exact meanings.

Truth: Conclusions are always tentative.

---

ations; that is, it has more utility. Research on effective teaching, for instance, has identified general teaching behaviors—such as close supervision, meaningful praise, and appropriate types of questions—that are positively related to student achievement for most if not all teachers. Thus we can think about a single effective principle of instruction that can be learned and applied rather than trying to indicate a separate one for each teacher.

However, practitioners may, if they don't fully understand a theory, indiscriminately apply it. A good example is the well-known theory of positive reinforcement—that behavior followed immediately by positive reinforcement will increase the frequency of the behavior in similar circumstances—which is used in many situations. However, some well-intentioned teachers (as well as managers, parents, and others) do not differentiate among different types of reinforcement. In some situations some types of positive "extrinsic" reinforcement, such as rewarding a student who gets a good grade with extra recess, may reduce, rather than increase, the frequency of behavior. Some teachers dole out smiling faces, thinking that they are reinforcing a behavior, when in fact they may be reducing it. Thus practitioners need to be careful not to oversimplify theories. Moreover, theories may not accommodate individual differences and the complexity of teaching-learning situations. What may work in general, for most individuals in most settings, may not work with specific types of individuals in specific situations.

APPLYING SCIENTIFIC INQUIRY TO EDUCATION

The basic purpose of scientific inquiry is to provide sound explanations that can become knowledge, and the investigator employs a systematic series of steps to complete the research. These steps, which can be thought of as the process or method of scientific inquiry, are associated with questions that help judge the quality of the research and, hence, the credibility of the results. The goal of the researcher is to obtain credible answers to research questions by designing, conducting, and reporting research that will be viewed by others as trustworthy, that is, as being reasonable and making sense. The sequence of steps and questions is summarized in Figure 1.1. Each step in the process is important and contributes to the overall credibility and usefulness of the research. This book is organized around these steps and questions in the context of educational studies to provide the knowledge and skills that will lead to sound overall judgments about credibility and usefulness. The steps and questions introduced are elaborated on in later chap-

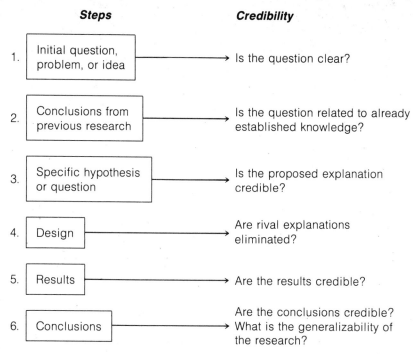

Figure 1.1 A framework for understanding the steps of scientific inquiry.

ters, but it is helpful to understand from the beginning the nature of the process that is presented throughout the book.

The first step is that the investigator faces an obstacle to effective decision making or understanding or identifies an idea or question that warrants further thought. This can be thought of as a general problem, question, or idea, a curiosity that begins the process. The next step, to review previous research on the topic, means finding relevant research, analyzing it, and relating it to the initial question. The credibility of the results depends in part on how well the investigator connects the study to already established knowledge.

Following the review the researcher formulates a specific research hypothesis or question. The hypothesis is an informed guess about the answer to the question, a hunch based on related literature and professional judgment. A question is warranted when the nature of the original idea or problem does not lend itself to a hypothesis (e.g., describing teachers' attitudes toward merit pay). The design of the study is based on what will be an adequate test of the hypothesis or what will answer the question. It includes the subjects, situations, measures, and procedures. A carefully designed study will be structured so that the explanation provided is the most credible one to explain the results. Here the reader searches for "rival" explanations, often a result of faulty methodology, that may mitigate the credibility of the explanation offered. Examples of rival explanations include experimenter bias, differential loss of subjects in different groups or between a pretest and posttest, selection bias, and changes caused by factors that are not controlled.

The credibility of the results builds on previous aspects of the study, focusing on the reasonableness of the results in light of previous research and the extent to which rival explanations are eliminated. The evaluation of the conclusions, in turn, also builds on previous credible judgments. Finally, judgments are made on the **generalizability** of the research, that is, whether the explanations are useful in other situations, with other subjects, times, treatments, and measures. In other words, can the conclusions be generalized to other people in other contexts? The explanation may be true in one situation, with one group of people, but not true in other situations with different people. This is an important concern for educational research since educators are interested in applying the results to particular groups and circumstances. Table 1.2 summarizes common factors affecting generalizability.

Generalizability: Use of results in other situations with other individuals

Two further points should be stressed. First, reasonably credible explanations and results are necessary to be able to generalize. Second, we should not be overly strict in judging generalizability. For example, if we dismiss the findings of effective teaching practices because the characteristics of the teachers sampled do not match our teachers exactly (e.g., average age in the sample is 32; average age of our teachers is 28), we are probably being overly strict in our judgment. On the other hand, it is best to be cautious in applying the findings of research done with college students to

Table 1.2 FACTORS AFFECTING GENERALIZABILITY

Factor	Description
Subjects	Characteristics of subjects such as socioeconomic status, age, gender, race, and ability. Whether and how subjects are selected from a larger population. Conclusions based on group averages assumed true for individuals or subgroups within the sample. Subjects' awareness of the research.
Situation	Characteristics of the setting in which the information is collected, e.g., naturally occurring or contrived; time of day; surroundings.
Time	Some explanations change over time, e.g., years or decades.
Treatments	Characteristics of the way in which an experimental treatment is conceptualized and administered.
Measures	Nature of and type of measures used to collect information.

middle school students. In other words, we need to be reasonable and use good common sense in generalizing.

TYPES OF EDUCATIONAL RESEARCH

Educational research is the application of scientific inquiry to educational problems. Although all educational research shares the purpose, characteristics, and process of scientific inquiry, there are different types of educational research. Indeed, it is common to discuss educational research in the context of one of these types because it provides further information about the purpose and nature of the study. That is, it means more to say "experimental research" or "applied correlational research" than simply "research." We will consider the various types of educational research in this section.

Educational research: Scientific inquiry applied to educational problems.

Two Traditions of Research: Quantitative and Qualitative

Increasingly in recent years educational research is described as quantitative or qualitative. These terms refer to two different research traditions, each with its own terminology, methods, and techniques. For many decades most educational research was based on the **quantitative** tradition, that is, what is known as a positivist philosophy of how we generate new knowledge. As reflected in the methods of the basic sciences and psychology, the positivist believes that there are facts with objective reality that can be expressed numerically. Consequently, there is a heavy reliance on numbers, measurement, experiments, and numerical relationships and descriptions. Until the mid 1970s the vast majority of studies in education was quantitative in nature. Today it is becoming more and more common to read studies that are qualitative, or at least have some qualitative features.

Quantitative: Emphasizes numbers, measurements, deductive logic, control, and experiments.

   Qualitative research stresses a phenomenological model in which reality is rooted in the perceptions of the subjects. There is a focus on understanding and meaning through verbal narratives and observations rather than through numbers. Qualitative research usually takes place in naturally occurring situations, as contrasted with quantitative research, which exhibits control and manipulation of behaviors and settings. Table 1.3 summarizes the major features of these two traditions. Note the different terms that are used to refer to qualitative research. As we will see in later chapters, there are different types of both quantitative and qualitative research. Although there is a greater emphasis on qualitative methods today

Qualitative: Emphasizes natural settings, understanding, verbal narratives, and flexible designs.

Table 1.3   CHARACTERISTICS OF QUANTITATIVE AND QUALITATIVE
RESEARCH[a]

	Quantitative	Qualitative
Other terms or phrases associated with the approach	Positivist Experimental Hard data Statistical	Naturalistic Field research Ethnographic Phenomenological Anthropological Ecological
Key concepts	Variable Operationalized Controlled Reliable Valid Statistically significant Replicated Hypothesized	Meaning Understanding Social construction Context Situation
Academic affiliation	Agriculture Psychology Political science Economics Basic sciences	Anthropology History Sociology

Goals	Test theory
	Establish facts
	Show relationships
	Predict
	Statistically describe
		Ground theory
		Develop understanding
		Describe multiple
		   realities
		Capture naturally
		   occurring behavior

Design	Structured Predetermined Formal Specific	Evolving Flexible General
Data	Quantities Counts Measures/instruments Numbers Statistics	Verbal descriptions Field notes Observations Documents
Techniques or methods	Experiments Quasi-experiments Structured observations Structured interviews Surveys	Observation Participant observation Open-ended interviewing Review of documents and artifacts

(*continued*)

Table 1.3   (*continued*)

	Quantitative	Qualitative
Role of researcher	Distant Short term Detached Uninvolved	Close Long term Involved Empathic Trusting Intense
Data analysis	Deductive Statistical	Inductive Ongoing Stress models, themes, and concepts

[a] Adapted from Bogdan and Biklen, 1982.

than in the past, most educational research reported in journals and presented at conferences is quantitative. Consequently, the focus of this book is also on quantitative methods.

Basic Research

Basic research (also called pure or fundamental research) has as its primary purpose the development of theories. The goal of basic research is to understand and explain, to provide broad generalizations about how phenomena are related. It is not concerned with applying the results to practical situations. Basic research is often conducted in highly controlled, contrived settings. Examples include studies of how the memory system works, language development, and social development. By definition, little educational research is basic, although educational researchers can and do conduct and use basic research.

Basic research: Formulates and refines theories.

Applied Research

The purpose of **applied research** is to test theories and other ideas in the context of naturally occurring educational settings. It is usually focused on a problem that needs to be solved to improve the practice of education. The results are immediately and directly relevant to educational decision making. To the extent that general theories are tested, the results may be generalized to many different educational settings. For example, based on theories of human memory developed through basic research, a new curriculum may

Applied research: Improves practice and solves practical problems.

be tested for improved retention of science concepts among sixth-graders. Other examples of applied research in education are studies comparing different teaching styles, identifying characteristics of effective schools, or examining the effect of lengthening the school day on student achievement.

Action Research

Action research is a specific type of applied research. Its purpose is to solve a specific classroom problem or make a decision at a single local site. The goal is to improve practices immediately within one or a few classrooms. Teachers are often involved in action research. These studies can be very useful, and in fact will be well within your capabilities by the time you finish this book. For example, if you are a teacher and want to see if a new way of assigning spelling homework results in higher test scores, you may want to design a study to investigate your new type of assignment.

Action research: Studies specific classroom problems.

Evaluation Research

Evaluation research is directed toward making decisions about the effectiveness or desirability of a program. The purpose is to make judgments about alternatives in decision-making situations. In most cases evaluation research is focused on a specific location or type of program and involves judgments about such questions as these: Which reading curriculum should be implemented? Did the new program work? Should the district build two small schools or one large school? What is the impact of increased technology on student and teacher knowledge and attitudes? Often such questions require research methods that are unique to each situation. Evaluation research has formalized these methods to build a vast literature on program evaluation that integrates different research methods with evaluation models. Like research, evaluation studies use principles of scientific inquiry.

Evaluation research: Judgments for decision making.

Nonexperimental Research

The previous types of educational research are distinguished primarily by differences in purpose, the reasons for conducting the study. We now turn toward differences based on the methodology used in the research. Nonexperimental, as contrasted with experimental research, is a major methodological distinction. **Nonexperimental research** is inquiry in which the investigator has no direct control over what is studied, either because it has already occurred

Nonexperimental research: No manipulation of factors.

or because it cannot be controlled. In other words, in nonexperimental research the investigator is unable to manipulate any factors or phenomena. This characteristic has important implications for conclusions drawn. It usually means that the study can describe something or uncover relationships between two or more factors. Nonexperimental studies can be classified as descriptive, analytical, or causal comparative. Descriptive research includes studies that provide simple information (e.g., How do teachers define critical thinking?) and relationships or correlations, which tie two or more factors together (e.g., Do teachers in different grade levels have the same or different definitions of critical thinking?). Other questions that exemplify descriptive research are these: What is the relationship between physical conditioning and academic achievement? Are parents in favor of career ladders for teachers? Is there a correlation between creativity and self-esteem? How do high school counselors spend their time during the school day?

Analytical research includes historical, linguistic, philosophical, and legal analyses that rely on deductive reasoning to establish important relationships and conclusions. Causal comparative studies (also called *ex post facto* studies) describe relationships between something that occurred in the past and subsequent responses in such a way that it may be possible to draw causal relationships between them. For example, do students who took typing in seventh grade have more positive attitudes than students who did not take typing?

Experimental Research

In **experimental research** the investigators have control over one or more factors in the study. That is, they can "manipulate" a factor and then see what will happen to the responses of subjects as a result. The purpose of manipulating a factor is to investigate its causal relationship with another factor. For example, some investigators may be interested in studying the causal relationship between time on task and achievement. They manipulate the former by having one group of children spend a small amount of time on the subject and a second group a large amount of time. The investigators determine (manipulate) whether children are engaged a small or large amount of time. If the children who are engaged a longer amount of time show higher achievement than the other children, time on task may be causally related to achievement.

There are different types of experimental research, depending on specific characteristics of the design. These types will be covered in Chapter 8. At this point it is important to remember that in an experiment the investigator determines what will happen to the

Experimental research:
Manipulation of factors that may affect subjects' behavior.

subjects in order to examine causal relationships between what is manipulated and the subjects' responses.

FORMAT TO REPORT EDUCATIONAL RESEARCH

Every year millions of dollars are spent on educational research and millions more on related research in psychology, sociology, and other social sciences. Every year hundreds of research reports and articles are published. One of the primary objectives of this book is to enable you to become an intelligent reader of these reports. A research report is a document, usually a paper or article, that sets forth the research problem, what the researcher has done to collect data, how the data are analyzed and interpreted, and the conclusions. In other words, the report is a summary of what was done, how it was done, why it was done, and what was discovered. Most reports follow a standard format or organizational structure, as summarized in Figure 1.2. These parts are discussed briefly and are identified in actual articles in Chapter 12.

Title and Author(s)

The research report typically begins with the title and names of the author(s). The professional affiliation of the author(s) is provided in many reports, particularly published articles. Good titles tell the reader something about the major factors and type of subjects that are studied.

Title and author(s)
Abstract
Introduction
    Context for the research
    General research problem
    Significance of the research
    (Specific research question)
Review of literature
Specific research question or hypothesis
Method and design
    Subjects
    Instruments
    Procedures
Results
Discussion
Conclusions
References

Figure 1.2 Format of research reports

Abstract

Although many reports, especially journal articles, follow the title and author with an abstract, some do not. The abstract in journal articles is typically 50 to 200 words long and is often set in smaller type than the rest of the article. The abstract is a brief summary of the entire study, including the problem, methods used, and major findings. By reading the abstract you will usually learn enough to decide whether or not to read the entire report.

Introduction

The introductory section is usually one to several paragraphs in length, including a statement of the context for the research, its significance, and the general or specific research problem investigated. The context provides background information relating the study to broader areas. It also indicates briefly the development of the research problem. The significance of the research, a statement about how the results will be useful, can be thought of as a justification, need, or reason for conducting the research. Almost all reports include a statement that indicates the research problem of the study. This statement can be broad or specific, and sometimes both a broad and a more specific problem are included. The problem indicates concisely and as clearly as possible the focus of the study, what the researcher hopes to discover. Most general problems are stated near the beginning of the report, and more specific problems just before the review of literature, but there is no consistency of level of specificity or location across different articles and reports.

Review of Literature

Although the introductory section may include some references to other research or literature, a more formal review of literature begins after the research problem. The review, one to several paragraphs long, summarizes and analyzes previous research on the same problem. A good review critiques the studies and shows how the findings relate to the problem being investigated.

Specific Research Question or Hypothesis

Often, but not always, a specific research question or hypothesis will follow the review of literature. A hypothesis is an informed guess or prediction about the results; it indicates before the study is carried out what the results will be. A hypothesis follows the review of literature because it is based on what previously completed, related studies have found.

Method and Design

In this section the researchers indicate who was studied, how the information was obtained, and in the case of an experiment, any treatments or manipulations. The first part of the section usually describes the subjects, individuals the researcher observes or obtains information from in order to address the research problem. The report will describe the characteristics of the subjects and indicate whether they have been selected from a larger group. The second section focuses on the instrumentation used to gather information from the subjects, including a description of the instruments and an evaluation of their reliability and validity. In some reports this section will also describe how the instrument was administered; in others, this information is provided in the third section, procedures. The procedures section may also include a summary of how the data were collected and, in experimental studies, will indicate how the manipulations were carried out. The researchers may also discuss the design of the study and materials used, and they may indicate how precautions were taken to reduce bias or otherwise improve objectivity.

Results

This section indicates how the researchers analyzed the data and shows the results. There are often tables and graphs to summarize large amounts of data succinctly. This section should be an objective reporting of what was found, without interpretation or discussion.

Discussion

This is the section in which the investigators explain their results. The data are interpreted in light of other research and possible weaknesses in the methodology of the study.

Conclusions

Conclusions are summary statements that reflect the overall answers to the research questions or whether or not the research hypotheses are supported. The conclusion is an inference derived from the results, weaknesses in the study, and relationship of the results to previous literature. Conclusions should be limited to what is directly supported by the findings and what is reasonable, given other research. Implications and recommendations are often included in this section, although the investigators need to be careful not to overgeneralize.

References

This is a listing of the sources cited in the report. The style of listing references will vary, the most common being APA (American Psychological Association). A bibliography includes sources that are not cited in the report but are used by the authors.

OUTLINE SUMMARY

1. Sources of knowledge for making educational decisions
   A. Personal experiences
      (1) Essential to good education
      (2) Enhanced by research findings
      (3) Limited to our own experiences
      (4) Possibly inaccurate or biased
   B. Tradition
      (1) Sometimes helpful
      (2) May stifle new knowledge and practices
   C. Authority
      (1) Expertise necessary
      (2) May be wrong or conflicting
      (3) Analysis needed
   D. Scientific approach
      (1) Objective, systematic, testable
      (2) Verifiable, public process
2. Scientific inquiry
   A. Systematic method; can be used in education
   B. Purposes
      (1) Explains phenomena to understand and predict
      (2) Provides a basis for description and causality
   C. Characteristics
      (1) Objectivity, control of bias, willingness to alter beliefs, verification, induction, precision, truth
      (2) Not strictly adhered to in educational research
   D. Theories
      (1) General explanations of behavior
      (2) Wide generalizability
      (3) Situation specific application

3. Applying scientific inquiry to education
   A. Series of steps and questions
      (1) Initially based on literature
      (2) Designed to answer the question
      (3) Rival explanations sought
      (4) Overall credibility based on results and other research
   B. Generalizability
      (1) Based on characteristics of subjects, situation, time, treatments, measures
      (2) Should not be overly strict
      (3) Depends on credible results
4. Types of educational research
   A. Quantitative
      (1) Relies on numbers, measurements, objectivity
      (2) Researcher detached
      (3) Design predetermined
      (4) Data analyzed deductively
   B. Qualitative
      (1) Relies on personal descriptive observations
      (2) Researcher involved with subjects
      (3) Flexible, evolving design
      (4) Data analyzed inductively
   C. Basic research—to understand and explain
   D. Applied research—immediately useful to educational practices
   E. Action research—useful to specific classrooms or schools
   F. Evaluation research—helps makes decisions about program effectiveness
   G. Nonexperimental
      (1) Descriptive, with no direct control
      (2) Correlational—to describe relationships
      (3) Analytical—based on nonnumerical description
   H. Experimental
      (1) Studies cause-and-effect relationships
      (2) Manipulates factors that affect subjects
5. Format to report educational research
   A. Summary of what was done, how, with whom, why
   B. Abstract—summary of entire report
   C. Introduction—reasons and general question
   D. Review—analysis of related literature
   E. Method—subjects, instruments, procedures
   F. Results
   G. Discussion—explanation and interpretation of results
   H. Conclusions—summary inferences from results

STUDY QUESTIONS

1. What are some important ways in which educational knowledge is obtained? What are the strengths and weaknesses of different sources of knowledge?

2. How is a scientific approach to inquiry different from inquiry based on personal experience?

3. In what ways can explanation of educational phenomena improve teaching and learning?

4. In what ways can theories be useful in education? What are some limitations of theories?

5. What are the steps of scientific inquiry? Why are questions used as a part of the overall framework?

6. What is necessary for a study to be judged credible?

7. Why are principles of generalizability important in interpreting research? Can you think of research findings that have been overgeneralized?

8. What are the differences between qualitative and quantitative approaches to research?

9. How can research you have read be classified as basic, applied, evaluation, or action research? Is it experimental or nonexperimental?

10. What is the essential difference between experimental and nonexperimental research?

11. Read some research studies and identify the various sections, that is, introduction, review of literature, results, and so on.

Chapter
2

Variables, Research Problems, and Hypotheses

In the first few paragraphs of an article you will learn about the purpose of the research. To understand the purpose you will need to be able to identify and interpret the research problem. This step requires an acquaintance with variables, essential concepts in conceptualizing and communicating research.

VARIABLES IN EDUCATIONAL RESEARCH

One of the most used terms in research is *variable*. A **variable** is a label or name that represents a concept. Concepts are nouns that stand for a class of objects, such as *tree, house, desk, teacher, creativity,* and *school*. Researchers use *variable* rather than *concept* because most of what is studied varies, that is, contains variations that can be described numerically or categorically. Thus, a variable is a type of concept that can take on different values or have categories. For example, the concepts intelligence, achievement, social class, and cognitive style contain a range of values, which is often expressed numerically. However, many variables are better described as containing two or more categories, for example, male and female, cooperative versus individualized instruction, beginning teachers with or without student teaching experience. There are

Variable: A concept that contains variations.

also variables that can be identified but may not be expressed numerically or have categories. These variables are single factors that affect research, such as experimenter bias or subject awareness of being studied.

Constitutive and Operational Definitions

A precise definition of each variable communicates clearly the intent of the researcher and enhances the usefulness of the results. Vague definitions are difficult to interpret and usually lead to less meaningful results. Two types of definitions are commonly used in research, constitutive and operational. A **constitutive definition** uses other words and concepts to describe the variable. For example, *attitude* may be defined constitutively as "a predisposition to respond favorably or unfavorably toward a person, object, or event," and the variable *value* may be "the degree to which an event is perceived to be positive or negative." Constitutive definitions are important in communicating what is being investigated, but they may not indicate precisely what the variables mean. Another type of description, called an operational definition, is needed to provide this more precise meaning.

Constitutive definition: Uses words or concepts.

An **operational definition** indicates the "operations" that are performed to measure or manipulate the variable. It is essential to understand operational definitions because researchers will use different ways of measuring or manipulating the same variable. Hence the meaning of the results depends on understanding the operational definition, not simply the more generic meaning implied by the term. Suppose you are interested in learning about the relationship between parenting styles and childrens' loneliness. There are many different definitions and ways of measuring both variables, and you would need to examine the questions asked and the way the responses were scored to know what a particular researcher means. Or consider the variable socioeconomic status (SES), commonly used in research, in which the terms *high*, *middle*, and *low* often describe categories. These terms are meaningful only if you know the rules for classifying subjects as high, middle, or low. In fact in different studies the procedure for obtaining what is termed high SES can be quite different, resulting in a subject classified as high in one study and middle in another. Thus, to some extent, operational definitions are arbitrary and often are not explicitly stated. If you are interested in knowing whether cooperative or individualized methods of teaching are most effective in promoting student achievement, knowing simply that a study of these two methods showed cooperative methods to be better is not sufficient.

Operational definition: Uses techniques that measure or produce.

You need to know how the terms *cooperative, individualized,* and *achievement* are determined or measured.

Following are some examples of variables, with corresponding constitutive and operational definitions:

Variable	Constitutive definition	Operational definition
Self-concept	Characteristics used to describe oneself	Scores on the Coopersmith Self-Esteem Inventory
Intelligence	Ability to think abstractly	Scores on the Stanford-Binet
Teacher with-it-ness	Awareness of student involvement and behavior	Results of the Robinson Scale of teacher with-it-ness

Types of Variables

There are several types of variables in educational research. We will consider the most important: independent and dependent, extraneous and confounding, and continuous and categorical. Other types of variables will be summarized briefly.

Independent and Dependent Variables   In much of our research one variable precedes, either logically or in time, another variable. The variable that comes first and influences or predicts is called the **independent variable.** The second variable, the one that is affected by or is predicted by the independent variable, is the **dependent variable.** In an experiment at least one independent variable is the presumed cause of differences between groups on the dependent variable. The independent variable is the antecedent; the dependent variable is the consequence. Predictions are made from independent variables to dependent variables. When we say, "If X then Y," X is the independent variable and Y is the dependent variable. When we control which students receive particular teaching methods (antecedent), we may see the effect on achievement (consequence). Teaching method is the independent variable; achievement is the dependent variable. In educational research, teacher behavior, methods of instruction, curriculum, individual characteristics of students, socioeconomic status, and peer group behaviors are common independent variables, and achievement, attitudes, values, self-concept, and social development are common dependent variables (these may also be independent variables, depending on the study).

Independent variable: Precedes, influences, or predicts the results.
Dependent variable: Affected by or predicted by the outcome.

In nonexperimental research the independent variable cannot be manipulated or controlled by the investigator. Such variables may still be considered independent if they clearly precede the dependent variable. For example, a study of the effect of school size (independent variable) on achievement (dependent variable) may locate and use large, medium, and small schools, although it cannot manipulate or alter the size of a particular school. However, it is clear that school size precedes achievement. In correlational studies several nonmanipulated variables may be considered independent because they precede the dependent variable. For example, a school administrator may need to predict teaching effectiveness to hire the best teachers. Several variables are available for each candidate, including grade point average, supervisor's comments about student teaching, and an interview. If these variables are used to predict the outcome (effectiveness as a teacher), they are independent variables.

In some nonexperimental research it is difficult to label variables as independent or dependent, for example, in relationship studies in which one variable does not precede the other. For instance, a study of the relationship between critical thinking and creativity may be conducted to show they are distinct, unrelated concepts. In this case neither is an independent or dependent variable; there are simply two variables in the study. Other nonexperimental, descriptive research may compare groups of subjects, and often the variable used to classify the groups is considered independent. For example, a descriptive study of the attitudes of school principals toward school financing might divide the principals into groups depending on the size and location of each school. Here attitudes would be the dependent variable and size and location of schools the independent variables.

Extraneous and Confounding Variables   An **extraneous variable** affects the dependent variable but is unknown or not controlled by the researcher. These variables change the results and "mess up" the study. In designing research, investigators try to control or account for whatever extraneous variables may be present. As a reader and consumer of research it is very important for you to identify extraneous variables that may be related to the results. A **confounding variable** is a type of extraneous variable that varies systematically with the independent variable. For instance, suppose you find a study comparing two methods of teaching reading, a totally phonics approach and a combined phonics/comprehension approach. Two classrooms are used in the study, one classroom implementing

Extraneous variable: Source of error affecting the results.

Confounding variable: Varies systematically with the independent variable.

each approach. If different teachers are in each class, "teachers" is a confounding variable because the style, personality, and knowledge of each teacher is confounded with the treatments and will affect reading scores (dependent variable) in addition to the methods of instruction. So if one group of students did score better than the other, you would not know if it was because of the method or the teacher. Throughout the rest of the book further types of extraneous variables will be identified, and examples will show how they affect the research.

Continuous and Categorical Variables   A **continuous variable** (or measured variable) can theoretically take on an infinite number of values within a given range of scores. In other words, the value of a continuous variable could be any point on a continuum. The values are rank-ordered, from small to large or low to high, to indicate the amount of some property or characteristic. Common continuous variables in educational research are achievement and aptitude test scores; self-concept; attitude and value measures; and height, weight, and age. A **categorical variable** is used to assign an object or person to a group that is defined by having specified characteristics. The most simple type of category has two groups (dichotomous), such as male/female, high/low, white/black, and morning/afternoon. Other categorical variables can have three or many more categories, for example, grade level, nationality, occupation, and religious preference. It is also common to use continuous scores to create categories. For instance, socioeconomic status is generally used as a continuous variable, but the scores can be grouped into categories such as high, middle, and low SES. Thus the designation of continuous or categorical variable may depend on how the researcher uses the scores. The same variable can be continuous in one study and categorical in another. Also, although most dependent variables are continuous, both independent and dependent variables can be either continuous or categorical.

Continuous variable: Infinite values within a range.

Categorical variable: Groups defined by specific characteristics.

Other Types of Variables   In the research literature you may encounter additional types of variables, and you will need to be at least familiar with the terms. An **intervening variable** (or latent variable) is an internal, unobservable trait or process, within the subjects, that accounts for observable behavior. It is presumed or inferred from a measure of something and often operates between an independent and dependent variable to explain relationships. Psychologists refer to intervening variables as hypothetical constructs—something inside or within an individual that is abstract.

Intervening variable: Unobservable trait that influences behavior.

Examples of intervening variables include creativity, learning, motivation, hostility, and anxiety. These are not undesirable in a study but exist to explain more fully the process of change and relationship. For example, a study may examine the effect of a new type of reinforcement (independent variable) that motivates students (intervening variable) and results in greater achievement (dependent variable).

A **control variable** is built into the design of a study so that it will not be an extraneous variable. Control variables are often included as independent variables. For example, in a study of the effect of different teaching methods on achievement you may be concerned about how the cognitive style of the students affects the results. If you divide the group of students into different types of cognitive style first, and then examine the effect of each method, cognitive style becomes a control (and independent) variable. (In this type of design the control variable, cognitive style, could also be termed a blocking variable.) Control variables can also be accounted for by being held constant (e.g., using only students with one type of cognitive style) or by being adjusted for statistically.

Control variable: Built into the design.

An **organismic variable** (also called subject, status, measured, attribute, or assigned variable) is a characteristic of the subject that cannot be manipulated, such as height, weight, intelligence, gender, SES, and cognitive style. These are usually independent or control variables. Some independent variables, like anxiety, can be either manipulated or organismic, depending on the design of the study. Others, like intelligence, will always be organismic.

Organismic variable: Describes a stable characteristic of subjects.

RESEARCH PROBLEMS

A clear, concise statement of the purpose of a research investigation is important for two reasons. First, it provides a focus for the researcher and is an essential initial step in the investigation. Second, it gives the reader and user of research important information. It helps the reader decide quickly if the research is pertinent or interesting and makes the research much easier to understand.

The statement of purpose is often referred to as the research problem, and some researchers think of the research problem as synonymous with a very specific, focused problem statement. Actually there is a wide range of specificity in problem statements, and sometimes you will find that range in the same article or report. At one end of the spectrum is a general statement of purpose that indicates the goal or broad objectives of the study. Here are some examples: 148,335

College of St. Francis Library
Joliet, Illinois

EXAMPLES: GENERAL STATEMENTS OF PURPOSE

The purpose of this research is to study adolescent loneliness.

This research will investigate the social integration of retarded adults.

The goal of this study is to ascertain what teachers think critical thinking is.

The purpose of this study is to investigate the memory processes of students.

This study investigates the relationship between creativity and intelligence.

In each case you have a general idea of what will be studied, but these statements lack clarity, are ambiguous, and do not provide sufficient information. They are fine as a beginning statement of purpose, but they eventually need to be more specific and focused.

At the other end of the specificity continuum are statements that contain more detail and information than is necessary. As a result, they are difficult to understand. An extreme example would be the following:

EXAMPLE: TOO SPECIFIC RESEARCH PROBLEM

The purpose of this study is to investigate whether seventh- and eighth-grade male and female teachers who teach in a predominantly middle-class school in a western Michigan suburb who are identified by principal ratings and the Teacher Effectiveness Inventory, given in the fall semester by trained observers, will have students who, matched by ability when entering school in the fall, differ in the level of achievement in mathematics and language arts as measured by the Iowa Test of Basic Skills.

In the middle of the spectrum you will find the majority of research problem statements, those that contain sufficient detail and information in a sentence that is clear and succinct. Following are some examples from published articles:

EXAMPLES: GOOD RESEARCH PROBLEM STATEMENTS

"The purpose of this paper is to examine the effectiveness of a teacher intervention strategy for enhancing social play in relationships between severely or profoundly retarded children and nonhandicapped peers." (Cole, 1986, p. 201)

"The purpose of this study was to examine the impact of systematic cooperative learning and test-taking strategies on one component of academic performance, the recall of text material." (Lambiotte et al., 1987, p. 52)

"The purpose of this study was to examine the relationships among locus of control beliefs, feelings of efficacy, and perceptions of stress of teachers in an urban, multilateral school district." (Parkay, Greenwood, Olejnik, and Proller, 1988, p. 14)

"The purpose of this investigation was to examine a series of expectations about the effects of training intermediate grade children in the use of self-directed critical thinking." (Hudgins and Edelman, 1988, p. 262)

"Our study examined the effects of dyad reading on the achievement of 32 poor readers in the second grade." (Eldredge and Quinn, 1988, p. 42)

"The purpose of this study was to investigate, using qualitative research methods, teachers' perceptions of factors related to work stress. The study was designed to focus on the general question, What do teachers mean when they identify work-related factors as sources of stress?" (Blase, 1986, p. 14)

"To what extent are there differences in the amount of time allocated to instruction in specific subject matter areas for LD, emotionally/behaviorally disturbed (EBD), educable mentally retarded (EMR), and nonhandicapped students?" (Ysseldyke, Thurlow, Christenson, and Weiss, 1987, p. 45)

"Are individual differences among teachers in their differential behavior toward higher and lower achieving students consistent enough to suggest distinct patterns of teaching?" (Mitman, 1985, p. 150)

You will encounter many degrees of specificity and clarity in problem statements. General statements are often found in the first few paragraphs of the study. They are sufficient as an orientation to the research, but a more specific, yet concise and clear statement, either in the introduction or later in the article after the review of literature, is necessary. In Table 2.1 there are problems written in both general and specific language. The specific problems are good because they summarize several aspects of the study, including the type of research (experimental, relationship, or descriptive), independent and dependent variables, and subjects. Each of these will be considered in greater detail in discussing criteria for evaluating problems.

Sources for Research Problems

How does a researcher begin to develop a good problem? Several sources are commonly used to begin the process of problem formulation. It should be noted that coming up with a good research problem is usually a rather arduous and time-consuming task. Initial ideas that seem promising typically need revision as literature related to the idea is analyzed and implications for research design are clarified. Often initial ideas are completely discarded and the researcher starts over with a new idea. Many researchers begin to identify a topic by reading current books and journals in their area and by talking with knowledgeable professionals about current problems or issues. Once a very broad area of interest is identified, further reading usually leads to a more specific research problem. Additional factors influence the feasibility of the proposed study,

Table 2.1   RESEARCHABILITY OF PROBLEMS

Nonresearchable	Researchable
Should we teach sex education in elementary schools?	What is the difference in knowledge and attitudes of fifth-graders taught sex education compared to fifth-graders who are not taught sex education?
Do teachers need to have courses in test construction?	Will the classroom testing procedures used by teachers who take a course in test construction differ from those of teachers who have not had the course?
Should the school day be longer?	What is the relationship between length of the school day and SAT scores of high school students?
Should learning-disabled students be mainstreamed in English as well as in physical education?	What is the effect of mainstreaming fourth-grade learning-disabled students into English classes on the self-concept, attitudes, and achievement of all students?

such as cost, the ability and training of the investigator, and the availability of subjects.

Although there is no single strategy for identifying research problems that works best for all investigators, several sources have been useful to most.

Investigator's Interests and Experiences   Some of the best sources of ideas come from the interests and practical experiences of the investigator. A teacher encounters many problems and questions daily that may lead to researchable problems. There may be concerns about teaching methods, grouping, classroom management, tests, individualization, grades, standardized test data, or a multitude of everyday experiences. Administrators may face problems in scheduling, communicating to teachers, providing instructional leadership, generating public support, or handling serious discipline. University professors may see that student teachers are encountering difficulties that need to be resolved. In addition to personal experiences, each of us has interests and knowledge about our profession that can yield good problems. It may be a topic that we are curious about or have read about, or we may have a long-standing interest in certain areas.

Applying Theory   A very common source for research problems is a theory that has implications for educational practice. One approach is to take a theory in a related area, such as psychology or sociology, and develop a problem that extends it to an educational setting. A good example is research on leadership styles. The psychological research has established that there are clear differences among autocratic, participatory, and laissez-faire leadership styles in the outcomes of small groups and business settings. Would the same be true of principal leadership for student achievement? Other examples would be using theories of reinforcement, attitude development, information processing, and communication. In each case the theories suggest implications that can be further researched in educational settings. Another way to apply theories is to directly test, revise, or clarify an existing educational theory. Here the intent is to develop and change the theory rather than to test its implications.

Replication   An excellent type of study is one that replicates previous research, that is, repeats a completed study with relatively minor changes that will further contribute to our knowledge. It may seem that replication would not add new knowledge, when in fact just the opposite is true. Progress in building a body of knowledge depends on a series of replications to verify and extend the initial findings. One of the weaknesses in educational research is that there have been too few replications. Borg and Gall (1989) summarize four reasons for conducting replication studies:

1. To check the findings of a major or milestone study. Replications can confirm or disconfirm the validity of a study that produces new evidence or that reports findings that challenge previous research or theory.

2. To check the validity of research findings with different subjects. Replications often use the same procedures but change the type of subjects used to see if the original findings hold for different subjects. For example, much of Kohlberg's initial research on moral development was with men. A good replication study would ascertain whether the findings would hold up for women as well. Studies that are originally limited in scope can justifiably be replicated to extend the findings to other people and conditions.

3. To check trends or change over time. Replications can be used effectively to see if initial findings hold over time. This type of replication is done with attitudes, values, achievement, and other areas where trend data are important. For instance, the National Assessment of Educational Progress (NEAP) has measured the performance of 9, 13, and 17 year old school children in key subjects since 1969. Every two years the same questions are asked, which provides a very nice assessment of changes in student performance over time.

4. To check important findings using different methodologies. It is possible that a research finding may be unduly influenced by the way a variable is measured. For example, there are many ways to measure critical thinking. A particular study may report a "significant" result using one way to measure critical thinking, but the result may be limited to the way it was measured. Thus, a useful replication would repeat the study but change the instrumentation. The same is true for procedures in a study. Research that replicates and changes what may be faulty methods, like the way a treatment is administered, or what the experimenter says to the subjects, or other conditions, may change the results. A related reason to replicate is to use different statistics to analyze the data.

Clarification of Contradictory Results   There are seemingly contradictory findings in many cases in the literature. Some studies indicate one conclusion, and other studies, of the same thing, come to an opposite conclusion. These apparent contradictions present very good opportunities for research. For instance, research on the effect of between-class ability grouping (tracking) on student achievement is mixed. Some studies indicate that it promotes higher overall achievement, whereas other studies conclude that it makes no difference on student achievement but has adverse attitudinal and social effects. Why are there contradictions? By examining the studies, discrepancies in methodology or populations may be found that suggest needed research to explain the contradictions.

CONSUMER TIPS
Criteria for Evaluating Research Problems

A good research problem clearly, explicitly, and concisely communicates to the reader and user of research the specific question addressed in the study. The following criteria can be used to judge how well the problem accomplishes this purpose.

1. **The problem must be researchable.** A researchable problem is one that can be answered by collecting and analyzing data. Problems that are concerned with value questions or philosophical ideas are not researchable in the sense that a specific question has a correct answer. There are many interesting questions in education that require value or ethical analyses, but to be able to conduct research the question must lend itself to the systematic process of gathering and analyzing data. Table 2.1 presents some examples of nonresearchable problems that are rephrased to be researchable.

2. **The problem should be important.** The results of research need to have theoretical or practical importance. Problems that have already been well researched or are trivial should be avoided. Most studies that make contributions are original in purpose and/or method. Theoretical importance is determined by the contribution of the study to existing knowledge. Are the results meaningfully related to what is already known? Do the results add new knowledge or change the way we understand phenomena?

Practical importance suggests that the results will have immediate use in day-to-day activities or decisions. How will the results be used? All too often the answer to this question is not carefully thought out; as a result a lot of data are gathered but not utilized.

3. **The problem should indicate the type of research.** The language used in the research problem should indicate whether the study provides a simple description, a relationship, or a difference.

A simple description is implied from such problems as these: How many third-graders have computer experience? What criteria are most important in placing mentally retarded children? What are the social and personality characteristics of gifted children? How do children react when parents separate? A relationship describes something and also indicates how two or more variables may be related. It can be expressed statistically as either a correlation coefficient or in differences between categories of the independent variable. For example, the following problems imply a relationship that probably uses some type of correlation coefficient.

EXAMPLES: RELATIONSHIP PROBLEMS THAT INDICATE CORRELATIONAL STUDIES

What is the relationship between achievement and self-concept?

Is there a relationship between effort in doing an assignment and attitudes about it?

Can leadership potential be predicted from high school grades, recommendations, and participation in extracurricular activities?

Other relationship problems analyze the differences between levels of the independent variable.

EXAMPLES: RELATIONSHIP PROBLEMS THAT INDICATE STUDIES OF DIFFERENCES

How do males and females differ in their attitudes toward freedom of the press?

Are elementary school teachers different from secondary school teachers in assertiveness?

What is the difference between sixth-, seventh-, and eighth-graders' self-concept of ability?

Some research problems imply more than a simple relationship. They suggest a particular type—a *causal* relationship. Here the intent of the research is to test a cause-and-effect relationship between the independent and dependent variables. This category includes all experimental research and some types of nonexperimental research. Typically, differences are emphasized in the problem statement, and often the word *effect* is used. (Unfortunately some relationship studies that are not causal still use the term *effect*, which may be misleading; e.g., What is the effect of socioeconomic status on career aspirations? A more accurate statement is what is the relationship between socioeconomic status and career aspirations?) Here are some difference questions that imply cause-and-effect relationships:

EXAMPLES: PROBLEMS THAT INDICATE CAUSE-AND-EFFECT RELATIONSHIPS

Will method A result in higher achievement than method B?

Is there a difference in attitude between students having peer teaching compared to students who have traditional instruction?

What is the effect of small-group instruction on the reading achievement of second-graders?

---

4. **The problem should specify the population.** The population is simply the people that the researcher wants to investigate. A good research problem identifies, with a few words, the most important distinguishing characteristics of the population. Too much detail about the subjects will unnecessarily repeat the full description in the subjects section of the research report. Hence the description of the population in the research problem should be concise yet informative. Here is a problem that is too vague about the population:

Do children who practice with calculators achieve more than those who do not practice with calculators?

Here is the same problem with a description that is too specific:

Do fourth-grade, low-SES, low-ability students from Carpenter Elementary School who practice with calculators achieve more than those who do not practice with calculators?

A good level of specificity would be this:

Do low-ability, low-SES fourth-graders who practice with calculators achieve more than those who do not practice with calculators?

5. The problem should specify the variables. A good problem statement of a relatively simple study will name the variables and how they may be related in a single sentence. Often these will be independent and dependent variables. Variables are described, like the population, with a moderate level of specificity. "A study of the effect of teacher workshops" is far too general; in fact there is no dependent variable at all. "A study of the effect of teacher workshops on teacher morale as measured by the Smith Morale and Attitude Scale" does provide a dependent variable, but there is more detail than necessary and still the problem does not communicate much about the independent variable (workshop). Here the design of the study will contribute to the description of the independent variable. If two groups of teachers are being compared, one who attends the workshop and one who does not, a better, more informative problem would be "Is there a difference in the morale of teachers attending a teacher workshop compared to teachers who do not attend?" The independent variable is more than just named; it is described.

Research problems that are more complex, because of having several independent and/or dependent variables, may need to be stated in more than one sentence. The first sentence typically includes either the main variables or a general term to represent several variables, followed by one or more sentences that describe all the variables.

EXAMPLE: RESEARCH PROBLEM IN MORE THAN ONE SENTENCE

The purpose of this study is to investigate the relationship between measures of aptitude and attitudes toward college among high school students. The measures of aptitude include scores from the SRA and SAT, high school grade point average, and class rank. Attitudes toward college are assessed by the Canadian College Attitude Scale, which reports four subscale scores: motivation, academic versus social climate, reputation, and expectations for success.

In this study there are four independent and four dependent variables, and it would be cumbersome to try to include all of them in one sentence.

6. The problem should be clear. The importance of a clear, concise research problem cannot be overemphasized. One purpose of the research problem is to communicate the purpose of the study, a result that occurs only if the reader's understanding of the purpose is consistent with the researcher's. Also a clear research problem reflects clear thinking by the researcher. A clear problem includes terms that are not ambiguous. Ambiguity is seen when different people, reading the same thing, derive different meanings from what is read. If a term or phrase can mean several things, it is ambiguous. Terms such as *effect, effective, achievement, aptitude, methods, curriculum,* and *students,* by themselves, are ambiguous or vague. The terms are too general and should be replaced or modified so that the meaning is clear. A vague statement such as "what is the effect of sex education?" needs much more specificity. What is meant by "effect" and "sex education"? What grade level? What type of study is it? It is also best to avoid technical language or jargon that may not be well understood by others, unless the report is intended to be read only by other professionals in a specific field. A successful problem indicates unambiguously the what, who, and how of the research by using declarative sentences such as "The purpose of this study is to . . ." or questions such as "What is the relationship between . . ."; "Is there a difference between . . ."; "How do . . ."; "What is. . . ." Either type of sentence is acceptable, and you will find both in the literature.

HYPOTHESES

Hypotheses are educated "guesses" or tentative explanations about a correct solution to a problem, descriptions, possible relationships, or differences. In research, a hypothesis is the expectation or prediction of the investigator about what the results will be. It is a conjectural statement of the researcher's expectations about how the variables in the study are related. In short, a hypothesis is a prediction that is made prior to data collection.

Hypotheses: Tentative predictions or expectations.

Why Researchers Use Hypotheses

Researchers use hypotheses because they serve a number of important purposes:

1. The hypothesis provides a focus that integrates information. We often have hunches about predictions, based on experience, previous research, and the opinions of others. By forming a hypothesis the researcher synthesizes the information to make the most accurate prediction possible. Usually the researcher draws heavily on the related literature. If the hypothesis does not follow from or is not logically related to the previous literature, the importance or contri-

bution of the research is questionable. The overall credibility of the study is diminished.

2. The hypothesis is testable. It provides a statement of relationships that can be tested by gathering and analyzing data.

3. The hypothesis helps the investigator know what to do. The nature of the hypothesis directs the investigation by suggesting appropriate sampling, instrumentation, and procedures. It helps the researcher keep a focused, specific scope that is not too general.

4. The hypothesis allows the investigator to confirm or disconfirm a theory. Hypotheses help advance knowledge by refuting, modifying, or supporting theories.

5. The hypothesis provides a framework for developing explanations that can be scientifically investigated. Explanations that are not contained in a hypothesis are metaphysical in nature and are not subject to scientific verification.

6. When supported, the hypothesis provides evidence of the predictive nature of the relationship between the variables. Knowledge of a tested, confirmed prediction is more powerful evidence than an unconfirmed, untested observation of the relationship.

7. Hypotheses provide a useful framework for organizing and summarizing the results and conclusions of the research. They help the reader understand the meaning and significance of the study.

Types of Hypotheses

There are two ways to classify hypotheses: whether the hypothesis is derived from inductive or deductive logic, and whether the hypothesis is stated as a *research* or *statistical* hypothesis. We will briefly consider both ways of classification.

An inductive hypothesis is formed from a researcher's observations of behavior. The observations are synthesized to form tentative explanations about how the behaviors are related to one another and to other variables such as teaching methods, curriculum materials, and teacher behavior. In fact, teachers provide a rich source for inductive hypotheses because they can use their experience and knowledge to formulate hypotheses that may explain observed relationships. A limitation of inductive hypotheses is that because they depend on local data and idiosyncratic observations, the generalizations are often restricted and hard to relate to a broader theory or established body of applied research.

Deductive hypotheses are derived from theory, and thus the testing of them contributes to a better understanding of the theory or its application. The findings are integrated with existing facts and theories, which helps build a meaningful body of knowledge. For example, the theory of positive reinforcement suggests that teachers should reward desirable behavior. This principle has generated a great amount of research based on deductive hypotheses. From the general theory we have built a larger knowledge base that includes the effects of intrinsic and extrinsic reinforcement, praise, tokens, behavior modification, immediate and delayed reinforcement, and self-reinforcement.

Hypotheses are also classified as research or statistical. A **research hypothesis** is a conjectural, declarative statement of the results the investigator expects to find. Research hypotheses are sometimes referred to as working or substantive hypotheses. Most research hypotheses are directional, in which the nature of the expected relationship is stated. For example,

> **Research hypothesis:** Statement of expected results.

Fifth-grade students participating in a computer-aided mathematics lesson will demonstrate higher achievement than students using a traditional paper-and-pencil lesson.

In a study of relationships the research hypothesis might be:

There is a positive relationship between time on task and achievement.

A research hypothesis is used when the investigator anticipates the specific outcome of the study, for example, which group will score higher than the other, an increase or decrease in scores, a positive or negative relationship, more or less of something, and so forth.

Research hypotheses can also be nondirectional. The researcher believes there will be a difference or relationship, but is unsure about the nature of it; for example,

There will be a difference in achievement when comparing individually tutored children to those receiving group tutoring.

Such nondirectional research hypotheses are not very common. Usually either previous research or the experiences and intuition of the investigator suggests a direction.

The **statistical hypothesis** is a statement of a relationship or difference that can be tested statistically. Statistical hypotheses are usually stated in what is called the "null" form. A **null hypothesis** is a statement that the differences or relationships have occurred because of chance. Normally this is a statement of no difference or relationship. The null hypothesis is tested, and its acceptance or nonacceptance provides support or no support for the research hy-

> **Statistical hypothesis:** Statistical statement of possible results.
>
> **Null hypothesis:** Statistical statement of no relationship.

pothesis. The statistical procedures used to test the null hypothesis are discussed in greater detail in Chapter 9. At this point it is important to understand that we do not test the research hypothesis; we accept it when the null hypothesis is rejected. We do it in this way because researchers do not prove true an expected result. Rather, they can tentatively accept the research hypothesis when the statistical test shows that the null hypothesis, which is assumed to be true before the test, can be rejected. Table 2.2 shows the relationship among research problems, research hypotheses, and null hypotheses. The investigator begins with a problem, forms a research hypothesis based on a review of literature and/or personal experiences, forms the null hypothesis, tests the null hypothesis, and accepts or fails to accept the research hypothesis. Often there will not be an explicit null hypothesis in an article or report; rather it is usually implied in the statistical test. The research hypothesis is also implied but not stated in some articles.

Table 2.2 RELATIONSHIP OF RESEARCH PROBLEMS, RESEARCH HYPOTHESES, AND NULL HYPOTHESES

Research problem	Research hypothesis	Null hypothesis
What is the effect of a mainstreaming workshop on the attitudes of teachers toward mainstreaming?	Teachers' attitudes toward mainstreaming will improve as a result of attending a workshop on mainstreaming.	There is no difference in teachers' attitudes toward mainstreaming measured before a workshop on mainstreaming compared to their attitudes after the workshop.
Is there a relationship between teachers' attitudes toward the curriculum and student achievement?	There is a positive correlation between teachers' attitudes toward the curriculum and student achievement	There is no correlation between teachers' attitudes toward the curriculum and student achievement.
Is there a difference in achievement between students who are given highly detailed written comments on their work compared to students who are given grades only?	Students receiving highly detailed written comments on their work will show higher achievement than students given grades only.	There is no difference in achievement between students receiving highly detailed comments about their work compared to students receiving grades only.

CONSUMER TIPS
Criteria for Evaluating Research Hypotheses

1. The research hypothesis should be stated in declarative form. Since the research hypothesis is a possible explanation it must be written in the form of a declarative sentence. A question cannot be a hypothesis.

2. The research hypothesis should be consistent with known facts, previous research, and theory. The research hypothesis should follow from other studies and established theories. In general, it should not contradict previous research but rather should build on related literature; the results should contribute to the established body of knowledge. It is best for the research hypothesis to follow the review of literature. The reader should be able to understand why a particular hypothesis is put forth.

3. The research hypothesis should follow from the research problem. It is confusing to use variables in the hypothesis that have not been identified by the research problem. A general problem may include several variables, and thus several research hypotheses are used to indicate all of the anticipated relationships.

4. The research hypothesis should state the expected relationship between two or more variables. A hypothesis must have at least two variables and must indicate how the variables are related. A study that analyzes the relationship by a correlation coefficient will use the terms *positive relationship* or *negative relationship*. In a study that analyzes differences between groups, the relationship may be expressed as a difference (more or less, higher or lower). In either case an expected relationship is stated. Most research hypotheses conjecture the relationship between two variables. It can be awkward and confusing to include more than two variables in one sentence, with the exception of studies that have several dependent variables and one independent variable (e.g., Students in the cooperative class will show more positive attitudes toward learning, higher achievement, and more prosocial behavior than students in the individualized class.)

5. A research hypothesis should be testable. As pointed out previously, being testable means being verifiable in the sense that data can be obtained to determine whether or not the hypothesis can be supported. It is a matter of measuring the variables in such a way that the hypothesis can be confirmed or not confirmed. Thus the variables must be measurable, and the researcher must be able to obtain data that represent values of the variables. The researcher must therefore include operational definitions of the variables (not necessarily as part of the hypothesis statement but perhaps following the hypothesis). Stated differently, the variables must be amenable to operational definitions that can be applied by using an instrument or observations to collect data. For example, the hypothesis "Children taking a unit on nutrition will be more healthy" is not testable because "more healthy" is difficult to operationalize and measure, and it would be almost impossible to attribute better health to the unit on nutrition.

6. **The research hypothesis should be clear.** Similar to the terminology used in research problems, words, phrases, and descriptions in the research hypothesis should be unambiguous. A clear hypothesis is easier for the reader to comprehend and easier for the researcher to test. Vague terms and jargon should be avoided.

7. **The research hypothesis should be concise.** Consistent with criteria for research problems, hypotheses should be sufficiently detailed to communicate what is being tested and, at the same time, be as succinct as possible. A concise hypothesis is easier to comprehend. Often it is desirable to break down a long hypothesis into several shorter hypotheses to be as brief as possible in each sentence.

OUTLINE SUMMARY

1. Variables
   A. Concepts that vary numerically or by categories.
   B. Definitions.
      (1) Constitutive.
      (2) Operational.
   C. Types of variables.
      (1) Independent.
      (2) Dependent.
      (3) Extraneous.
      (4) Confounding.
      (5) Continuous.
      (6) Categorical.
2. Research problems.
   A. Range from general to specific.
   B. Sources for research problems.
      (1) Interests and experience of the investigator.
      (2) Application of theory to an educational problem.
      (3) Replication of previous studies.
      (4) Results of previous research that indicates contradictory conclusions.

    C. Criteria for evaluating research problems.
      (1) Researchable through the collection and analysis of data.
      (2) Theoretically or practically important.
      (3) Indicate whether the study is descriptive, a relationship, or causal.
      (4) Indicate population.
      (5) Indicate independent and dependent variables.
      (6) State in clear and concise language; vague terms should be avoided.
3. Hypotheses.
    A. Tentative predictions before data are gathered.
    B. Purposes.
      (1) Relate previous literature and experience to the problem.
      (2) Provide relationships that can be tested.
      (3) Focus the research.
      (4) Help in confirming or modifying theory.
      (5) Help in summarizing the results.
    C. Types of hypotheses.
      (1) Inductive hypotheses.
      (2) Deductive hypotheses.
      (3) Research hypotheses.
      (4) Null hypotheses.
    D. Criteria for evaluating research hypotheses.
      (1) State in declarative form.
      (2) Consistent with and build on previous research and theory.
      (3) Follow the research problem and review of literature.
      (4) State expected relationships.
      (5) Testable.
      (6) Clear and concise.

STUDY QUESTIONS

1. Why is it important to have operational definitions of variables?

2. What is the difference between an operational and constitutive definition?

3. What is the difference between independent and dependent variables?

4. Under what research circumstances would it be difficult to identify separate independent and dependent variables?

5. Give some examples of extraneous variables.

6. When is an extraneous variable a confounding variable?

7. Give some examples of continuous and categorical variables.

8. How is it possible for a research problem to be too specific?

9. What important sources can researchers draw on to identify significant research problems?

10. Under what circumstances are replication studies significant?

11. What are the criteria for evaluating research problems?

12. Why is it important for research problems to be clear and concise?

13. What are some reasons for using hypotheses in research?

14. What is the difference between research and null hypotheses?

15. Give some examples of research and null hypotheses.

16. What are the criteria for evaluating research hypotheses?

Chapter
3

Locating and Reviewing Related Literature

The second major section of a research article is the review of literature. The review provides an important link between existing knowledge and the problem that is being investigated. A good review enhances the credibility of the research, whereas a poor review diminishes credibility. Thus it is important for you to be able to judge the quality of the review. It is also important for you to be able to locate research that is related to a problem or issue. In this chapter we will discuss the purposes of the review in greater detail, summarize the steps needed to review the literature on a specific topic, and identify criteria for a critique.

THE PURPOSE OF REVIEWING RELATED LITERATURE

Broadly stated, the purpose of the review is to relate previous research to the problem under investigation. A discussion of more specific purposes follows.

Refining the Research Problem

Initial research problems tend to be general and somewhat tentative. At this stage the researcher thinks that the problem may be profitable but needs to be more specific and more limited. By reviewing related studies and discussions of research in that area, the investigator learns how others have defined the general problem in more specific ways. Ideas and examples are found that help delimit the problem, and concepts and variables are clarified as the researcher finds operational definitions.

The process of refining a research problem can be frustrating. Typically, an initial problem that seems to have merit needs to be changed as the researcher reviews previous studies in the area. A new problem is formulated, and often it too needs revision as further literature is reviewed. This process can be repeated many times as more and more literature is reviewed, and although it can be frustrating, it is a necessary part of sound research.

Developing Significance for the Research

It is important for research to be significant or meaningful, to make a contribution to existing knowledge or practice. Previous knowledge indicated by existing research provides a broader context, allowing the researcher to link the proposed study to accumulated knowledge to indicate specifically how it will add to, expand, and build on this base. Previous studies will help the researcher identify new directions worth pursuing, and unnecessary duplication can be avoided. It also helps the researcher interpret findings so that the conclusions are meaningful. By placing new results in the context of previous results, potential merit is enhanced. Without the foundation that is provided by the review, the results are less likely to be significant.

Identifying Methodological Techniques

By learning about the specific methods other researchers have employed to select subjects, measure variables, and implement procedures, an investigator can identify approaches that may be useful. Both successful and unsuccessful methods are usually found, and both will help the investigator identify new ideas and avoid past mistakes or difficulties. Often, methodological weaknesses can suggest a need for research to be replicated with improvements in specific methods.

Identifying Contradictory Findings

A review of the literature may uncover studies or theories that contradict one another. Researchers find this a fruitful area in which to conduct subsequent studies. Possible reasons for the inconsis-

tency, such as using different types of subjects, measures, or procedures, can be identified, and research can be designed to resolve
the contradiction. Such studies provide very significant contributions to knowledge.

Developing Research Hypotheses

A sound research hypothesis is usually based on a review of literature. Previous studies in related areas may suggest a specific
result, and the hypothesis should be consistent with these studies.
When there are few or no closely related studies, existing theories
should be used to justify a particular hypothesis. Thus, the literature
provides a basis for the hypothesis by either theory or more specific
facts established by other studies. If educational studies or theories
are not clearly related, the researcher should look to other fields of
study, such as psychology, sociology, or communication. Often theories in these fields can serve as the basis for the hypothesis.

Learning About New Information

A review of literature almost always leads to new information and
knowledge, either in the topic of interest or in unrelated areas.
Often, while searching the literature for one topic you will come
across interesting and useful research in other areas. In fact, it usually requires discipline to refrain from following a lead that is interesting and perhaps relevant in important ways but is not related
to the problem or issue of initial interest. You will also learn about
journals, books, and other sources that you were unfamiliar with or
which may be recently published.

STEPS TO REVIEW RELATED LITERATURE

A set of sequential steps will increase the quality of the research
reviewed and lessen the time necessary to locate the most appropriate studies. This sequence is also appropriate for learning about
recent research in an area. Any search of literature should be preceded by complete familiarization with the library you will use. It
is best to have someone who can orient you to the library, showing
you where reference materials and journal indexes are located. If
possible, a librarian who is assigned to or who knows about educational literature should be found, and you should feel free to ask
questions whenever necessary. Searching literature can be quite
time-consuming, and a good librarian is there to help you. Also, do

not be too discouraged if the library does not have a particular book or issue of a journal. Most libraries have an interlibrary loan procedure, which will allow you access to almost any source, including copies of journal articles.

Step One: Locate Existing Reviews and Other Information in Secondary Sources

A **secondary source** is one that reviews, summarizes, or discusses someone else's research. Secondary sources are good to start with because they provide an overview of the topic, often citing relevant research studies. Some examples of secondary sources are textbooks, scholarly books devoted to a particular topic, reviews of research in books or journals, yearbooks, encyclopedias, and handbooks. We will look at these sources in greater detail. One word of caution, however, about secondary sources: Since they combine the information from other secondary sources and actual studies, it is possible that the author did not accurately report the research. Furthermore, the "review" may be selective to support a particular point of view, or the author may inadvertently fail to locate important studies.

Secondary source:
Summarizes, reviews, or discusses original research.

Textbooks   Textbooks provide a nontechnical overview of several topics within a particular field of study. Hence, there are textbooks in most major fields of education, for example, educational psychology, reading, special education, measurement and evaluation, learning, early childhood education, counseling, and administration. These texts are located through the subject index of the appropriate catalog. Catalogs are in the form of cards, microfiche, or on-line computer, depending on the library. The limitation of textbooks is that they are often basic and general and may not have the necessary detail. Textbooks are also out of date in the sense that the research cited may have been conducted several years before the book was available.

Scholarly Books   Scholarly books are written on many topics that you would find in a textbook. These books are intended for other researchers and professionals in the area and consequently are usually more sophisticated, having more details about the research. Scholarly books can be located through the library's catalog, professors, publishers' advertisements, publishers' catalogs, journals, and conference proceedings. Following are some examples:

EXAMPLES: SCHOLARLY BOOKS

Ames, C., & Ames, R., eds. *Research on Motivation in Education: Goals and Cognitions.* New York: Academic Press, 1989.

Baron, J. B., & Sternberg, R. J. *Teaching Thinking Skills: Theory and Practice.* New York: Freeman, 1987.

Cooper, H. M. *Homework.* White Plains, NY: Longman, 1989.

Cormier, S. M., & Hagman, J. D., eds. *Transfer of Learning: Contemporary Research and Applications.* New York: Academic Press, 1987.

Damon, W., *The Moral Child: Nurturing Children's Natural Moral Growth.* New York: Macmillan, 1990.

Gottfried, A. E., & Gottfried, A. W. *Maternal Employment and Children's Development: Longitudinal Research.* New York: Plenum, 1988.

Hannum, W. H., & Stuck, G. B. *Computers and Effective Instruction.* White Plains, NY: Longman, 1989.

Kurfiss, J. G. *Critical Thinking: Theory, Research, Practice, and Possibilities.* ASHE-ERIC Higher Education Report #2, 1988.

Liebert, R. M., & Sprafkin, J. *The Early Window: Effects of Television on Children and Youth,* 3rd ed. New York: Pergamon Press, 1988.

Morris, R. J., & Blatt, B., eds. *Special Education: Research and Trends.* New York: Pergamon Press, 1986.

Sternberg, R. J., ed. *The Nature of Creativity: Contemporary Psychological Perspectives.* Cambridge, Eng.: Cambridge University Press, 1988.

Encyclopedias   Encyclopedias, with short summaries of many topics, are good sources during the initial stages of a review. In education, one encyclopedia is usually recommended: The *Encyclopedia of Educational Research,* 5th ed. (1982), offers over 2,000 pages of reviews in all areas of education. A new edition of this encyclopedia should be published in the mid-1990s. Other encyclopedias, most of which are more specialized, include the *International Encyclopedia of Education, Encyclopedia of Comparative Education and National Systems of Education, Encyclopedia of Educational Evaluation, Encyclopedia of Psychology,* and *International Encyclopedia of Teaching and Teacher Education.*

Reviews, Handbooks, and Yearbooks   A number of sources have
comprehensive, up-to-date reviews on specific topics. Many of
these reviews are in books or monographs that are published annually, although different subjects are reviewed each year. Following is a list of the sources used to locate reviews of literature.

**EXAMPLES: REVIEWS, HANDBOOKS, AND
YEARBOOKS**

Annual Review of Psychology.

Educational Leadership. Monthly journal that includes syntheses
of research in many issues on varied topics.

Educational Psychology Review. A new journal that reviews topics
related to educational psychology.

*The Educator's Desk Reference: A Sourcebook of Educational In-
formation and Research* (1989). Good source for bibliographies,
reference books, and journals.

Educators' Handbook: A Research Perspective (1987). Helps educators locate information on effective schools and teaching.

Fourth Review of Special Education (1980). *First, Second,* and *Third
Reviews* are also good.

Handbook of Behavior Therapy in Education (1988).

Handbook of Reading Research (1984).

Handbook of Research on Educational Administration (1988).

Handbook of Research on Teaching, 3rd ed. (1982). Excellent
source for reviews on topics related to teaching; earlier editions
are also excellent.

Handbook of Special Education: Research and Practice (1987–
1988). Three volumes.

International Handbook of Bilingualism and Bilingual Education
(1988).

International Handbook of Women's Education (1989).

NSSE Yearbooks. National Society for the Study of Education; excellent overviews of varied topics.

Research Guide for Studies in Early Childhood (1988).

Review of Educational Research. A journal published quarterly on
various topics.

Review of Research in Education. A book published annually; each volume contains different topics.

The Second Handbook on Parent Education (1988).

Yearbook of Adult and Continuing Education.

Yearbook of Special Education.

Table 3.1 summarizes examples of some of the topics reviewed by four secondary sources related to effective teaching.

In searching for reviews of research you may come across **meta-analysis,** a review that synthesizes previous studies quantitatively. It is a relatively new procedure that uses statistical methods to combine systematically the results of a number of studies of the same problem.

Meta-analysis: A quantitative review of previous studies.

The first step in meta-analysis is data collection, which in this case refers to specifying the studies that will be included. Thus, the "data" are what is reported in existing studies, including the criteria that are used to select the studies, such as the years and sources. The second step is to review each study and record results and other characteristics. The final step is to use one of several statistical techniques to combine the results of all the studies. Often, the overall finding of the analysis is referred to as *effect size.* In the following example, excerpts from a meta-analysis illustrate each of these steps.

EXAMPLE: META-ANALYSIS RESEARCH

"The purpose of this paper is to integrate statistically the results of the literature on teacher expectations. . . . Standard search procedures were used to locate studies, and 47 were found. The results . . . are not generalisable to the dissertation literature after 1977, as those studies were not located in time for inclusion. Both experimental studies . . . and nonexperimental studies were read and coded on the following dimensions: publication status, research design, type of expectation or label . . . type of subjects, and type of effect used as the dependent variable. . . . The dependent variables were converted into effect sizes (δ) — standardised mean differences between the high expectancy group and the low expectancy group" (M. L. Smith, 1980, pp. 53–54).

Most meta-analyses reported in reputable journals are characterized by a comprehensive search of the literature and sound sta-

Table 3.1   TOPICS REVIEWED IN SELECTED SECONDARY SOURCES

Source	Topics reviewed
Review of Research in Education, Vol. 15 (1988–1989)	Improving Thinking Through Instruction
	Adult Literacy Education
	Grouping Children for Learning
	Cooperative Activities in the Classroom
	Schooling in Mathematics and Science
Review of Educational Research, Vol. 58, 1 (1988)	Supervision of Counselors and Teachers
	Acquisition of Teaching Skills
	Test Anxiety
	Timing of Feedback and Learning
	Extracurricular Influences in Secondary School
Educators' Handbook: A Research Perspective (1987)	Mathematics Learning and Teaching
	Research on Reading
	Teaching Writing
	Teaching Science
	Mainstreaming
	Gifted and Talented
	Teacher-Principal Relationships
	School Effectiveness Research
	Parenting
	Stress and Burnout
	Teaching Social Studies
	Teaching with Computers
	Teacher Planning
	Classroom Management
Handbook of Research on Teaching, 3rd Ed. (1986)	Syntheses of Research on Teaching
	Teachers' and Students' Thought Processes
	Teacher Behavior and Student Achievement
	Classroom Organization and Management
	Media in Teaching
	School Effects
	Adapting Teaching to Individual Differences Among Learners
	Teaching Creative and Gifted Learners
	Teaching Bilingual Learners
	Teaching Mildly Handicapped Learners
	Early Childhood and Elementary School Teaching
	Teaching Reading
	Teaching Written Composition
	Teaching Mathematics
	Teaching Natural Sciences
	Teaching Art
	Teaching Social Studies
	Moral and Values Education

tistical procedures. However, because this type of review has only recently been published, there are some questions about its credibility. For example, what sense would it make if all studies, whether poorly conducted or well conducted, are included in the synthesis? That is, what criteria should be used to include studies in the review? As we will see later in this chapter, an important component of a good review is an analysis, as well as a summary, of the literature.

Step Two: Identify Key Terms

Once a search of secondary sources is completed and the research problem is refined, the investigator needs to make a list of key terms that represent the problem. This step is accomplished by identifying the most important terms in the problem and then thinking of other terms that are closely related. These terms are then located in indexes to find related literature. The indexes organize the literature by subject and author, and at this stage of the review the investigator finds the key terms in the subject section of the index. For most searches of educational literature, the investigator is well advised to use special thesauruses that are available to help select the most appropriate key terms. The *Thesaurus of ERIC Descriptors* is a listing of the terms used in indexes of educational research. It organizes the descriptors alphabetically and defines each one so that the investigator can match his or her definition to the one used in the indexes. Once the investigator has identified the best thesaurus descriptors, they are used to continue the search. The thesaurus also indicates terms that are closely related to the descriptors. For example, suppose your research problem is the following: The purpose of this study is to investigate the effect of teaching styles on student achievement. Key terms are *teaching style* and *student achievement*. Figure 3.1 shows how *teaching style* is entered in the thesaurus. You will note that this term has been used as an ERIC descriptor since 1966, 771 times in the index CIJE and 737 times in the index RIE (CIJE and RIE are defined in the next section). The entry shows how the descriptor is defined, a broader descriptor (Teaching Characteristics), and several descriptors related to it. It is best to use some of the related terms as descriptors in your search since their definitions may be closer to what you mean by *teaching styles* than the definition in the ERIC system. Related terms are also used when an exhaustive search of the literature is required. The only way to know if a descriptor will be useful in identifying literature related to your problem is to use it to locate articles and reports and examine the titles and abstracts. If they seem to be promising, it is probably best to use that descriptor.

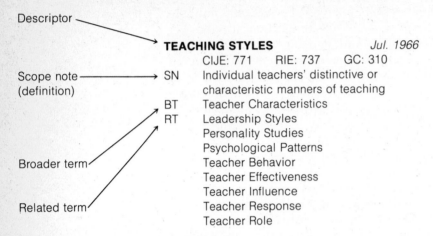

Descriptor

Scope note
(definition)

Broader term

Related term

TEACHING STYLES *Jul. 1966*
CIJE: 771 RIE: 737 GC: 310
SN Individual teachers' distinctive or
characteristic manners of teaching
BT Teacher Characteristics
RT Leadership Styles
Personality Studies
Psychological Patterns
Teacher Behavior
Teacher Effectiveness
Teacher Influence
Teacher Response
Teacher Role

Figure 3.1 Sample thesaurus entry.

If your problem is psychologically oriented and you may be using psychological literature, it would be best to consult the *Thesaurus of Psychological Index Terms* to use the index *Psychological Abstracts*. Since the terms in this index are different from those in educational indexes, the key terms must be appropriate to the index.

Step Three: Identify the Appropriate Journal Indexes and Abstracts

Many indexes may be used to locate research on education. The most useful and comprehensive is *Current Index to Journals in Education* (CIJE). **CIJE,** published monthly by the Educational Resources Information Center (ERIC), provides abstracts of almost 800 journals and periodicals. The abstracts are written by personnel in 16 clearinghouses. Each clearinghouse focuses on an area of education, for example, teacher education, elementary and early childhood education, handicapped and gifted children, reading and communication skills, and urban education. The clearinghouses also abstract unpublished reports and provide very useful bibliographies, reviews, newsletters, and bulletins. CIJE includes a subject and author index, a main entry section of abstracts, and an index of journal contents.

CIJE: *Current Index to Journals in Education.*

ERIC also publishes the index *Resources in Education* (**RIE**), which abstracts research reports not published in journals. These would include, for example, papers presented at conferences and meetings, federally funded project reports, and documents prepared by state education agencies.

RIE: *Resources in Education (not journal articles).*

Education Index provides bibliographic information for about 300 periodicals. Since it does not include abstracts, and all of its research journals are also in CIJE, CIJE is the best index to use. The only reason to use *Education Index* is to search for literature published before 1969, when CIJE was initiated.

Psychological Abstracts is a monthly publication covering almost 1,000 journals, books, and other documents. It is useful for a search of a topic that is related to psychology, such as counseling, intelligence, group dynamics, or information processing. Similarly, *Sociological Abstracts*, which is published five times a year, is useful for topics that may be related to sociology, such as urban education.

There are also a number of specialized indexes and abstracts, the most relevant of which for educational research follow.

EXAMPLES: SPECIALIZED INDEXES AND ABSTRACTS

Adolescent Mental Health Abstracts

Business Education Index

Canadian Education Index

Dissertation Abstracts International

Educational Administration Abstracts

Educational Technology Abstracts

Exceptional Child Education Resources (formerly *Exceptional Child Education Abstracts*)

Higher Education Abstracts (formerly *College Student Personnel Abstracts*)

Nutrition Abstracts and Reviews

Physical Education Index

Reading Abstracts

Research into Higher Education Abstracts

Resources in Vocational Education

Social Science Citation Index

Sport and Fitness Index

State Education Journal Index

Step Four: Search Indexes for Primary Sources

The ultimate objective in a review of literature is to identify primary sources that investigate a problem or idea of interest. **Primary sources** are original articles and reports in which researchers communicate directly to the reader the methods and results of their study. It is important to read primary sources because they allow a more informed judgment about the quality and usefulness of the information. An analogy in literature is reading a book as it was originally written by the author. Cliff Notes and other summaries are analogous to secondary sources.

Primary sources: Articles that report original research.

Primary sources are reported in a wide variety of journals. In fact there are hundreds of journals, which differ greatly in quality. To help you understand these differences, consider how articles get published. The most common procedure is for the authors to write a manuscript that will be submitted to a journal for publication. If the format and topic of the article are appropriate, the editor will usually send the manuscript to two or three reviewers and/or associate or assistant editors to be evaluated. The journal is said to be **refereed** if this procedure is followed. A **nonrefereed** journal does not use external reviewers to evaluate the manuscript. The evaluation is structured so that the reviewers, who are "experts" in the topic investigated, comment on the significance of the problem, methodology, data analysis, contribution of the findings and conclusions, and other criteria. Usually the reviewers are asked to recommend that the manuscript be published as submitted, revised and resubmitted, or rejected. Rarely do they recommend to publish as submitted.

Refereed: Sent to reviewers for an evaluation.

Nonrefereed: Not reviewed by outside experts.

The strength of the refereed review process is that helpful suggestions will improve the quality of the manuscript. Some journals use a blind refereed process to control for reviewer bias. A blind review is one in which the name of the authors of the manuscript are omitted, which supposedly reduces subjectivity. Clearly a blind review process is desirable and is usually used by journals that have a reputation for publishing high-quality articles. In the "publish or perish" culture of higher education it is naturally more prestigious to be published in higher-quality journals. The result is that many more manuscripts are submitted than are actually accepted. Indeed, the rejection rate is often used, justifiably so, as a barometer of quality. Table 3.2 summarizes some of these differences for some educational journals.

Remember that there are hundreds of journals, some of which are published primarily for financial reasons, and much of what is published is seriously flawed. Certainly just because it *is* published does not mean that it is good research, so you may be well advised

Table 3.2 DESCRIPTIONS OF SELECTED EDUCATIONAL JOURNALS

Journal	Circulation	Approx. no. articles per year	Referenced	No. references per manuscript	Manuscripts reviewed blindly	% Manuscripts accepted	Publishes invited articles	Invited articles reviewed
Action in Teacher Education	3,500	14	Yes	2	Yes	20	Yes	Yes
American Biology Teacher	7,000	115	Yes	2–3	Yes	50	Yes	Yes
American Educational Research Journal	N/A	48	Yes	2	Yes	15	No	—
Child Development	8,500	200	Yes	2–3	Yes	10–15	Yes	Yes
The Clearing House	2,500	129	—	—	—	—	—	—
Education	3,000	88	Yes	2	No	25	Yes	No
Educational Forum	48,000	45	Yes	3–4	Yes	10	Yes	Yes
Educational Leadership	98,000	160	Yes	3	Yes	10	Yes	No
Educational Record	10,000	32	No	0	No	20	Yes	Yes
Journal for Research in Mathematics Education	N/A	50	Yes	4–6	Yes	17	No	Yes
Journal of Educational Psychology	N/A	90	Yes	3	Yes	20	Yes	Yes
Journal of Educational Research	3,200	48	Yes	2	No	18–20	No	Yes
Journal of Experimental Education	1,600	40	Yes	2	No	25	No	—
Journal of Reading	19,000	90	Yes	2	Yes	15	Yes	Yes
Journal of Research in Science Teaching	2,000	90	Yes	2–3	Yes	40	Yes	Yes
Phi Delta Kappan	145,000	180	Yes	2–3	Yes	5	Yes	No
Principal	25,000	60	No	0	No	10	Yes	Yes
Reading Research Quarterly	9,700	28	Yes	3	Yes	15–23	Yes	Yes
The Reading Teacher	48,000	90	Yes	2	Yes	15	Yes	Yes
Review of Educational Research	N/A	25	Yes	2–3	Yes	13.5	No	—
School of Science & Mathematics	5,400	120	Yes	2–3	No	40–55	Yes	Yes
Teachers College Record	3,200	40	Yes	2	Yes	15–25	Yes	No

Source: Adapted from K. T. Henson (1988). Writing for education journals, Phi Delta Kappan, 69, 752–754.

to learn which journals in your area are regarded as high-quality publications. A good source for learning about the journals is *Education Journals and Serials: An Analytical Guide* (Collins, 1988), which summarizes 800 different educational and education-related journals. It is organized by subject area (e.g., adult and continuing education, teaching methods, music, reading and language arts, simulation and gaming, and special education) and has an annotated summary of each journal.

The search for primary (and secondary) sources is made in one of three ways: manually, by on-line computer, and by compact disc computer. Although the strategy for searching is basically the same for the three approaches, we will look at each one.

Manual Search   To conduct a manual search, select the most recent available index. Using the subject headings in the index, which are organized alphabetically, find the key terms you have previously identified. The index will list, by title, published articles that are related to the key term. Read through the list of titles and determine which of the articles may be useful for the review. Pertinent information is recorded such as the name of the author(s) and journal, volume, number, date of publication, and pages. If an abstract of the article is available in the index it will provide further information about the relevance of the article. Often the title is not a good indication of what is in an article. Repeat this procedure for related terms in the index until you have noted all potentially relevant articles. Then find the next most recent index and repeat the process. Continue with as many indexes as necessary to generate a list of as many as 30 possible references. An exhaustive search will often have many more than 30. You may need to use indexes that go back 10 or more years to locate a sufficient number of articles.

An example of what you will find in CIJE for *teaching styles* is shown in Figure 3.2. Depending on what you need to relate to teaching styles, some of the articles will be more relevant than others. For instance, if your interest is in relating styles to achievement for elementary school teachers, you would not be interested in the articles published in journals related to college teaching (e.g., *College Teaching* and *Teaching English in the Two-Year College*) or titles clearly indicating that the article concerns secondary-level or college students. In this particular index only a few of the articles listed seem related to elementary teaching styles, and none are clearly related to elementary students' achievement. This is not an uncommon occurrence in searching the literature. Often you will find only 1 or 2 promising articles out of 10 or 20. You then need

Teaching Styles

Gambling with Students' Minds, Lives, and Futures: Time for New Techniques. *Clearing House* v60 n6 p284–86 Feb 1987　　EJ 350 532

Research: Wondering Why in Weyauwega, WI. *Journal of Reading* v30 n8 p752–55 May 1987　　EJ 350 586

A Profound Proposal for Reform in Composition Instruction: The C-Team. *Teaching English in the Two-Year College* v14 n2 p137–41 May 1987　　EJ 350 629

Training and Coaching Beginning Teachers: An Antidote to Reality Shock. *Educational Leadership* v44 n5 p34–36 Feb 1987　　EJ 350 644

A Comparison of Activity Structures During Basic Skills and Problem-Solving Instruction in Seventh-Grade Mathematics. *American Educational Research Journal* v23 n3 p393–414 Fall 1986　　EJ 351 734

Managing the Classroom: A Matter of Style. *Techniques* v3 n1 p42–50 Jan 1987　　EJ 352 422

Get Them Involved! Styles of High- and Low-Rated Teachers. *College Teaching* v35 n1 p13–15 Win 1987　　EJ 352 714

Determinants of Teacher Work: Some Causal Complications. *Teaching and Teacher Education* v3 n1 p55–60 1987　　EJ 353 192

Who Determines Teacher Work? The Debate Continues. *Teaching and Teacher Education* v3 n1 p61–64 1987　　EJ 353 193

In Celebration of the Teacher. *Action in Teacher Education* v9 n1 p75–79 Spr 1987　　EJ 353 204

Reflecting on Reflective Teaching. *Journal of Teacher Education* v38 n2 p33–39 Mar–Apr 1987　　EJ 353 251

Are Methods of Enhancing Creativity Being Taught in Teacher Education Programs as Perceived by Teacher Educators and Student Teachers? *Journal of Creative Behavior* v21 n1 p22–33 1987　　EJ 353 987

A Study of the Relationship between Instrumental Music Teachers' Modeling Skills and Pupil Performance Behaviors. *Bulletin of the Council for Research in Music Education* n91 p155–59 Spr 1987　　EJ 354 810

Introduction and Integration of Classroom Routines by Expert Teachers. *Curriculum Inquiry* v17 n2 p135–76 Sum 1987　　EJ 355 424

Relationship between Perceived Learning Style and Teaching Style of Junior College Educators. *Community/Junior College Quarterly of Research and Practice* v11 n3 p169–77 1987　　EJ 355 870

Teachers' Political Knowledge and Attitudes. *Social Studies Teacher* v8 n4 p7 Apr–May 1987　　EJ 356 189

Is Queen Victoria Lecturing Today? Teaching Human Sexuality Using Famous Personalities. *Teaching Sociology* v15 n3 p257–62 Jul 1987　　EJ 357 378

"Entre libre" dans la classe ("Entre Libre" in the Classroom). *Francais dans le Monde* n210 p69–74 Jul 1987　　EJ 358 152

Figure 3.2 Sample CIJE entry.

to go to different years or months of the index and related terms to locate 15 to 30 articles that seem promising.

Once you have the completed list, you must determine if the library you are using has the journals. For those the library carries, ask a librarian how to retrieve the issues that contain the articles you need. This step will save you a lot of time. Some journals are bound by volume in stacks that are available to you, others are in microfiche, and in many libraries journals are accessible only to librarians. In most searches some of the articles you need will not be available in your library. You may need to check with other local libraries (by phone first) or use interlibrary loan. Another way to obtain the article is to write to the author and request a reprint. The reference librarian can help you locate the address.

On-line Computer Search   Most university and public libraries and many public school systems have access by computer to many of the same indexes that you can search manually. Although a brief manual search is recommended to make sure that your key terms are accurate, a computer search can save a great deal of time and provide a more comprehensive search. A computer search allows you to use combinations of key terms that cannot be used in a manual search, enabling you to focus the search much more and identify articles that are directly relevant to your problem. One type of computer search is called on-line because the librarian uses a telephone line to connect a computer at the library with another computer that holds the index in what is called a **data base.** Several data bases can be accessed, depending on your problem. For educational research the Lockheed DIALOG data base contains most of the indexes needed, such as CIJE and RIE.

Data base: Computerized library of resources.

Working with a librarian, use the key terms to select descriptors that can be used in the search. The descriptors are combined by using *and* and/or *or*, connectors that will broaden or reduce the search. *And* will reduce the search because the computer will look for articles that are categorized by all the descriptors indicated. For example, a search of *teaching style and elementary teaching* would have fewer references than only *teaching style* (*teaching style* by itself would include elementary, middle and high schools, and colleges and universities). The *or* connector increases the number of references because the computer searches for articles that have any of the descriptors listed. If you use *teaching style or teacher sensitivity,* the search would find articles cataloged by either term. The *or* connector is used with related terms in the thesaurus, whereas the *and* connector is used between independent and dependent variables and with descriptors that will limit the search to a particular grade level or subject.

Once all possible descriptors and combinations have been identified, begin the computer search by indicating the number of references in the data base for each descriptor and combination. For example, for *teaching styles*, there are 1,725 articles in CIJE. Generally you want to try several different combinations of descriptors to see how many articles are in the data base and then use the combination that gives you a reasonable number of articles closest to your specific research problem or topic. You can further reduce a large number of identified articles by telling the computer to list articles appearing in particular years and/or journal titles, by limiting the number to the most recent 20 or 30 articles (or however many you want), or by limiting the search to major descriptors. As many as six major descriptors are assigned to each article to identify the main focus; minor descriptors are used for less important aspects and features such as grade level and type of research.

Your librarian will know how to conduct the computer search and will try several approaches before asking for the final set of references to be printed. Usually, a sample of the articles identified through certain combinations of descriptors is reviewed to make sure that the complete set actually printed is what you need. Since an on-line search can be costly, it is important for you to prepare the possible key terms and combinations before attempting to access the data base. A librarian who is skilled in educational computer searches is invaluable and should be consulted when possible. Once the final set of articles is identified, the computer can print, either in your library or at another location, the basic bibliographic information or an abstract. Naturally printing abstracts is more expensive, but the abstract will give you a much better feel for the relevance of the article. You then review the titles and/or abstracts that are printed to determine which articles you will locate in journals for the complete report.

Compact Disc Computer Search   Recent technological advances now allow libraries to have complete data bases on discs kept in the library and accessed through computer hardware in the library. This development allows the librarian or the researcher the flexibility of searching by computer without having to be connected on-line to another computer in a different location. Without the ongoing costs associated with on-line searching, it is possible to try many different descriptors and combinations and have the printed titles and abstracts available immediately. Most compact disc computers are open to students and faculty, so you can essentially do your own computer search. Most libraries that have ERIC on compact disc will also have PsycLit, a data base that contains citations and articles in psychology and related disciplines from over 1,400 journals and other serial publications. PsycLit is a computerized version of *Psychological Abstracts*. Both the ERIC and PsycLit data bases are updated quarterly. Manual copies of the indexes are updated monthly. The specific procedures for accessing the data bases will vary from one library to another, so it is necessary to consult guidelines and directions at the library you are using.

Step Five: Summarize and Analyze Primary Source Information

Once you locate the primary source, the article or report that contains the original data collection and analysis, you will need to read it and summarize the information it contains. It is useful to have a strategy for recording notes on the article as you read it. An efficient approach is to record your notes on index cards (I find the 5-×-8 size best) because after all the articles are reviewed the cards can be easily organized in different ways. Begin by reading the abstract of the article, if there is one, and the purpose or research problem. Then read the results and decide if it is worthwhile to read the article more carefully and take notes on it. Do not be too discouraged if some of the articles you locate are not useful. Part of the process of reviewing literature is to locate and read many more articles than you will eventually use.

After you decide to use the article, begin taking notes by writing complete bibliographic information, preferably in the style you will use in writing; summarize the research problem as briefly as possible; and underline or circle the independent and dependent variables. Next indicate in outline form the subjects, instruments, and procedures used and then summarize the results and conclusions. On the other side of the card record interesting or insightful quotations; indicate any weakness or limitations in the methodology, analysis of data, or conclusions; and indicate how the study may be related to your problem. You will find it useful to develop a code for indicating your overall judgment of the article. If you find it closely related to your problem and highly credible, you might give the article an A; if somewhat related and credible, a B; and so on. It will also help to develop a code that indicates the major focus of the study by topic or descriptor. For example, in reviewing studies on teacher awareness you may find that some studies examine the effect of awareness on student achievement, some focus on strategies to improve awareness, and others emphasize different approaches to awareness depending on the type of students in the classroom. Each of these could have a code or notation on the card, such as "effect on ach.," "improv. awareness," and "approaches."

Step Six: Organize the Review

Although the review of literature can be organized in different ways, the most common approach is to group together studies that investigate similar topics or subtopics. This process is initiated by coding the studies as you read them; then the articles with the same code are put in one pile, those of another code in a second pile, and so forth. The different topics are then put in order, usually from articles related to the problem in a more general way first to articles specifically related to the problem. Within each topic it may be possible to organize the studies by date, with the most recent studies last. This arrangement gives the reader a sense of the development of the research over time. In fact in many articles with a specific problem, the entire review will be organized chronologically. The review should not be organized by study or article, in which each paragraph in the review deals with a different study. Studies that are only generally related should be summarized briefly. If several of these studies have similar results they should be grouped together; for example, "Several studies have found that teacher expectations are related to student achievement (Smith, 1978; Tyler, 1985; Wylie, 1983)." Most reviews select representative general studies; there is no attempt to do an exhaustive review of all studies. However, exhaustive reviews may be necessary for theses, dissertations, and other major projects.

For studies that are closely related to the problem, you should begin with a brief summary and then analyze the studies. The analysis is important because it suggests that the researchers are not simply accepting the studies as credible; they are examining the methodology of the studies critically to make better judgments about the contribution of the results. A critical examination enables the researchers to show the relationship of the proposed or current study to previous literature. This step is essential for the results to contribute to our knowledge. It also generates many good ideas that will improve subsequent research. Therefore, the third step in reviewing closely related studies is to indicate explicitly how the reviewed study is related to the present research. For a few studies, then, those that are closely related to the problem, there should be three elements: a summary of the study reviewed, an analysis of the study, and a summary of how the study relates to the research problem or purpose of the manuscript. It is also advisable to avoid long quotations and the same wording in discussing each study, for example, "A study by Brown (1987) indicated that . . ."; "A study by Smith (1979) indicated that . . ."; "A study by Jones (1969) showed that. . . ." Quotations in general should be used sparingly and only when a special or critical meaning could not be indicated

(text continues on page 64)

Dimensions of Attributions

Summary of
previous research

In describing the nature of attributions that are relevant to educational settings, Weiner (1979) has advanced a three-dimensional typology of attributions. The first of the three dimensions, *locus of causality*, was first introduced by Heider (1958), who suggested that the attributions people offer as explanations for behaviors and events emphasize· factors that originate within the person or arise from environmental sources. As examples of possible causal factors, Heider mentioned ability, effort, task difficulty, and luck and pointed out that the first two causes are internal factors, whereas the second two causes are external factors. Weiner, Russell, and Lerman (1978, 1979) later found that the locus of causality dimension is closely related to affective reactions that follow test feedback. Individuals who attribute their success to external factors report feelings of gratitude, surprise, and thankfulness, whereas those who emphasize internal factors report pride, confidence, and satisfaction. Failing students, on the other hand, experience guilt, regret, and aimlessness when they blame themselves, and anger, surpise, and hostility when they externalize their failure.

Just as luck is an external factor and ability is an internal one, luck also fluctuates more than ability, suggesting that a second dimension—*stability of causes*—should be considered when describing attributions (e.g., Frieze & Weiner, 1971; Weiner, 1972; Weiner et al., 1971).

Analysis of
previous research

Although Heider did not emphasize the stability dimension as much as the locus of cause dimension, subsequent studies of changes in expectations after success and failure indicated that the expectancy shifts which follow feedback are closely linked to stability (e.g., Feather & Simon, 1971; McMahan, 1973; Weiner et al., 1971). For example, in one study (Weiner, Nierenberg, & Goldstein, 1976) subjects who believed they had done well on a task were asked to report their expectations concerning future performances as well as estimate the cause of their success. Although positive increases in expectations were not related to the locus of the cause, expectancy incre-

Figure 3.3 Review of literature. (*Source:* D. R. Forsyth and J. H. McMillan (1981). Attributions, affect, and expectations: A test of Weiner's three-dimensional model, *Journal of Educational Psychology,* 73, 393–396.)

ments were associated with the perceived stability of the causal factor. When subjects attributed their success to such factors as ability or the nature of the task, their expectations for success increased, whereas subjects who attributed their success to luck or effort reported less positive expectancies.

To circumvent the methodological difficulties with unitary cause scales, the current investigation assessed attributional dimensions using a technique developed by Seligman, Abramson, Semmel, and von Baeyer (1979). In this technique, individuals rate the influence of causes in terms of the conceptual dimensions themselves. For example, rather than assuming that an attribution to ability reflects an emphasis on internal rather than external factors, these researchers ask participants to indicate the extent to which an outcome was caused by "something about you or something about other people or circumstances" (Seligman et al., 1979, p. 243). Initial findings indicate that the dimensional bipolar scales are accurate measures of conceptually meaningful dimensions and yield results that are comparable to those of other assessment techniques (Seligman et al., 1979; Weiner, 1980). Furthermore, multidimensional scaling and factor analytic studies of the actual dimensions underlying unitary causal judgments show that bipolar dimensional ratings are highly correlated with the cognitive dimensions that actually underlie respondents' unitary cause judgments (Meyer, 1980; Passer, Kelley, & Michela, 1978).

Predictions. Given the persistent findings in many areas attesting to the dramatic impact of perceived control, it was hypothesized that people who attributed their outcome to controllable factors would experience more positive affective reactions than individuals who feel they cannot control the causes of their performance. In addition, although successful students should feel better—in terms of affect—than failing students (e.g., Bailey, Helm, & Gladstone, 1975; McMillan & Sprat, Note 1), the locus of attributed cause should moderate the magnitude of this effect. After success, internal attributions should be associated with more positive affective reactions, whereas negative affective reactions should be related to internal attributions for failure.

Relates previous research to current study

Figure 3.3 (*continued*)

by your own words. You should use short sentences and transition sentences so there is a logical progression of ideas and sections. Many of these suggestions are illustrated in Figure 3.3, which is an excerpt of a review of literature from a published article.

The length of the review depends on the type of study, whether or not it is published, and the topic that is researched. An exploratory study may have a limited review, whereas an exhaustive review in a theses or dissertation can be as long as 30 or 40 typed pages. A lengthy review needs major and minor headings and periodic summaries.

CONSUMER TIPS
Criteria for Evaluating the Review of Literature

When reading and evaluating the review of literature section of research studies or reports several criteria should be considered.

1. The review of literature should adequately cover previous research on the topic. In reading research in an area you are familiar with, you will be able to judge the scope of the review. Were important studies ignored? Does the number of studies in the review reflect research activity in that area? Often you will realize that there is far more research in an area than indicated by the review. Do the authors of the article cite mainly their own research? Although it is sometimes quite appropriate for authors to use their own work as a major part of the review, it may also indicate investigator bias. If the authors limit their review to their own studies and do not include other related research, the credibility of the study could justifiably be questioned.

2. The review of literature should cite actual findings from other studies. It is important for the review to be based on the empirical results of previous research, not on opinions of others about previous research or on the conclusions of previous research.

3. The review of literature should be up to date. The studies reviewed should include the most recent research on the topic. This does not mean that older studies are not relevant, however. Sometimes the best and most relevant research has been conducted decades ago.

4. The review of literature should analyze as well as summarize previous studies. The analysis may be a critique of methodology or inappropriate generalizations, an indication of limitations of the study (e.g., to certain populations, instruments, or procedures), or a discussion of conflicting results.

5. The review of literature should be organized logically by topic and not by author. A review that has one paragraph for each study usually fails to integrate and synthesize previous research.

6. The review of literature should briefly summarize minor studies and discuss in detail major studies. Minor studies are those that are related to one or two aspects of the study. Major studies are directly relevant to most aspects of the study or have important implications.

7. The review of major studies should relate previous studies explicitly to the research problem or methods. What is the implication of the review? How can it be helpful and improve subsequent research?

8. The review of literature should provide a logical basis for the hypothesis. If there is a hypothesis, it should be based on the review. There should be a clear connection among the problem, review, and hypothesis.

9. The review of literature should establish a theoretical framework for the problem. For basic and most applied research the review should provide the theoretical context for the study, thereby enhancing the significance of the findings.

10. The review of literature should help establish the significance of the research.

OUTLINE SUMMARY

1. Good reviews enhance credibility of the findings.
2. Purposes.
   A. Relate previous studies to the problem under investigation.
   B. Help to focus and refine the research problem.
   C. Develop significance for the problem under investigation.
      (1) Justifies conducting the research.
      (2) Shows how existing knowledge is improved.
   D. Identify previously used methods of investigation to avoid past mistakes and provide ideas for further studies.
   E. Identify contradictory results of previous research.
   F. Provide a basis for the research hypothesis.
   G. Save time by providing insights, ideas, and successful methods.
   H. Lead the researcher to new information and knowledge.
3. Steps in reviewing related literature.
   A. Find a librarian to help.
   B. Secondary sources.

       (1) Summarizes original research.

       (2) Found in textbooks, scholarly books, encyclopedias, reviews in journals or books, handbooks, and year-books.

       (3) Meta-analysis.

  C. Identify key terms with appropriate thesaurus of descriptors.

  D. Identify journal indexes and abstracts.

       (1) ERIC includes CIJE and RIE.

       (2) *Psychological Abstracts*.

       (3) Other specialized abstracts and indexes.

  E. Search indexes for primary sources.

       (1) Original research.

       (2) Quality varies—some refereed with blind review; others are nonrefereed.

       (3) First search manually by key terms in the subject index.

       (4) Search by computer, either on-line or compact disc, using key terms and appropriate connectors.

  F. Summarize primary studies on note cards.

  G. Write the review.

       (1) Organize by topic or chronologically.

       (2) Summarize somewhat related studies briefly.

       (3) Summarize, analyze, and relate studies that are closely related.

       (4) Most reviews are selective, not exhaustive.

4. Evaluate reviews with the following criteria:

  A. Does it adequately cover previous research?

  B. Are actual findings from other studies cited?

  C. Is it up to date?

  D. Does it analyze as well as summarize other studies?

  E. Is it logically well organized and easy to follow?

  F. Are major studies reviewed in detail?

  G. Does the hypothesis follow from the review?

  H. Is a theoretical framework established?

  I. Does it help to establish the significance of the study?

STUDY QUESTIONS

1. What are the major purposes of the review of literature?

2. How can the review help the researcher refine an initial research problem?

3. Why does previous research help establish the credibility of the findings of a study?

4. Why is it sometimes helpful to find contradictory findings in previous research?
5. How can the review save the researcher time?
6. How can the review improve proposed methodology?
7. What are the steps in conducting a review of literature?
8. What is the difference between a secondary and primary source?
9. What are some examples of useful secondary sources?
10. What secondary sources are relevant to your field of study?
11. What is a meta-analysis?
12. What is the procedure for identifying key terms?
13. What is the difference between CIJE and RIE?
14. What are the steps in finding articles through an index like CIJE?
15. What makes some journals better than others?
16. What are the steps of writing a review of literature? How should the review be organized?
17. What are the criteria for evaluating a review of literature?

Chapter
4

Subjects and Sampling

The third major part of research reports is the methodology or methods section. As noted in Chapter 1, the first subsection of the methodology section describes the subjects from whom data are collected. The manner in which subjects are selected has important implications for identifying factors that affect subject performance and for generalizing the results. Hence it is necessary to understand who the subjects are and how they were selected.

INTRODUCTION TO SAMPLING

What Is a Subject?

A **subject** is an individual who participates in a research study or is someone from whom data are collected. In experiments, for example, each person who is given a treatment and whose behavior is measured is considered to be a subject. The term *subject* may also identify individuals whose behavior, past or present, is used as data, without their involvement in some type of treatment or intervention. For instance, a researcher might use last year's fourth-grade test scores as data, and each fourth-grader included is considered to be a subject. In qualitative research individuals are identified as participants rather than subjects.

Subject: Person from whom data are collected.

What Is a Population?

A **population** is a group of elements or cases, whether individuals, objects, or events, that conform to specific criteria and to which we intend to generalize the results of the research. This group is also referred to as the target population or universe. The specification of the population begins with the research problem and review of literature, through which a population is described conceptually or in broad terms, for example, seventh-grade students, beginning teachers, principals, special education teachers, and so forth. A more specific definition is then needed, based on demographic characteristics. These characteristics are sometimes referred to as delimiting variables. For example, in a study of first-grade minority students, there are three delimiting characteristics: students, first grade (age), and minority. Further delimiting variables should be added to provide as precise a definition as possible. What about geographic region, socioeconomic status, gender, type of community, and types of schools? Are both public and private students included? How is "minority" defined? It is also important to distinguish the target population from a list of elements from which a group of subjects is selected, which is termed the survey population. In a study of beginning teachers, the target population may be beginning teachers across the United States, in all types of schools. The survey population may be a list of beginning teachers that was obtained from four states. Although the intent may be all beginning teachers, the results are limited, or delimited, to beginning teachers in the four states. Thus, generalization from subjects to populations should be based on the survey population.

Population: Persons to whom results can be generalized.

What Is a Sample?

The **sample** is the group of elements, or a single element, from which data are obtained. Although the phrase "the sample included . . ." is used to discuss the characteristics of the people or events in the sample, the nature of the sampling procedure is usually described by one or more adjectives, such as *random* sampling or *stratified random* sampling. These types of sampling procedures are defined, with illustrations from actual studies, in the following section. It is important for the researcher to define as specifically as possible both the sampling procedure and the characteristics of the sample used in the study. Here is an example of a good description of the sample.

Sample: Group of subjects from whom data are collected.

EXAMPLE: DESCRIPTION OF A SAMPLE

"The sample for this study consisted of nine seventh-grade mathematics teachers and their students. All teachers had volunteered for the study and each teacher received a $100 stipend. The teachers taught in four public schools in a medium-sized Western city, a low-middle to middle class community with a small proportion of minorities. According to a school district brochure, the district had approximately 32,000 students in 42 elementary schools, 9 middle schools, and 9 high schools during the school year the study was conducted.

The class sizes ranged from 16 to 34. There were 5 female and 4 male teachers. The teachers had an average of approximately 11 years of teaching experience (range = 2–26). Of these 11 years, 8 were as math teachers (range = 2–22) and 6 were as middle-school math teachers (range = 2–10). All had secondary certification, and 4 had Master's degrees in Administration. One of the teachers had a math major in college, 6 a math minor, and 2 had no special training in math." (Burns and Lash, 1986, p. 395)

TYPES OF SAMPLING PROCEDURES

The purpose of sampling is to obtain a group of subjects who will be representative of the larger population. The degree of representativeness is based on the sampling technique employed. We will first describe different sampling procedures and then consider the strengths and weaknesses of each in obtaining a representative sample.

Probability Sampling

In social science and educational research it is usually impractical and unnecessary to measure all the elements in the population of interest. Typically, a relatively small number of subjects or cases is selected from the larger population. The goal is to select a sample that will adequately represent the population, so that what is described in the sample will also be true of the population. The best procedure for selecting such a sample is to use **probability sampling,** a method of sampling in which the subjects are selected ran-

Probability sampling: Known probability of selection from the population.

domly in such a way that the researcher knows the probability of selecting each member of the population. Random selection implies that each member of the population as a whole or of subgroups of the population has an equal chance of being selected. As long as the number of cases selected is large enough, it is likely that a very small percentage of the population, represented by the sample, will provide an accurate description of the entire population.

It should be noted, however, that there is always some degree of error in sampling, and that error must be considered in interpreting the results of the sample. In probability sampling this calculation can be made very precisely with some statistical procedures. Consider a population of 1,000 third-graders, from which you will select randomly 5 percent, or 50, to estimate the attitudes of all the third-graders toward school. If the attitude score was 75 for the sample of 50 subjects, 75 can be used to estimate the value for the entire population of third-graders. However, if another sample of 50 students is selected, their score might be a little different, say 73. Which one is more correct? Since all 1,000 students have not been tested to obtain the result we do not know for sure, but the results can be used to estimate the error in sampling. This is basically the technique that political polls follow when it is reported that the vote is 45 percent ± 3. The plus or minus 3 is the estimate of error in sampling.

There are many types of probability sampling procedures. You will probably encounter four types in educational research: simple random, systematic, stratified, and cluster.

Simple Random Sampling   In simple random sampling every member of the population has an equal and independent chance of being selected for the sample. This method is often used with a small number in the population, for example, putting the names or numbers of all population members in a hat and drawing some out as the sample. If every member of the population can be assigned a different number, a table of random numbers can identify the population members that will make up the sample. This approach is not convenient if the population is large and not numbered. The most common way of selecting a random sample from a large population is by computer. There are computer programs that will assign numbers to each element in the population, generate the sample numbers randomly, and then print out the names of the people corresponding to the numbers.

Simple random sampling is illustrated in the following study of mothers' strategies for influencing their children's schooling.

Simple random sampling: Each member of the population has the same probability of being selected.

EXAMPLE: SIMPLE RANDOM SAMPLING

"We interviewed a sample of 41 mothers of eighth graders from one middle school. These mothers were randomly selected from a list of 129 mothers provided by the principal of the school." (Baker and Stevenson, 1986, p. 157)

Systematic Sampling   In systematic sampling every nth element is selected from a list of all elements in the population, beginning with a randomly selected element. Thus, if there is a need to select 100 subjects from a population of 50,000, every nth element would correspond to every 500th subject. The first element is selected randomly. In this example that would be some number between 1 and 500. Suppose 240 was randomly selected as a starting point. The first subject chosen for the sample would be the 240th name on a list, the next subject would be the 740th, then the 1,240th, and so on until 100 subjects were selected. Systematic sampling is virtually the same as simple random sampling. It is certainly much more convenient.

> **Systematic sampling:** Every nth member of the population is selected.

There is a possible weakness in systematic sampling if the list of cases in the population is arranged in a systematic pattern. For instance, if a list of fourth-graders in a school division is arranged by classroom and students in the classrooms are listed from high to low ability, there is a cyclical pattern in the list (referred to as periodicity). If every nth subject that is selected corresponds to the pattern, the sample would represent only a certain level of ability and would not be representative of the population. Alphabetical lists do not usually create periodicity and are suitable for choosing subjects systematically.

Stratified Sampling   A modification of either simple random or systematic sampling is first to divide the population into homogeneous subgroups and then select subjects from each subgroup, using simple random or systematic procedures, rather than the population as a whole. This is termed **stratified sampling**. The strata are the subgroups. Stratified sampling is used primarily for two reasons. First, as long as the subgroups are identified by a variable related to the dependent variable in the research (e.g., socioeconomic status in a study of achievement) and results in more homogeneous groups, the sample will be more representative of the population than if taken from the population as a whole. This result reduces error and means that a smaller sample can be chosen.

> **Stratified sampling:** Subjects are selected from strata or groups of the population.

Second, stratified sampling is used to ensure that an adequate number of subjects is selected from different subgroups. For example, if a researcher is studying beginning elementary school teachers and believes that there may be important differences between male and female teachers, using simple random or systematic sampling would probably not result in a sufficient number of male teachers to study the differences. It would be necessary in this situation first to stratify the population of teachers into male and female teachers and then to select subjects from each subgroup. The samples can be selected in one of two ways. A proportionate stratified sample is used when the number of subjects selected from each stratum is based on the percentage of subjects in the population that have the characteristic used to form the stratum. Thus, in the previous example, if 5 percent of the population of elementary teachers is male, 5 percent of the sample would also be male teachers. A second approach is to take the same number of subjects from each stratum, regardless of the percentage of subjects from each stratum in the population. This is referred to as disproportionate stratified sampling. It is used often because it ensures that a sufficient number of subjects will be selected from each stratum. For instance, if out of a population of 200 elementary teachers only 10 percent are male, a proportionate sample of 40 would include only 4 male teachers. To study male teachers it would be best to include all 20 male teachers in the population for the sample and randomly select 20 female teachers. When disproportionate sampling is used the results of each stratum need to be weighted to estimate values for the population as a whole.

In the following example disproportionate stratified sampling ensures that the same number of first- and third-graders are selected randomly.

EXAMPLE: STRATIFIED SAMPLING

"From a pool of all children who returned a parental permission form (more than 80% return rate) 24 first graders (10 girls, 14 boys; mean age, 6 years, 6 months), and 24 third graders (13 girls, 11 boys; mean age, 8 years, 8 months) were randomly selected." (Clements and Nastasi, 1988, p. 93)

Cluster Sampling   When it is impossible or impractical to sample individual elements from the population as a whole, usually when there is no exhaustive list of all the elements, cluster sampling is used. **Cluster sampling** involves the random selection of naturally occurring groups or areas and then the selection of individual elements from the chosen groups or areas. Examples of naturally occurring groups would be universities, schools, school divisions, classrooms, city blocks, and households. For example, if there is a need to survey a state for the television viewing habits of middle school students, it would be cumbersome and difficult to select children at random from the state population of all middle-schoolers. A clustering procedure could be employed by first listing all the school divisions in the state and then randomly selecting 30 school divisions from the list. One middle school could then be selected from each division, and students selected randomly from each school. This is a multistage clustering procedure. Although cluster sampling saves time and money, the results are less accurate than other random techniques.

Cluster sampling: Naturally occurring groups are selected.

Nonprobability Sampling

In many research designs it is either unfeasible or unnecessary to obtain a probability sample. In these situations a nonprobability sample is used. A **nonprobability sample** is one in which the probability of including population elements is unknown. Usually, not every element in the population has a chance of being selected. It is also quite common for the population to be the same as the sample, in which case there is no desire to generalize to a larger population. In fact you will find that much of the educational research reported in journals, especially experimental studies, uses a group of subjects without reference to a larger population.

Nonprobability sample: Probability of selection not known.

Convenience Sampling   A convenience sample is a group of subjects selected because of availability, for example, a university class of a professor conducting some research on college students, classrooms of teachers enrolled in a graduate class, schools of principals in a workshop, people who decide to go to the mall on Saturday, or people who respond to an advertisement for subjects. There is no precise way of generalizing from a convenience sample to a population. Also, the nature of the convenience sample may bias the results. For example, if the available sample for studying the impact of college is the group of alumni who return on alumni day, their responses would probably be quite different from those of all alumni. Similarly, research on effective teaching that depends on teachers in a particular geographic area, because they are available, may result in quite different findings than research done in other geographic areas.

Convenience sample: Nonprobability available sample.

EXAMPLES: CONVENIENCE SAMPLES

"Participants in the study were sixth grade students enrolled in four classes at a public school in a suburb north of Minneapolis, Minnesota. Of the total number, 65 students were boys and 56 were girls. From the pool of 121 subjects, 7 were not included in the final analysis for various reasons, leaving 114 subjects." (Carrier and Williams, 1988, pp. 291–292)

"Twelve volunteer third-grade teachers and their students participated in the study. The teachers were employed in 10 public schools located in three school districts in suburban areas of northern California." (Mitman, 1985, p. 151)

"The initial group of subjects in this study was composed of 42 undergraduate secondary education students majoring in a variety of disciplines. They were about to be placed in classrooms to student teach for their first semester. Thirty-five of these students also participated in the concluding part of the experiment at the end of the semester, following a 10-week student teaching experience." (Tiene and Buck, 1987, p. 262)

"The study was conducted in a school system of approximately 2,800 elementary school students attending 6 schools. All kindergarten and first grade teachers using intraclassroom ability grouping were asked to participate. Of 22 teachers invited to participate, 20 agreed and were subsequently observed." (Haskins, Walden and Ramey, 1983, pp. 867–868)

Although we need to be very wary of convenience samples, often this is the only type of sampling possible, and the primary purpose of the research may not be to generalize but to better understand relationships that may exist. Suppose a researcher is investigating the relationship between creativity and intelligence, and the only available sample is a single elementary school. The study is completed, and the results indicate a moderate relationship: Children who have higher intelligence tend to be more creative than children with lower intelligence. Because there was no probability sampling, should we ignore the findings or suggest that the results are not valid or credible? That decision seems overly harsh. It is more reasonable to interpret the results as valid for children similar to those studied. If the school serves a low socioeconomic area, the results will not be as useful as those from a school that serves all socioeconomic levels. The decision is not to dismiss the findings but to limit them to the type of subjects in the sample. As more and more research accumulates with different convenience samples, the overall credibility of the results is enhanced.

Although it is not common for a researcher to state explicitly that a convenience sample was used, it will be obvious from the subjects subsection of the article. If some type of probability sampling procedure other than convenience sampling was used it will be described. Thus, in the absence of such particulars you can assume that the sample was an available one. The following examples are typical.

Purposive Sampling   In **purposive sampling** (sometimes referred to as judgment or judgmental sampling) the researcher selects particular elements from the population that will be representative or informative about the topic. Based on the researcher's knowledge of the population, a judgment is made about which cases should be selected to provide the best information to address the purpose of the research. For example, in research on effective teaching it may be most informative to observe "expert" or "master" teachers rather than all teachers. To study effective schools it may be most informative to interview key personnel, such as the principal and teachers who have been in the school a number of years. The use of "selected precincts" for political polls is a type of purposive sampling.

Purposive sampling is not widely used in quantitative studies. In qualitative research, on the other hand, some type of purposive sampling is almost always used. Purposive sampling is illustrated by the following excerpts.

Purposive sampling: Selection of particularly informative or useful subjects.

Quota Sampling   Quota Sampling is used when the researcher is unable to take a probability sample but still wants a sample that is representative of the entire population. Different composite profiles of major groups in the population are identified, and then subjects are selected, nonrandomly, to represent each group. A type of quota sampling that is common in educational research is conducted to represent geographic areas or types of communities, such as urban, rural, and suburban. Typically, a state is divided into distinct geographic areas, and cases are selected to represent each area. As in availability and purposive sampling, there is a heavy reliance on the decisions of the researcher in selecting the sample, and appropriate caution should be used in interpreting the results.

Quota sampling: Nonrandom sampling representative of a target population.

EXAMPLES: PURPOSIVE SAMPLING

"Introductory psychology students (N = 210) volunteered to take the Dogmatism Scale (Form E) for experimental credit. From the upper and lower quartiles on the Dogmatism Scale, 44 high and 44 low dogmatic subjects were selected for the experiment." (Rickards and Slife, 1987, pp. 636–637) Notice also that this is a convenience sample.

"Four second-grade and two first-grade teachers from public schools in the San Francisco Bay Area participated in the study. All were women with at least 10 years of teaching experience at the elementary level. Teachers were recruited to include as wide a range of backgrounds and approaches in the teaching of mathematics as possible. Some were recommended by their principals as being strong mathematics teachers who had been involved in various inservice and curriculum development activities. Others agreed to participate in the study because they were interested but did not consider themselves to be particularly outstanding mathematics teachers." (Putnam, 1987, pp. 17–18)

"Six schools were selected from the 26 in the district. Selection was governed by the need to capture the variability of retention practices within the district. For example, two schools with high-retaining and three with low-retaining kindergartens were selected, along with one school that had a developmental kindergarten and a transition (between kindergarten and first grade) class." (Smith and Shepard, 1988, p. 311)

HOW SUBJECTS AND SAMPLING AFFECT RESEARCH

In reading and interpreting research you will need to be conscious of how the sampling procedures might have affected the results and how the characteristics of the subjects affect the usefulness and the generalizability of the results.

Knowledge of Sampling Procedures

To understand how sampling may affect research it is essential to know the characteristics of different sampling procedures. This knowledge will help you interpret the sample that is used. You should first be able to identify the sampling procedure and then evaluate its adequacy in addressing the research problem and in supporting the conclusions. It will be helpful to know the strengths

Table 4.1   STRENGTHS AND WEAKNESSES OF SAMPLING METHODS

Method of sampling	Strengths	Weaknesses
Probability		
Simple random	1. Usually representative of the population 2. Easy to analyze and interpret results 3. Easy to understand	1. Requires numbering each element in the population 2. Larger sampling error than in stratified sampling
Systematic	1. 1, 2, and 3 above 2. Simplicity of drawing sample	1. Periodicity in list of population elements
Proportionate stratified	1. 1, 2, and 3 of simple random 2. Allows subgroup comparisons 3. Usually more representative than simple random or systematic 4. Fewer subjects needed 5. Results represent population without weighting	1. Requires subgroup identification of each population element 2. Requires knowledge of the proportion of each subgroup in the population 3. May be costly and difficult to prepare lists of population elements in each subgroup
Disproportionate stratified	1. 1, 2, 3, and 4 of proportional stratified 2. Assures adequate numbers of elements in each subgroup	1. 1, 2, and 3 of proportional stratified 2. Requires proper weighting of subgroup to represent population 3. Less efficient for estimating population characteristics
Cluster	1. Low cost 2. Requires lists of elements 3. Efficient with large populations	1. Less accurate than simple random, systematic, or stratified 2. May be difficult to collect data from all elements in each cluster 3. Requires that each population element be assigned to only one cluster

(continued)

Table 4.1   (*continued*)

Method of sampling	Strengths	Weaknesses
Nonprobability		
Convenience	1. Less costly	1. Difficult to generalize to other subjects
	2. Less time-consuming	2. Less representative of an identified population
	3. Ease of administration	3. Results dependent on unique characteristics of the sample
	4. Usually assures high participation rate	
	5. Generalization possible to similar subjects	
Purposive	1. 1, 2, 3, 4, and 5 of convenience	1. 1, 2, and 3 of convenience
	2. Adds credibility to qualitative research	
	3. Assures receipt of needed information	
Quota	1. 1, 2, 3, 4, and 5 of convenience	1. 1, 2, and 3 of convenience
	2. More representative of population than convenience or purposive	2. Usually more time-consuming than convenience or purposive

and weaknesses of each sampling procedure, as summarized in Table 4.1.

Volunteer Samples

A continuing problem in educational research, as well as in most social science research, is the use of volunteers as subjects. It is well documented that volunteers differ from nonvolunteers in important ways. Volunteers tend to be better educated, higher socioeconomically, more intelligent, higher in need of social approval, more sociable, more unconventional, less authoritarian, and less conforming than nonvolunteers. Obviously, volunteer samples may respond differently than nonvolunteers because of these differences.

One way volunteers are used is in survey research. The researcher typically sends questionnaires to a sample of individuals and tabulates the responses of those who return them. Often the percentage of the sample returning the questionnaire will be 50 to 60 or even lower. In this circumstance the sample is said to be biased in that the results may not be representative of the population. Thus, the nature of the results depends on the types of persons who respond, and generalizability to the target population is compromised. The specific effect that a biased sample has on the results depends on the nature of the study. For example, a study of the relationship between educational level and occupational success would be likely to show only a small relationship if only those who are most successful respond. Without some subjects who are not successful in the sample, success cannot be accurately related to the level of education. If a survey of teachers is conducted to ascertain their general knowledge and reading and writing skills, the results would probably be higher than the true case because of the tendency of volunteers to be better educated.

Volunteers are commonly used in research because the availability of subjects is often limited by time and resources. There have been thousands of studies with teachers who volunteer their classes for research. Much research on school-age children requires written permission from parents, and this necessity can result in a biased sample. Suppose a researcher needed parents' permission to study their involvement in the education of their children. Chances are good that parents who are relatively involved would be most likely to agree to be in the study, affecting a description of the nature of parental involvement for all students.

Sample Size

An important consideration in judging the credibility of research is the size of the sample. In most studies there are restrictions that limit the number of subjects, although it is difficult to know when the sample is too small. Most researchers use general rules of thumb in their studies, such as having at least 30 subjects for correlational research, and at least 15 subjects in each group in an experiment. In surveys that sample a population, often a very small percentage of the population must be involved, for example, less than 5 or even 1 percent. Of course if the survey sample is too small, it is likely that the results obtained cannot characterize the population. Formal statistical techniques can be applied to determine the number of subjects needed, but in most educational research these techniques are not used.

In educational research a major consideration with sample size is concluding that a study with a relatively small sample that found no difference or no relationship is true. For example, suppose that you are studying the relationship between creativity and intelligence and, with a sample of 20 students, found that there was no relationship. Is it reasonable to conclude that in reality there is no relationship? Probably not, since a significant reason for not finding a relationship is because such a small sample was used. In addition to the small number of subjects, it is likely that there may not be many differences in either creativity or intelligence, and without such differences it is impossible to find that the two variables are related. That is, with a larger sample that has different creativity and intelligence scores, a relationship may exist. This problem, interpreting results that show no difference or relationship with small samples, is subtle but very important in educational research since so many studies have small samples. As we will see in Chapter 9, it is also possible to misinterpret what is reported as a "significant" difference or relationship with a very large sample. Also, a sample that is not properly drawn from the population is misleading, no matter what the size.

Subject Motivation

Sometimes subjects will be motivated to respond in certain ways. Clues for this phenomenon will be found in the description of how the subjects were selected. For example, if a researcher was interested in studying the effectiveness of computer simulations in teaching science, one approach to the problem would be to interview teachers who used computer simulations. The researcher might even want to select only those science teachers who had used the simulations more than two years. It is not hard to understand that the selected teachers, because they had been using the simulations, would be motivated to respond favorably to them. The response would be consistent with the teachers' decision to use simulations. Psychology students may be motivated to give inaccurate responses in studies conducted by their psychology professor if they do not like the professor, or they may respond more favorably if they want to help a professor they like.

Sampling Bias

In selecting a sample from a population there is always some degree of sampling error. This error is the discrepancy between the true value of a variable for the population and the value that is calculated from the sample, and it is expected and precisely estimated as part of sampling. A different type of error is due to **sampling bias,** a type of sampling error that is controlled or influenced by the researcher to result in misleading findings. Occasionally researchers will de-

Sampling bias: Sampling error caused by the researcher.

liberately skew the sampling. The most obvious deliberate bias is selecting only those subjects that will respond in a particular way to support a point or result. For instance, if a researcher is measuring the values of college students and wants to show that the students are concerned about helping others and being involved in community service, bias would result if the researcher deliberately selected students in education or social work and ignored majors that might not be so altruistically oriented. Selecting friends or colleagues may also result in a biased sample. An even more flagrant type of bias occurs when a researcher discards some subjects because they have not responded as planned or keeps adding subjects until the desired result is obtained. Sampling bias also occurs nondeliberately, often because of inadequate knowledge of what is required to obtain an unbiased sample and the motivation to "prove" a desired result or point of view. In qualitative studies the researcher needs to be particularly careful about possible unintended bias because the sampling changes during the study.

Bias can also result from selecting subjects from different populations and assigning them to different groups for an experiment or comparison. Suppose a researcher used graduate sociology students to receive a treatment in an experiment and graduate psychology students as a control group. Even if the samples were selected randomly from each population, differences in the populations, and consequently samples, in attitudes, values, knowledge, and other variables could explain why certain results were obtained.

CONSUMER TIPS
Criteria for Evaluating Subjects Sections of Reports and Sampling Procedures

1. **The subjects in the study should be clearly described, and the description should be specific and detailed.** Demographic characteristics, such as age, gender, socioeconomic status, ability, and grade level must be indicated, as well as any unique characteristics, for example, gifted students, students enrolled in a psychology class, or volunteers.

2. **The population should be clearly defined.** It is especially important to provide a specific definition of the population in studies using probability sampling. Vague descriptions, such as "retired workers" or "high-ability students" should be avoided. The characteristics of each stratum in a stratified sampling procedure should also be included.

3. **The method of sampling should be clearly described.** The

specific type of sampling procedure, such as simple random, stratified, cluster, or convenience, should be explicitly indicated in sufficient detail to enable other researchers to replicate the study.

4. The return rate should be indicated and analyzed. In studies that survey a population, the return rate of questionnaires should be indicated. If the return rate is less than 60 percent, the researcher should analyze the implications of excluding a significant portion of the population. This step is accomplished by comparing the nonrespondents to those who returned the questionnaires to determine if there are significant differences between the groups.

5. The selection of subjects should be free of bias. The procedures and criteria for selecting subjects should not result in systematic error. Bias is more likely when a researcher is "proving" something to be true, in convenience samples, and when volunteers are used as subjects.

6. Selection procedures should be appropriate for the problem being investigated. If the problem is to investigate science attitudes of middle school students, it would be inappropriate to use high school students as subjects. If the problem is to study the characteristics of effective teaching, the work of student teachers would probably not be very representative of effective teaching behaviors.

7. There should be an adequate number of subjects. If the sample is selected from a population, the sample size must be large enough to represent the population accurately. There must also be a sufficient number of subjects in each subgroup that is analyzed. Studies with small samples that report no differences or no relationships should be viewed with caution since a higher number or a better selection of subjects may result in meaningful differences or relationships. Studies that have a very large number of subjects may report "significant" differences or relationships that are of little practical utility.

8. Qualitative studies should have informative and knowledgeable subjects. Since the purpose of qualitative research is to understand a phenomenon in depth, it is important to select subjects that will provide the greatest and richest information. The researcher should indicate the criteria used to select subjects, the reasons why these particular individuals were selected, and the strategies used for selecting subjects during the study.

OUTLINE SUMMARY

1. Subject selection.
   A. Participants from whom data are gathered.
   B. Population.

(1) Group to whom results are generalized.

(2) Described by delimiting variables.

C. Sample.

2. Procedures for selecting subjects.

A. Probability sampling.

(1) Subjects selected from a larger population.

(2) Always some error in sampling.

(3) Simple random sampling.

a. Every member of the population has the same chance of being selected.

b. Every member of the population must be numbered.

(4) Systematic random sampling.

a. Subjects are selected without numbering each member of the population.

b. Periodicity may cause bias in the result.

(5) Stratified random sampling.

a. Divides population into groups before sample selection.

b. Often provides a more accurate sample.

c. Desirable for comparing subgroups.

d. Proportionate or disproportionate selection.

(6) Cluster sampling.

a. Naturally occurring groups of subjects are selected at random.

b. Usually less accurate.

B. Nonprobability sampling.

(1) Very common and over time results in generalizable conclusions.

(2) Convenience samples.

(3) Purposive samples.

(4) Quota sampling.

3. Subjects and sampling procedures affect research in several ways.

A. Volunteer subjects.

B. Sample size.

C. Subject motivation.

D. Sampling bias.

4. Criteria for evaluating subjects sections of reports and sampling.

A. Clearly defined subjects, population, and sampling design.

B. Adequate and/or analyzed return rate.

C. Selection should be free of bias.

D. Selection should be appropriate to the problem.

E. Sample size should be adequate.

F. Qualitative research should use the most knowledgeable and informative subjects.

STUDY QUESTIONS

1. What is a sample and a population?

2. Why is it important to define the population as specifically as possible?

3. What is the difference between probability and nonprobability sampling?

4. When should a researcher use stratified random sampling?

5. How is cluster sampling different from stratified sampling?

6. Why should readers of research be cautious of studies that use a convenience sample?

7. What are some strengths and weaknesses of various types of sampling?

8. How can volunteer subjects cause bias in a study?

9. Why is sample size an important consideration in research that fails to find a "significant" difference or relationship?

10. In what ways can sampling be biased?

11. Give an example of a study that used both stratified and systematic sampling.

12. What is the difference between a convenience and a purposive sample?

13. What criteria should be used in judging the adequacy of a subjects section in a report or sampling procedure?

Chapter
5

Foundations of Educational Measurement

In this chapter we will review basic principles of measurement used to judge the adequacy of instrumentation. In the next chapter we will review the strengths and weaknesses of different types of instruments.

INTRODUCTION TO MEASUREMENT

Definition of Measurement

Most researchers define measurement as the assigning of numbers to indicate different values of a variable; some may also use it to refer to qualitative data collection as well. **Measures** are specific techniques or instruments used for measurement and generally refer to quantitative devices. These are often tests and questionnaires that provide objective and quantifiable data.

Measures: Instruments and techniques.

Two related terms, evaluation and assessment, are sometimes used interchangeably with measurement. However these terms usually mean something different. For most researchers, **evaluation** refers to procedures to collect information and use the information to make decisions. In this sense evaluation goes beyond measurement. Principles of measurement and specific instruments are part of evaluation, but other characteristics of research, such as sampling, design, and related literature, are also used to make deci-

Evaluation: Decisions based on measurement.

sions. For example, school districts routinely decide which particular textbooks will be adopted, a decision that may involve an evaluation of each potential textbook. Suppose teachers are surveyed for their opinions about the textbooks, and an instrument is constructed to measure these opinions. This is measurement. The results of the survey are combined with other information, such as the cost of the textbooks, recommendations from a parent committee, and research on the effects of different modes of presenting information, to make decisions about the textbooks. The entire process is one of evaluation.

Evaluation is also used to compare performance with an objective or standard. In this sense student achievement is evaluated by comparison to national norms or locally set standards of achievement (e.g., the dropout rate will be less than 4 percent; the percentage of high school students taking foreign languages will rise to 40 percent; the mean level of achievement of sixth-graders will be above the national mean). Other definitions of evaluation focus on professional judgment or a process in which a judgment is made about something. Such judgments may or may not involve measurement.

Assessment is a term that is also used in a variety of ways. The shorter term, *assess,* is a synonym for measure. When researchers say they "assessed" something, they mean that they measured it. Sometimes *assessment* means "evaluation," and sometimes it refers to the more specific process of diagnosis of individual problems.

The Purpose of Measurement for Research

Measurement is an essential link in research. The information collected through measurement provides the basis for the results, conclusions, and significance of the research. Thus, if the measurement is not accurate and credible, the research is invalid. Good research must have sound measurement. Stated differently, research is only as good as the measurement on which it is based. Measurement is an essential component of quantitative research because it provides a standard format for recording observations, performance, or other responses of subjects and because it allows a quantitative summary of the results from many subjects.

The purpose of measurement is to provide information about the variables that are being studied. In an experiment, the dependent variable is measured. In correlational research each variable is measured. Thus there is a close relationship between the names and definitions of the variables being studied and the nature of their measurement. In practice, the variable is defined by how it is measured (operational definition), not by how it is labeled or defined by the researcher. This distinction is especially important for consumers of research who want to be able to use the results. For example, if you were reading research on improving students' critical thinking, you would find that there are many different ways to define and measure critical thinking. It would be important to read the instruments section of the research to determine the specific manner in which critical thinking was measured to see how well it matches the critical thinking you want to promote with your students. It would not be advisable to scan the results of various studies and employ the teaching methods that seem to be effective without examining the measures used to assess critical thinking.

Scales of Measurement

Measurement involves the use of numbers to represent a variable. The manner in which the numbers are used to describe something determines the amount of information that is communicated. A useful classification of this process is referred to as scales of measurement. Because the scales are arranged hierarchically on the basis of how much information is provided, from low to high, they are often called levels of measurement. The scales are important for research because they help determine the nature of the measurement needed to answer research questions and the statistical analyses of the numbers generated by the measures. The four scales of measurement used in research are nominal, ordinal, interval, and ratio.

Nominal Scales   The simplest scale of measurement is termed nominal, or classificatory. A **nominal scale** is one in which the researcher assigns different numbers to mutually exclusive categories. Mutually exclusive categories are those in which all observations assigned to the same category have a similar characteristic, and they differ on the basis of a specific characteristic from observations in other categories. Examples of nominal data in research are males = 1, females = 2; minority = 1, white = 2; transfer = 1; nontransfer = 2. The numbers are assigned arbitrarily, without any value or order being placed in the categories. Numbers are used only for convenience. In fact *nominal* means "to name," and the use of nominal scales is a way to assign numbers to names.

Nominal scale: Numbers assigned to categories.

In research the term *nominal* is also used to describe the nature of the data that are collected. Data are referred to as nominal if the researcher simply counts the number of instances, or frequency of observations, in each of two or more categories. For example, counting the number of male and female students; the number of fifth-, sixth-, and seventh-graders; the number of times a teacher used different types of reinforcement; and the number of tenured and untenured teachers voting yes or no to a proposal to abolish tenure are frequency counts in different categories.

Ordinal Scales   An **ordinal scale** is one in which the categories are rank-ordered. Each category can be compared to the others in terms of *less than* or *greater than*, but there is no indication in an ordinal scale of the magnitude. In other words, they are ordered categories, without knowing how much less or greater than one category is from the others. A good example of an ordinal scale is the ranking of debate teams on their performance. The results show who is best, next best, and so forth, but we do not know the difference between rankings, for instance, between first and second best. Ordinal scales are used extensively in educational research because many of the traits measured can be defined only in terms of order. Students are thought of as more mature, more serious, more ethical, more altruistic, more cooperative, more competitive, more creative, having a more positive self-concept, having greater ability, and so forth. Thus the resultant scores from the measurement can be interpreted to mean that one score is higher or lower than another, but the degree of difference between different scores is not known.

Ordinal scale: Numbers rank-ordered.

Interval Scales   An **interval scale** is ordinal and has equal intervals between numbers. The characteristic of equal intervals allows us to compare directly one score to another. For instance, if John scores 90 on a test with an interval scale, June scores 80, and Tim scores 70, we know that the distance between Tim and John is twice the distance between John and June or between June and Tim. We also know that the distance between the scores of 50 and 60 is equal to the distance between 80 and 90. Although there is significant debate among measurement specialists about whether test scores and questionnaire results are ordinal or interval, most standardized test results are treated as interval scale data.

Interval scale: Equal intervals between numbers.

Ratio Scales   A **ratio scale** is one in which ratios can be used in comparing and interpreting the scores. This use is possible if the trait being measured has a true zero point; that is, none of the trait is present. Weight is an example of ratio data because there is a true value for zero, which corresponds to no weight at all, and there are equal intervals between different weights. We can say, for instance, that Fred, who weighs 150 pounds, is twice as heavy as

Ratio scale: Numbers expressed as ratios.

Mary, who weighs 75 pounds. Few, if any, measures in educational research are ratio in nature.

FUNDAMENTAL PRINCIPLES OF DESCRIPTIVE STATISTICS FOR UNDERSTANDING MEASUREMENT

Since measurement involves the manipulation of numbers, basic principles of descriptive statistics must be introduced now to understand subsequent principles of measurement presented in this chapter and in Chapter 6. This will be a conceptual, nontechnical introduction with a minimum of calculations.

Statistics are mathematical procedures used to summarize and analyze data. In quantitative studies, the data are collected by the researchers, who apply statistical techniques to better understand the meaning of the numbers. In this sense statistical procedures are applied after data collection to provide the results of the study. **Descriptive statistics** transform a set of numbers into indexes that summarize the characteristics of a sample. Common descriptive statistics include the frequency of scores, percentages, arithmetic mean, and standard deviation. These statistics communicate characteristics of the data as a whole and estimate the characteristics of the population. (The characteristics of a population are called *parameters* rather than statistics.)

Descriptive statistics also represent principles and are the basis for a vocabulary used in measurement. That is, a *distribution* can be a statistical result from a study, and it can also describe concepts related to measurement; for example, the distribution of scores from a norm-referenced test is normal and the distribution of scores from a criterion-referenced test is skewed. The emphasis in this chapter is on understanding the principles of descriptive statistics needed for measurement. Statistics that present results are summarized in Chapter 9.

> **Statistics:** Procedures that summarize and analyze quantitative data.

> **Descriptive statistics:** Summarizes a set of numbers.

Frequency Distributions

Suppose a researcher is interested in studying critical thinking with a class of eighth-graders. The researcher administers an instrument to measure critical thinking to 36 students and obtains the following scores, one for each student:

```
15 24 28 25 18 24 27 16 20 22 23 18
22 28 19 16 22 26 15 26 24 21 19 27
16 23 26 25 25 18 27 17 20 19 25 23
```

In this form it is difficult to understand how the students performed as a group or to have some idea of the number of students who obtained different scores. The initial procedure for understanding the results would be the creation of a **frequency distribution,** which organizes ungrouped data by indicating the number of times (frequency) each score was obtained. The scores are typically rank-ordered from highest to lowest, and the frequency of each score is indicated. The simplest type of frequency distribution is a frequency table, in which the values of the scores and the frequencies are listed vertically. Table 5.1 shows a frequency table for the set of critical thinking scores above (f means frequency). Another way to present the frequencies is to construct a two-dimensional graph, in which the possible frequencies are indicated on the vertical dimension and the possible scores are indicated on the horizontal dimension. The number of students who obtained each score is then indicated in the graph. In this graphic form the data can be presented as a frequency polygon or a histogram. A **frequency polygon,** illustrated in Figure 5.1 for the critical thinking scores, connects the observed frequencies with a line to show a picture of the distribution. A histogram is a type of bar graph, in which lines or bars represent each score or set of scores rather than lines connecting the frequencies of each score.

The shape of a distribution reveals some important characteristics of the scores: the most and least frequently occurring scores, whether the scores are bunched together or spread out, scores that

Frequency distribution: Indicates how often each score is obtained.

Frequency polygon: Graphic frequency distribution.

Table 5.1 EXAMPLE OF A FREQUENCY TABLE

Score	f
28	2
27	3
26	3
25	4
24	3
23	3
22	3
21	1
20	2
19	3
18	3
17	1
16	3
15	2

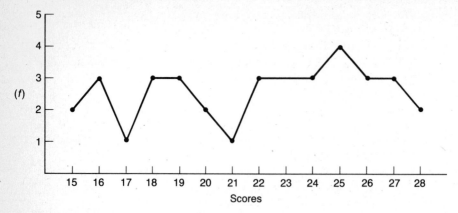

Figure 5.1 Example of a frequency polygon.

may be isolated from the others, and the general shape of the distribution. Figure 5.2 illustrates some common general shapes. The normal curve is perhaps most widely used. It is symmetrical and shaped like a cross section of a bell. It tells us that the majority of scores tend to cluster around the middle, with the same number of scores above and below the middle point. Because the normal curve characterizes many naturally occurring phenomena and has standard properties, it is used extensively for research and statistical procedures. In a flat, or rectangular curve, the scores are widely spread out from the middle. Distributions that concentrate scores at the high or low end of the distribution are called skewed. In a **positively skewed** distribution the scores are concentrated at the low end of the distribution; in a **negatively skewed** distribution the majority of the scores are at the high end of the distribution. A positively skewed distribution would result in a study of teachers' salaries if most of the salaries were low and a few of the salaries were high. Negatively skewed distributions are common in mastery testing, where typically most of the students score high and a few students score low.

Positively skewed: Large number of low scores; few very high scores.

Negatively skewed: Large number of high scores; few very low scores.

Measures of Central Tendency

Although it is very useful to know the pattern of the scores as indicated by the frequency distribution, it is also important to be able to use a single score to characterize the set of scores. Measures of central tendency provide statistics that indicate the average or typical score in the distribution. There are three measures of central tendency: mode, median, and mean.

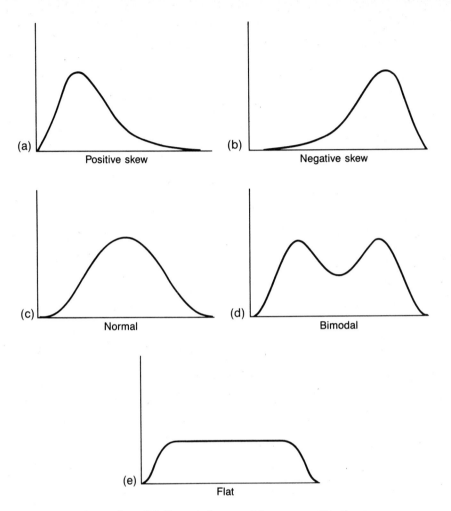

Figure 5.2 Examples of different shapes of frequency distributions.

Mode   The **mode** is simply the score in the distribution that occurs most frequently. It is a crude index of central tendency and is not used very much in research. Sometimes distributions have more than one most frequent score. Such distributions are bimodal, tri-modal, or multimodal. These terms describe a distribution that may technically have only one mode; for example, two scores in different parts of the distribution clearly occur more frequently than the rest in a bimodal distribution. There is no mode in distributions in which each score occurs the same number of times.

Mode: Score that occurs most frequently.

Median   The **median** is the middle score of the distribution, the point that divides a rank-ordered distribution into halves containing an equal number of scores. Thus 50 percent of the scores lie below the median and 50 percent lie above the median. The median is unaffected by the values of the scores. This characteristic is an advantage when the distribution contains atypically large or small scores, such as measures of "average" income and the "average" cost of a new house. The median is symbolized by *Mdn* or *M*.

Median: Score in the middle of the distribution.

Mean   The **mean** is the arithmetic average of all the scores in the distribution. It is calculated by summing all the scores in the distribution and then dividing this sum by the number of scores. For example, if a distribution contains the scores 5, 7, 8, 10, 10, 12, 14, 15, 15, 17, the mean would be 11.3 (5 + 7 + 8 + 10 + 10 + 12 + 14 + 15 + 15 + 17 = 113; 113/10 = 11.3). In the distribution of critical thinking scores in Table 5.1, the mean is 21.92 (789/36). The mean is used extensively in research, usually symbolized by $\overline{X}$ or *M* for the sample mean and μ for the mean of the population. The mean may be misleading as a typical score in distributions that contain extremely high or low scores because it is pulled toward the extreme scores. Thus, in a positively skewed distribution, like personal income, the mean income is higher than the most typical income because some very high incomes are used in the calculation. In this case the median income is more typical.

Mean: Arithmetic average of all scores.

Measures of Variability

Although a measure of central tendency is an excellent statistic of the most typical score in a distribution, to obtain a full description of the scores we also need to know something about how they tend to cluster around the mean or median. Measures of variability show how spread out the distribution of scores is from the mean, or how much dispersion or scatter exists in the distribution. If there is a large degree of dispersion, that is, if the scores are very dissimilar, we say the distribution has a large or high variability, or ariance. If the scores are very similar, there is a small degree of dispersion and a small variance.

The need for a measure of dispersion to describe a distribution is illustrated by comparing the different types of distributions in Figure 5.2. Distributions A, B, and C would have the same mean but represent quite different distributions. It is necessary to add a measure of variability to the mean to provide a more complete description. We will discuss two measures of variability, the range and the standard deviation, which provide more specific statistics than such general terms as *small, large, great,* or *little*.

Range   The **range** is simply the numerical difference between the highest and lowest scores in the distribution. It is calculated by subtracting the lowest score from the highest score. The range is a crude measure of dispersion because it is based on only two scores in the distribution, and it does not tell us anything about the degree of cluster. The range is particularly misleading in highly skewed distributions.

Range: Difference between the highest and lowest scores.

Standard Deviation   The measure of variability used most often in research is the **standard deviation,** a statistic that indicates the average distance of the scores from the mean of the distribution. It tells us, in other words, the "average" variability of the scores. It is calculated by first figuring the distance of each score from the mean. These are the deviation scores, which tell us how much each score deviates, or differs, from the mean. Then the deviation scores are averaged to determine a number that is called the standard deviation. In one sense, then, the standard deviation can be thought of as the average deviation.

Standard deviation: Average distance of the scores from the mean.

For any set of scores the standard deviation will be unique to the distribution of the scores. Thus, the standard deviation of one distribution may be .72; for another distribution, 16; and for yet another, 35. Once the standard deviation is computed, it is reported by indicating that 1 standard deviation equals a number; for example, 1 SD = 12.7, or 1 SD = 3.25 (Two other symbols are also used for standard deviation: s, which indicates the sample standard deviation, and the lowercase Greek letter sigma, σ, which indicates the population standard deviation).

The Standard deviation is particularly useful because of its relationship to the normal distribution. In a normal distribution, a specific percentage of scores falls within each standard deviation from the mean. For example, if the mean of a distribution is 40 and the standard deviation is 10, we know that about 34 percent of the scores of the distribution fall between 40 and 50. Similarly, we know that about 34 percent of the scores fall between 30 and 40. Thus, in normal distributions, regardless of the values of the scores, we know that about 68 percent of the scores fall between -1 and $+1$ SD (see Figure 5.3). Furthermore, we know that about 14 percent of the scores fall between $+1$ and $+2$ SD and between -1 and -2 SD, and that about 2 percent of the scores fall between $+2$ and $+3$ SD and between -2 and -3 SD. These properties of the normal curve and standard deviation, illustrated in Figure 5.3, allow researchers to compare distributions by knowing the standard deviations. Two distributions may have similar means, but if one has a standard deviation of 36 and the other 8, the former is far more variable.

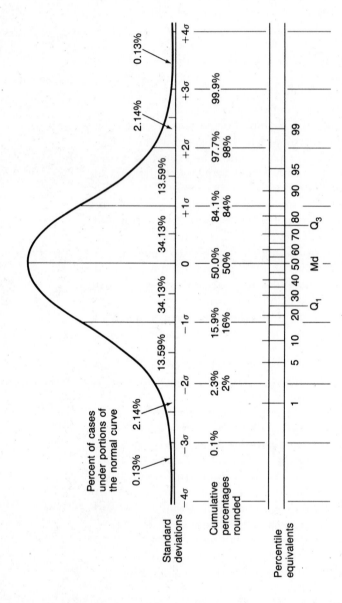

Figure 5.3 Normal probability curve. (*Source:* Harold G. Seashore (1980). Methods of expressing test scores, in *Test service notebook 148*. New York: The Psychological Corporation.)

Standard deviation is related to another important term in measurement, percentile rank. The **percentile rank** indicates the percentage of scores that is at or below a particular score. For example, if 17 is at the 64th percentile, 64 percent of the scores in the distribution are the same or lower than 17. In a normal distribution, a score at $+1\ SD$ is at the 84th percentile. In other words, 84 percent of the scores in a normal distribution are at or below $+1\ SD$. Similarly, $-1\ SD$ is at the 16th percentile, $+2\ SD$ is at the 98th percentile, and $-2\ SD$ is at the 2nd percentile (percentiles for the normal curve are indicated as cumulative percentages in Figure 5.3).

Percentile rank: Percentage of scores at or below a specified score.

Correlation

Frequency distributions, measures of central tendency, and measures of variability are used to summarize characteristics of one variable. However, in many instances it is useful to know the degree to which the scores of two or more variables are related. The most common approach to describing a relationship statistically is through correlation. A **correlation** is a measure of the relationship between two variables. A relationship means that the values of the variables vary together, that is, that the value of one variable can be predicted by knowing the value of the other variable. For example, we would expect that there is a relationship between age and weight, that by knowing a person's age we can predict, in general, the person's weight. Thus, we can predict that most ten-year-olds weigh more than most three-year-olds. In this case we have a **positive correlation,** in which an increase in one variable is accompanied by an increase in the other variable. This is also called a direct relationship. A positive correlation is illustrated graphically in the form of a scatterplot for age and weight in Figure 5.4. The values of each variable are rank-ordered, and the intersections of the two scores for each subject are plotted in the graph. Scatterplots are useful in identifying scores that lie outside the overall pattern, such as point I in Figure 5.4, and indicate whether the relationship is linear or curvilinear (see Figure 5.5). A positive correlation is indicated numerically by the correlation coefficient.

Correlation: Measure of relationship between two or more quantitative variables.

Positive correlation: Increases in one variable accompanied by increases in the other variable.

A **correlation coefficient** is a number between -1 and $+1$ that indicates the direction and strength of the relationship between two variables. The correlation coefficient is calculated by a formula and is usually reported as $r = .45$, $r = -.78$, $r = .03$, and so on. A positive correlation coefficient will have a positive value; for example, $r = .17$ or $r = .69$. The strength, or magnitude, of the relationship is the degree to which the variables are related. For a

Correlation coefficient: Number between -1 and $+1$ that indicates the direction and strength of the relationship.

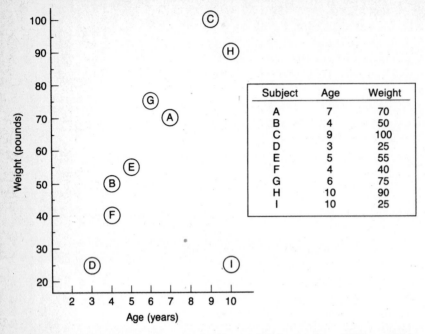

Subject	Age	Weight
A	7	70
B	4	50
C	9	100
D	3	25
E	5	55
F	4	40
G	6	75
H	10	90
I	10	25

Figure 5.4 Scatterplot. (*Source:* McMillan and Schumacher, 1989, p. 231.)

positive correlation the strength increases as the number increases. Hence a correlation of .85 is stronger than a correlation of .53, which is stronger than .37. In general, correlations between .10 and .30 are referred to as small or low positive relationships, .40 to 60 are moderate positive relationships, and .70 and above are high positive relationships.

A **negative correlation** indicates that as one variable increases, the other variable decreases. This is also referred to as an inverse relationship. Examples of negative correlations include the relationship between absenteeism and achievement and between amount of practice and number of errors in tennis. A negative correlation coefficient always has a negative sign ($-$). The strength of a negative relationship increases as the absolute value of the correlation increases. Thus, a correlation of $-.75$ is a stronger relationship than $-.52$. In other words, the strength of any relationship is independent of its direction. A correlation of $-.63$ indicates a stronger relationship than .35. Correlations between $-.10$ and $-.30$ are considered small; between $-.40$ and $-.60$, moderate; and between $-.70$ and -1.0, high. Correlations between $-.10$ and .10 generally indicate no relationship.

Negative correlation:
Increases in one variable accompanied by decreases in the other variable.

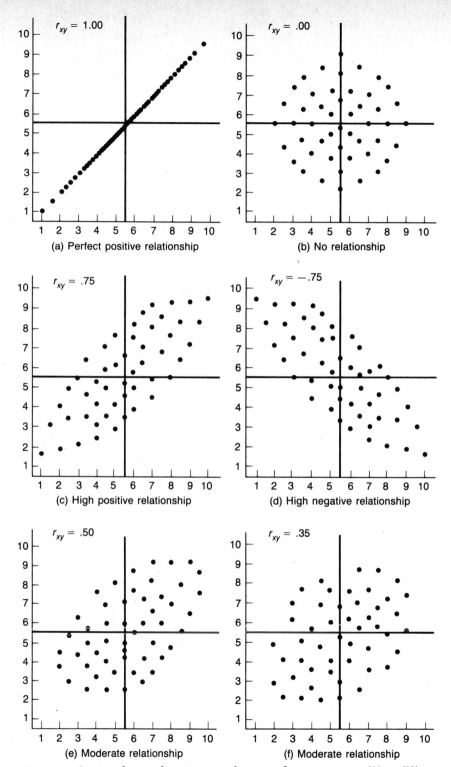

Figure 5.5 Scatterplots indicating correlations of various sizes ($N = 50$). (*Source:* W. A. Mehrens and I. J. Lehmann (1987). *Using standardized tests in education*, 4th edition, White Plains, NY: Longman, p. 49.)

VALIDITY OF EDUCATIONAL MEASURES

It has been noted that the credibility of research depends on quality measurement. If the measurement is not sound, the results are not useful. In this section we will discuss the first of two technical characteristics of measures used to judge overall quality and appropriateness—validity. The second important characteristic, reliability, will be reviewed in the next section.

Definition of Validity

Until recently, validity was defined as the degree to which an instrument measures what it says it measures or purports to measure. The emphasis was on judging the extent to which a test or questionnaire was valid. In 1985, however, measurement specialists from around the country agreed to a new, somewhat different definition. This definition emphasizes the use of test results rather than the test itself: **Validity** "refers to the appropriateness, meaningfulness, and usefulness of the specific inferences made from test scores. . . . The inferences regarding specific uses of a test are validated, not the test itself" (*Standards for Educational and Psychological Testing*, 1985, p. 9).

Validity: The extent to which inferences are appropriate and meaningful.

In other words, validity is a judgment of the appropriateness of a measure for the specific inferences or decisions that result from the scores generated by the measure. It is the inference that is valid or invalid, not the measure, because the same instrument can be valid in one circumstance or for one use and invalid for another. For example, tests of beginning teacher competency, such as the National Teacher Examinations, may be valid for judging how much a prospective teacher knows and understands about classroom management, child development, learning, motivation, and curriculum, but it may be invalid as a predictor of teaching effectiveness. Similarly, most standardized achievement tests are not valid for evaluating the effectiveness of a specific curriculum in a specific school because the test was constructed to measure a broad range of curricula, not a specific one. Standardized tests are appropriate for comparing general achievement with the achievement of others.

Types of Evidence for Judging Validity

Validity is established by presenting evidence that the inferences are appropriate. Although it is best for researchers to have several different types of evidence to be sure the inferences, which are the results of the research, are valid, there is great variation in what is reported in articles. There are three categories of evidence: content-related, criterion-related, and construct-related. You may recognize these terms as previously referring to types of validity. Each category represents a different type of evidence, and under ideal conditions the type of evidence used is consistent with the use of the results.

Content-Related Evidence   In general, **content-related evidence** demonstrates the extent to which the sample of items or questions in the instrument is representative of some appropriate universe or domain of content. This type of evidence is usually accumulated by having experts examine the contents of the instrument and indicate the degree to which they measure predetermined criteria or objectives. Experts are also used to judge the relative criticality, or importance, of various parts of the instrument. For example, to gather content-related evidence for a test of knowledge for prospective teachers, it is necessary to have experts examine the items and judge their representativeness (e.g., is a question about Piaget representative of what needs to be known about child development) and whether the percentage of the test devoted to different topics is appropriate (e.g., 20 percent of the test is on classroom management, but maybe it should be 40 percent). Content-related evidence is essential for achievement tests. Also, the domain or universe that is represented should be appropriate to the intended use of the results.

> **Content-related evidence:**
> Representativeness of larger domain.

Unfortunately, content-related evidence for validity is often not reported in research articles, usually because there is no systematic effort to obtain content-related evidence for locally devised instruments; when standardized instruments are used the reader must refer to previous research, reviews of the instrument, or technical manuals.

Criterion-Related Evidence   **Criterion-related evidence** pertains to the extent to which the test scores or other measures are related to other, independent measures. The independent measure is referred to as the criterion. For example, to provide criterion-related evidence for validity in establishing a new measure of intelligence, scores from the newly developed test could be correlated to scores from established intelligence tests like the Stanford-Binet or Wechsler Scales.

> **Criterion-related evidence:**
> Correlation with other measures or criteria.

Two approaches are used to obtain criterion-related evidence: predictive and concurrent. With predictive evidence, the criterion is measured at a time in the future, after the instrument has been administered. The evidence pertains to how well the earlier measure can predict the criterion behavior or performance. For instance, in gathering evidence on a new measure to select applicants for leadership positions, the scores on the instrument would be correlated with future leadership behavior. If persons who scored low on the test turned out to be poor leaders and those who scored high were good leaders, predictive criterion-related evidence would be obtained. With concurrent evidence, the instrument and the criterion are given at about the same time. Criterion-related evidence is often reported in research by indicating that a measure correlates with criteria that assess the same thing. For example, in a recent study on student prosocial behavior in the classroom, the researchers reported agreement between observers' and teachers' perceptions of prosocial behaviors.

EXAMPLE: CONCURRENT CRITERION-RELATED EVIDENCE FOR VALIDITY

"The teacher questionnaire measure of student cooperation showed a significant positive correlation . . . with the observation measure of Student Supportive and Friendly Behavior. . . . The questionnaire measure of student disruptiveness correlated negatively with observed Support and Friendly Behavior . . . Student Harmony . . . and Spontaneous Prosocial Behavior." (Solomon, Watson, Delucchi, Schaps, and Battistich, 1988, p. 536)

Construct-Related Evidence   Construct-related evidence demonstrates the degree to which a psychological construct can be inferred from the measure. Psychological constructs are characteristics that are not directly observable, such as attitudes, intelligence, motivation, self-concept, and creativity. They are theoretical constructions about traits and dispositions that affect behavior. Construct-related evidence is difficult to gather. Some of it is obtained by relating several measures of similar but different constructs, and some evidence is theoretical and logical rather than empirical. Often the extent of the construct-related evidence is expressed as a clear definition. Sometimes construct-related evidence is shown when the results are consistent with theory.

In a study on self-concept the authors refer to construct-related evidence by summarizing several points.

Construct-related evidence: Inference of a psychological construct.

EXAMPLE: CONSTRUCT-RELATED EVIDENCE FOR VALIDITY

"Factor analyses [a statistical procedure] have consistently identified the factors each is designed to measure ... whereas correlations among the factors are modest (median *rs* generally .2 or less) ... self-concept factors are significantly correlated with self-concepts in matching areas as inferred by teachers and significant others ... self-concepts in academic areas are substantially correlated with academic achievement, whereas nonacademic facets of self-concept are not." (Marsh, Smith, Marsh, and Owens, 1988, p 247)

Effect of Validity on Research

Validity must be established in the measurement of variables if the results of research are to have any value. Since validity implies proper use of the information that is gathered through measurement, it is necessary for both the investigators and consumers of the research to judge the degree of validity that is present, based on available evidence. In this sense, validity is a matter of degree and is not an all-or-none proposition. The investigators need to show that for the specific inferences they made in their study, there is evidence that validity exists. Consumers, however, may have their own uses in mind, and therefore need to base their own judgments on how they intend to use the results.

Does this statement suggest that validity must be established for each research situation and possible use? Such a requirement would add a considerable amount of data collection and analysis to each study, and is therefore impractical. In practice, it is necessary to generalize from other studies and research that interpretation and use are valid. This is one reason why already established instruments, for which some evidence on validity has probably accumulated, usually provide more credible measurement. Some researchers mistakenly believe, however, that because an instrument is established, it is "valid." Locally devised instruments, with no history of use or reviews by others, need to be evaluated with more care. Typically, when researchers use new instruments, greater attention is paid to gathering evidence for validity, and this evidence is reported as part of the research. You should be especially wary of research in which new instruments are used and evidence for validity is not presented. If an instrument has specific procedures for administration—for example, qualifications of the person who

administers it, directions, and time frame—the results are valid only
if these procedures have been followed. For instance, some instruments are appropriate for certain ages, and use with other ages
would be invalid.

Validity should be established before the data analyzed in the
research are collected. This is a major reason for a pilot test of the
instrument and procedures for administering it. The evidence
should be consistent with the use of the results. For example, if
you will use the results to determine which students have mastered
a body of knowledge, content-related evidence is necessary. If you
are examining a theory related to the development of cognitive
style, construct-related evidence is needed. Remember that your
use may be different than that of the researcher.

Although validity is a key concept in research, you will find a
great amount of variability in the amount of information found in
articles and research reports. It is not uncommon for there to be no
mention of validity. However, the most credible and usable research is conducted by persons who understand the importance of
validity, and address it.

RELIABILITY OF EDUCATIONAL MEASURES

An essential concept in understanding research is that what is measured is never a perfect indication of the trait, skill, knowledge,
attitude, or whatever is being assessed. There is always error in
measurement, and this error must be taken into consideration. It is
not a question of whether or not error exists, only what type and
how much. **Reliability** is the extent to which measures are free from
error. If a measure has high reliability, it has relatively little error,
and if it has low reliability, there is a great amount of error. Error
is measured by how consistent a person's score will be from one
occasion to the next.

Reliability: Consistency of scores.

Many factors contribute to the imperfect nature of measurement. There may be ambiguous questions or the students may not
be trying hard, may be fatigued or even sick, may be unfamiliar
with the types of questions asked, or may simply guess incorrectly
on most items. Sources of measurement error are listed in Table
5.2. Whatever the reasons, the student will perform somewhat differently on one occasion than on another. In other words, individuals will perform inconsistently to some degree from one occasion
to another. The researcher needs to indicate in specific, quantifiable terms the degree of error that exists.

Table 5.2   SOURCES OF MEASUREMENT ERROR

Sources associated with test construction and administration	Sources associated with the subject
Observer differences	Test anxiety
Changes in scoring	Reactions to specific items
Changes in directions	Illness
Interrupted testing session	Motivation
Race of test administrator	Mood
When the test is taken	Fatigue
Sampling of items	Luck
Ambiguity in wording	Attitudes
Misunderstood directions	Test-taking skills (test wiseness)
Effect of heat, lighting, ventilation of room	Reading ability

Source: Adapted from McMillan and Schumacher, 1989.

Types of Reliability

The actual amount of error in measurement is determined empirically through several types of procedures. As in validity, different types of evidence are used to indicate the error. These are called estimates of reliability. Each estimate measures certain kinds of errors. The estimates are reported in the form of a reliability coefficient, which is a correlation statistic that ranges between .00 and .99. If the correlation coefficient is high, say .78 or .85, the reliability is said to be high or good. Correlation coefficients below .60 generally indicate inadequate or at least weak reliability. We will consider five specific estimates of reliability: stability, equivalence, equivalence and stability, internal consistency, and agreement.

Stability   A **stability** estimate of reliability is obtained by administering one measure to one group of persons, waiting a specified period of time, and then readministering the same instrument to the same group of persons. The correlation of the two sets of scores is then calculated. This type of estimate is also called test-retest reliability. What is being measured is the consistency over time of the subjects' performance. If the trait or skill that is being measured changes between the first and second administration, the correlation, and the reliability, will be low. Consequently, stability estimates should not be used with unstable traits such as mood, and when it is used, any changes that may have occurred between the administrations should be noted. The value of the correlation will

Stability: Same instrument given twice.

also vary with the length of time between administrations. Other things being equal, a longer time interval will result in a lower correlation. It is therefore best to report the time interval with the correlation coefficient. On the other hand, if the interval is too short, subjects may remember their answers and simply reproduce them, making the reliability higher than it should be.

Stability estimates are rarely used with psychological measures because many of these instruments are reactive; persons taking them may change simply by answering the questions the first time. They are used for many aptitude tests, tests in the psychomotor domain, and some achievement tests. Stability estimates are written in a straightforward manner so that they are easy to identify.

EXAMPLE: STABILITY ESTIMATE OF RELIABILITY

"A sample of 73 students . . . was given the test twice 3 weeks apart without any intervention. The test-retest reliability coefficient was .79 for each grade level." (Ben-Chaim, Lappan, and Houang, 1988, p. 57)

Equivalence   A measure of **equivalence** is obtained by administering two forms of the same test to one group of persons, usually on the same day, and then correlating the scores from the two administrations. Each form of the test should be equivalent in content, mean, and standard deviation, although the specific questions would be different. This type of reliability estimate is often used in research on achievement when both a pretest, given before a treatment, and a posttest, given after a treatment, are administered to show how much the achievement of the subjects changed. Rather than giving the same test twice, the researcher gives alternate but equal tests. However, it may be difficult and time-consuming to develop two forms of a test.

Equivalence: Correlation of two forms of the same test.

Equivalence and Stability   An equivalence and stability estimate is obtained by administering to the same group of persons one form of an instrument and then a second form after a time interval. This method combines equivalence (alternate forms) with stability (time interval). Although this is the most stringent type of reliability estimate, it is not often employed. It is especially useful when researchers are concerned with long-range prediction (the strength of stability) and need to generalize to a large domain of knowledge or aptitude (the strength of equivalence).

Equivalence and stability: Two forms given at different times.

Internal Consistency   Internal consistency, the most widely used estimate of reliability, indicates the degree of homogeneity among the items in an instrument. Unlike the other estimates, only one form of an instrument is given once to one group of persons. This format results in one set of data, from which special computational formulas are applied to calculate correlations. There are three common types of internal consistency estimates: split-half, Kuder-Richardson, and Cronbach alpha. In split-half reliability the items in a test are divided into equal halves, and the scores of each person on the two halves are correlated for the reliability coefficient. The Kuder-Richardson method is used in tests for which there is a right and wrong answer to each item. It avoids problems of the split-half technique, such as knowing how to divide the test into equal halves, by calculating the average of all the correlations that could be obtained from all possible split-half estimates. This method is usually indicated as KR 20 or KR 21. The Cronbach alpha method is similar to the KR 20 but is used with instruments in which there is no right or wrong answer to each item. It is generally the most appropriate type of reliability for attitude instruments and other measures that contain a range of possible answers for each item.

Internal consistency is used when the purpose of an instrument is to measure a single trait. To allow calculation of the correlation, several items must measure the same thing. Thus in some instruments you may have taken, it seems as if the same questions are being asked over and over. To have internal consistency, a general rule of thumb is that there must be at least five questions about the same thing. In instruments in which there are subscales or subtests, a separate measure of internal consistency should be reported for each subscale. Of all the estimates, internal consistency is easiest to obtain and usually gives the highest reliability.

The accepted convention in reporting internal consistency is simply to state the type of method used and the correlation.

Internal consistency:
Correlation of items measuring the same trait.

EXAMPLES: INTERNAL CONSISTENCY ESTIMATES OF RELIABILITY

"The Cronbach's reliability coefficients for each group tested by sex and grade ranged from .72 to .86 on the pretest and from .82 to .88 on the posttest." (Ben-Chaim, Lappan, and Houang, 1988, p. 57)

"Internal consistency reliability (coefficient alpha) of this measure is .84 based on a sample of 42 students." (Woodward, Carnine, and Gersten, 1988, p. 78)

Agreement   There are three situations in which the traditional estimates of reliability are not appropriate. For these situations there is usually some type of coefficient of agreement, expressed as either a correlation or as a percentage of agreement. The first situation concerns establishing the reliability of observational measures. The usual procedure is to assess the extent to which different raters agree on what they observe. That is, when two or more raters independently observe the same behavior, will they record it in the same way? If they do, there is consistency in the measurement. If they record something different, however, there is low reliability. Typically, raters are trained until they reach a desired level of reliability before they observe in research. In a study on cooperative problem solving, the author uses both correlations and percentage of agreement to report interrater reliability.

EXAMPLE: INTERRATER RELIABILITY

"The pre- and posttests were marked by the field test teachers, following a training session that brought the teachers to an average interrater agreement between teachers of .88 . . . if the interrater agreement between teacher and trained marker was below 80%, the entire class was recoded . . . the average interrater agreement between markers was .97." (Ross, 1988, p. 580)

The second situation involves an insufficient number of items on an instrument measuring a single trait to compute an internal consistency estimate. In this circumstance, the researcher can use a method similar to stability by giving the instrument to the same group of persons twice. If there are only a few persons, say 15 to 20, the researcher can compute the percentage of responses that are the same rather than a correlation coefficient. This alternative is common in studies in which a new instrument has been developed and there has not been an opportunity to use a large number of persons in a pilot test.

Third, many achievement tests result in a skewed distribution of scores (e.g., criterion-referenced tests, discussed in the next chapter). With highly skewed distributions it is difficult to obtain a high correlation, and thus, most estimates of reliability would be low. With these types of tests a percentage of agreement is often used to show the number of persons who would be classified in the same way on a second test as they were on the first. Generally it is the consistency of the decision that would be made as a result of the

test rather than the scores themselves that is used to estimate reliability.

Effect of Reliability on Research

As with validity, the reliability of an instrument should be established before the research is undertaken, and the type of reliability
should be consistent with the use of the results. If you will use the
results for prediction or selection into special programs, stability
estimates of reliability are necessary. If you are interested in programs to change attitudes or values, internal consistency estimates
are needed. Reliability should also be established with individuals
who are similar to the subjects in the research. If previous studies
report good reliability with middle school students and you intend
to use the results with elementary school students, the reliability
may not be adequate. More commonly, reliability is reported with
the students used in the study. Failure to report reliability would
be cause to interpret the results with caution.

You will read some research in which reliability is not addressed, yet the results of the research show what are called "significant differences." This is an interesting situation in research
because it is more difficult to find differences between groups with
instruments that have low reliability. It is as if the differences were
observed despite what may have been low reliability. Of course it
is possible that the measurement was reliable, even though no reliability estimates were reported. This situation is likely to occur
in research in which the subjects are responding to questions so
straightforward and simple that reliability is "assumed." For example, in studies of students' perceptions of success or failure following performance on a test, the subjects are often asked to indicate on a scale from 1 to 10 (1 being a high degree of failure and
10 being a high degree of success) their feelings of success or failure. In much research the subjects report information such as age,
sex, income, time spent studying, occupation, and other questions
that are relatively simple. For these types of data, statistical estimates of reliability are generally not needed.

Several conditions affect reliability. One is the length of a test
or questionnaire: A longer test is more reliable than a shorter one.
Reliability is also a function of the heterogeneity of the group: It
is greater for groups that are more heterogeneous on the trait that
is being measured. Conversely, the more homogeneous the subjects, the lower the reliability. Reliability is also a function of the
nature of the trait that is being measured. Some variables, such as
most measures of achievement, have high reliabilities, whereas
measures of personality have lower reliabilities. Consequently, a

reliability of .80 or above is generally expected for achievement variables, whereas estimates of .65 are usually acceptable for measuring personality traits. By comparison, then, a personality instrument reporting a reliability coefficient of .90 would be judged excellent, and an achievement test with a reliability of .70 would be seen as weak. We need a much higher reliability if the results will be used to make decisions about individuals. Studies of groups can tolerate a lower reliability, sometimes as low as .50 in exploratory research. Measures of young children are usually less reliable than those of older subjects.

To enhance reliability, it is best to establish standard conditions of data collection. All subjects should be given the same directions, have the same time frame in which to answer questions at the same time during the day, and so on. Error is often increased if different persons administer the instruments. It is important to know if there are any unusual circumstances during data collection since these may affect reliability. The instrument needs to be appropriate in reading level and language to be reliable, and subjects must be properly motivated to answer the questions. In some research it is difficult to get subjects to be serious, for instance, when students are asked to take achievement tests that have no implications for them. Reliability can also suffer when subjects are asked to complete several instruments over a long period of time. Usually an hour is about all any of us can tolerate, and for younger children less than a half hour is the maximum. If several instruments are given at the same time, the order of their administration should not be the same for all subjects. Some subjects should answer one instrument first, and other subjects should answer the same instrument last. This is called counterbalancing the instruments. If several instruments are given and there is no counterbalancing, the results, especially for the instruments given at the end, should be viewed with caution.

Finally, reliability is a necessary condition for validity. That is, a measure cannot be valid unless it is reliable. However, a reliable measure is not necessarily valid. For example, I can obtain a very reliable measure of the length of your big toe, but that would not be valid as an estimate of your intelligence.

OUTLINE SUMMARY

1. Measurement
    A. Instrument and procedure for collecting information
    B. Used in evaluation

    C. Valid, reliable, and credible
    D. Scales of measurement
       (1) Descriptive of variables
       (2) Nominal scales—assign numbers to categories
       (3) Ordinal scales—rank-order categories
       (4) Interval scales—equal intervals between numbers
       (5) Ratio scales—express numbers as ratios
2. Descriptive statistics
    A. Indexes that summarize a set of numbers
    B. Frequency distributions
       (1) Frequency polygon
       (2) Normal distribution—bell-shaped and symmetrical
       (3) Skewed distributions—extreme positive or negative
           scores
    C. Measures of central tendency
       (1) Mode
       (2) Median
       (3) Mean
    D. Measures of Variability
       (1) Range
       (2) Standard deviation
    E. Correlation
       (1) Scatterplots
       (2) Correlation coefficients—range between -1 and $+1$
           and are numerical indexes
       (3) Strength
       (4) Positive
       (5) Negative
       (6) Curvilinear
3. Validity
    A. Appropriate use of test results
    B. Types of evidence
       (1) Content-related evidence—representativeness de-
           termined by expert judgment.
       (2) Criterion-related evidence—either predictive or
           concurrent, involves another criterion.
       (3) Construct-related evidence—used with psychologi-
           cal constructs not directly observable
    C. Inferences—valid or invalid
    D. Established before data collection
4. Reliability
    A. Error—always present
    B. Estimates amount of error
       (1) Stability

(2) Equivalence
(3) Internal consistency
(4) Agreement
C. Necessary for validity
D. Established before data collection
E. Improved by longer tests and heterogeneous subjects

STUDY QUESTIONS

1. How is measurement different from evaluation and assessment?
2. Why is measurement important in determining the quality of educational research?
3. What is the purpose of different scales of measurement?
4. What is the difference between nominal and interval scales of measurement?
5. In what ways are descriptive statistics useful in research?
6. Give some examples of different types of frequency distributions.
7. What are the common shapes of frequency distributions?
8. What are the special properties of a normal distribution?
9. In what ways are the mode, median, and mean different?
10. Explain the concept of standard deviation. Why is it important for research?
11. What is the relationship between the standard deviation and percentile rank?
12. Why is a scatterplot important in examining relationships?
13. Give some examples of positive and negative correlations.
14. Define validity and reliability. How are they related?
15. What types of evidence are used for validity?
16. Describe some factors that should be considered when evaluating validity.
17. What are the types of reliability?
18. How is error in measurement related to reliability correlation coefficients?
19. In what ways can different factors affect reliability?

Chapter
6

Types of Educational Measures

Researchers select from a large number of different types of educational measures to gather data. The choice of the researcher depends on the research problem, the advantages and disadvantages of each type of measure, and practical constraints. As a consumer of research it is important for you to understand the strengths and weaknesses of different approaches to measurement and how the results of different kinds of instruments should be interpreted. In this chapter the most common types of educational measures are reviewed with an emphasis on the interpretation and use of scores. You will also note that each technique has unique characteristics that affect the way validity and reliability are established and evaluated.

CLASSIFYING EDUCATIONAL MEASURES

Educational measures can be classified in three ways. A major distinction is between what has been termed "cognitive" and "noncognitive" measures. Cognitive measures focus on what a person knows or is able to do mentally. They include achievement and aptitude tests, measures of critical and creative thinking, and cognitive style. The emphasis is on what the person can process mentally with respect to knowledge of facts and problem solving. Cognitive measures are further differentiated by being either norm- or criterion-referenced. This characteristic, which is discussed in more detail later in this chapter, has important implications for interpreting results. Noncognitive measures include personality, attitude, value, and interest inventories. These instruments require some degree of cognitive processing, but the emphasis is on affective, or emotional, "feelings" and intuitions.

A second major factor in distinguishing educational measures is whether the instrument is commercially developed (often referred to as "off the shelf") or developed locally by the researcher ("home grown"). Most commercially prepared instruments will have more extensive use, information on reliability and validity, and specific directions for administration and scoring. Locally developed instruments are often better suited to applied research but may lack technical qualities. Both cognitive and noncognitive instruments may be either commercially prepared or locally developed.

A third important difference in educational measures is whether the subject is answering questions directly or the information is gathered without direct interaction with the subjects. Most tests, questionnaires, and interviews rely on information provided by the subjects. They are often called "self-report" instruments. Other measures, such as many observational devices, do not require subjects' responses to specific questions. Self-report measures are sometimes adversely affected by subject awareness and demands by the researcher.

TESTS

A **test** is an instrument that presents to each subject a standard set of questions that requires the completion of a cognitive task. The answers to the questions are summarized to obtain a numerical value that represents a cognitive characteristic of the subjects. All tests measure performance at the time the test is given. Tests differ in how the results are used, in their development, and in the types of validity and reliability that are established. The major differentiating characteristics are whether tests are norm- or criterion-referenced, achievement or aptitude, or standardized or locally developed.

Test: Standard questions of cognitive knowledge or skills.

Norm- and Criterion-Referenced Tests

A critical aspect of testing is in the interpretation of the results. When a score is obtained, what does it convey? How do you interpret it? What does it mean when the average score is 70 percent correct? Measurement specialists have identified two approaches to interpretation to derive accurate meaning from the scores. In **norm-referenced** interpretation, individual scores are compared to the scores of a well-defined norm or reference group of others who have taken the same test. There is less emphasis on the absolute amount of knowledge or skill demonstrated. What matters most is the comparison group and the capability of the test to distinguish between individuals on the trait being measured. For example, Bill's score of 55 in mathematics may place him above 60 percent of all other students who took the test, or Mary's score may place her in the top 10 percent. The score is the relative "standing" of the subject, compared to a previously determined "norm" group, a group of others who took the test at the same time.

> **Norm-referenced:** Tests that compare subjects with others.

Because the purpose of a norm-referenced test is to differentiate between individuals, it is desirable to obtain a group distribution of scores that shows a high variance. It would be impossible to say much about relative standing when the scores are all about the same. To achieve high variability, the test items are often fairly difficult. For instance, in many standardized achievement tests it is not uncommon for students around the middle of the distribution to answer only 50 percent of the items correctly. Easy items, ones that most know the answer to, and very hard items, ones that few can answer correctly, are used sparingly. Thus some content may not be covered on the test, which would affect the interpretation of the results. High variability is good when the researcher is looking for relationships between the test results and other variables. In fact, correlations require each variable to have wide ranges of results. This is one reason that much research investigating relationships with achievement uses norm-referenced tests. These are the types of tests that are most likely to provide data that will result in significant correlations.

It is also necessary to attend carefully to the nature of the norm or reference group in interpreting the results. Proper interpretation requires knowing what the scores are being compared against. It is like being in a class with an instructor who grades on the curve. If the class contains mostly very bright, motivated students, you can learn a lot and still "look" bad by comparison. On the other hand, if you are in a class with students who have low ability and are unmotivated, you can "look" good even though you have not learned much. Standardized tests usually report national norms, so that the score is compared to students across the nation. However there are different ways of obtaining a "national" sample. Often, for instance, minority groups are oversampled. A proper interpretation is therefore possible only if the characteristics of the norm group are understood. Also, evidence of reliability and validity established with the norm group may not be appropriate for individuals not represented in the norm group.

The purpose of a **criterion-referenced** test is to show how an individual compares to some established level of performance or skill. Here the score is interpreted by comparison to a standard or criterion rather than to the scores of others. The result is usually reported either as a percentage of items answered correctly or as pass/fail. Examples of criterion-referenced measurement include grading scales, such as 95 to 100 = A, 88 to 94 = B, and so on, and minimum competency tests, in which the emphasis is often on making sure that students know certain concepts and principles and have certain skills. An important characteristic of most criterion-referenced tests is that the results show a highly negatively skewed distribution. This characteristic lessens variability, which may make it difficult to find relationships between the test results and other variables. Another feature of criterion-referenced tests is that when pass/fail or some other "mastery" decision is made, professional judgment is used to set the passing or mastery score. There are many different ways to make these professional judgments, with quite different results. A related term, *domain-referenced* testing, indicates the degree to which a larger "domain" of knowledge is demonstrated by those being tested.

Criterion-referenced: Tests that compare subjects with a standard of performance.

Standardized Tests

A **standardized test** has uniform procedures for administration and scoring. Directions specify the procedures for giving the test, such as qualifications of the person administering the test, time allowed to answer the questions, materials that can be used by the subjects, and other conditions. The scoring of responses is usually objective, which means that there are specific instructions for how to score that do not involve personal judgments of the testers. Scoring is usually a count of the number correct. Most standardized tests have been administered to a norming group, which is helpful in interpreting the results. They are prepared commercially by experts in measurement, which usually means that careful attention has been given to technical aspects such as cultural bias, reliability, validity, clarity, and item analysis.

Standardized test: A test with uniform procedures for administration and scoring.

These tests are intended to be used in a wide variety of settings; obviously the test publisher wants to sell as many tests as possible. The traits and skills measured are usually defined in broad, general terms. Consequently, the test may not be specific enough for use in a particular setting. For example, suppose a teacher is investigating the effect of different instructional methods on eleventh-grade students' achievement in English. A standardized test of English may be available but may not be consistent with the specific reading materials this teacher intends to use. In this case the standardized test would not be sensitive enough to the different materials to show positive results. Thus there is a trade-off in using standardized tests for classroom-oriented research: Although there may be established technical qualities, the test may not focus directly on what is being studied.

Standardized Achievement Tests   A standardized achievement test is commercially prepared, with the characteristics previously indicated, and measures present knowledge and skills of a sample of relevant content. The emphasis is on recent school learning, what has been learned by the student, measuring proficiency in one or more areas of knowledge.

Standardized achievement test: Tests content area knowledge or skill.

There are several types of standardized achievement tests. Some, diagnostic in nature, identify specific strengths and weaknesses in a particular discipline or area. Some measure achievement in a single subject, such as reading or mathematics. Survey batteries are achievement tests that survey a number of different subjects. These are the type most commonly given to assess students' progress in several subjects. Most standardized achievement tests are norm-referenced, although some are criterion-referenced. Some focus on recall and recognition of specific facts, concepts, and principles, and others measure skills and application of knowledge.

The type of achievement test selected (diagnostic, survey battery, etc.) depends on the purpose of the study. If the investigation is concerned with a single subject, a test that measures only that area, rather than a comprehensive battery of many different subjects, would be preferable. If there is a desire to compare schools on achievement, a norm-referenced achievement test would be preferred. Broad evaluations of school performance are best assessed with survey batteries.

It is critical to assess evidence for content validity when using an achievement test. This assessment should include judgments about the relevance of the content that is in the test as well as judgments about whether the curriculum that may be investigated as an independent variable emphasizes the content that is in the test. Such judgments are usually made by examining each of the items in the test to determine their relevance to what is being taught and to the specific purpose of the research. It is also important to select a test that has an appropriate degree of difficulty for the students. A test that is either too easy or too hard will not have the variability that is needed to show relationships with other variables.

When existing standardized achievement tests do not match well with the purpose of the research, a locally developed test is needed. These are often called teacher-made, or informal, tests for examining classroom learning. There are important differences between standardized and locally developed achievement tests, as summarized in Table 6.1.

Standardized Aptitude Tests   A standardized aptitude test is a commercially prepared measure of knowledge or skills that is used to predict future performance. The difference between an achievement and an aptitude test is in the way the results are applied. The actual items can be very similar, especially in tests for young children. Often the terms *intelligence* and *ability* are used interchangeably with *aptitude*. Actually *aptitude* is a more general term that refers to the predictive nature of the instrument. Intelligence tests measure a particular type of aptitude, which is defined by the content of each specific test. Intelligence usually means some indication of the capacity of an individual to understand, process, and apply knowledge and skills in thinking or problem solving. It involves many different aptitudes together.

Standardized aptitude test: Predicts future performance.

Because of the negative connotation of intelligence tests, many publishers today use the terms *ability* or *academic aptitude* in names of the tests, for example, the Otis-Lennon School Ability Test and the Cognitive Abilities Test. The basic structure and content of these tests is much the same as when they were referred to as intelligence tests. Such tests are widely used in education and are useful in predicting many different tasks. Some of them, as those just mentioned, are given to large groups of students; others, like the Stanford-Binet and the Wechsler Scales, are given on an individual basis. For research, both individual and group tests are common, and for both types it is important for the person administering the test to be properly qualified.

There are also a large number of aptitude tests that measure specific kinds of aptitudes, such as vocational, clerical, law school, medical school, mechanical, critical thinking, and creative thinking tests. These tests are most useful when the purpose of the research is to focus on a particular type of aptitude. A few aptitude tests are batteries that assess many aptitudes at once. For example, the Differential Aptitude Tests (DAT) measure eight aptitudes: verbal reasoning, numerical ability, abstract reasoning, clerical speed and accuracy, mechanical reasoning, space relations, spelling, and language use. These tests have been useful in predicting both scholastic and vocational success.

Since aptitude tests are concerned with predicting future behavior, it is important to establish predictive criterion-related evidence for validity. It is also wise to have a stability estimate of reliability. These technical qualities are especially important if the tests will be used to select individuals for a special program and

Table 6.1   CHARACTERISTICS OF STANDARDIZED AND INFORMAL
            ACHIEVEMENT TESTS

	Standardized achievement tests	Informal achievement tests
Learning outcomes and content measured	Measure outcomes and content common to majority of United States schools. Tests of basic skills and complex outcomes adaptable to many local situations; content-oriented tests seldom reflect emphasis or timeliness of local curriculum.	Well adapted to outcomes and content of local curriculum. Flexibility affords continuous adaptation of measurement to new materials and changes in procedure. Adaptable to various-sized work units. Tend to neglect complex learning outcomes.
Quality of test items	General quality of items high. Written by specialists, pretested, and selected on basis of effectiveness.	Quality of items is unknown unless test item file is used. Quality typically lower than standardized because of teacher's limited time and skill.
Reliability	Reliability high, commonly between .80 and .95; frequently is above .90.	Reliability usually unknown; can be high if carefully constructed.
Administration and scoring	Procedures *standardized;* specific instructions provided.	Uniform procedures favored but may be flexible.
Interpretation of scores	Scores can be compared with those of norm groups. Test manual and other guides aid interpretation and use.	Score comparisons and interpretations limited to local school situation.

Source: N. E. Gronlund, and R. L. Linn (1990). *Measurement and evaluation in teaching,* 6th ed. New York: Macmillan, p. 269.

more than can be accommodated have applied or may be eligible. Almost all aptitude tests are standardized.

Interpreting Test Scores

The distinction between norm- and criterion-referenced tests is of major importance in interpreting test scores. Although the basic provisions of each approach to interpretation have been previously summarized, you will come across types of test scores that will have specialized meanings. Two of the most common are standard scores and grade equivalents.

Standard Scores   Most publishers of standardized, norm-referenced tests report at least two types of scores. One is the actual number of items correct, the raw score, and another is calculated from these raw scores, the standard score. **Standard scores** are transformed raw scores that have a distribution in the same shape as the raw score distribution but with a different mean and standard deviation. The most basic standard score is called a linear z score. A z score has a mean of 0 and a standard deviation of 1. The formula is

$$z = \frac{\text{raw score} - \text{mean}}{\text{standard deviation}}$$

Many other derived standard scores are then calculated from z scores, such as SAT and IQ scores. Two important points should be remembered regarding the interpretation of these types of standard scores. First, the unit of standard deviation is determined arbitrarily and does not reflect "real" differences between subjects. For instance, the SAT has a standard score mean of 500 and a standard deviation equal to 100. One subject may score 550 and another may obtain 590, but the 40-point difference is only in standard score units. In fact the 40 points may represent a difference of only a few correct answers. Second, in small distributions and in any raw score distribution that is not normal, scores are sometimes "normalized," that is, forced into a normal distribution and reported as standard scores. This practice may distort the meaning of the scores. Despite these limitations, however, standard scores are often used in research because the data are in a form that can be used in statistical analyses of the results. Also with standard scores, it is easier to compare groups who have taken different tests, such as consecutive years of third-grade achievement.

Standard scores: Raw scores transformed to a standard scale.

Grade Equivalents   Grade equivalents (GEs) are a popular type of score for reporting achievement. However, they are often misinterpreted. A **grade equivalent** score indicates how an individual compares with others in a normative group in terms of grade level. For example, a student who scores 5.0 has achieved the median score for all beginning fifth-graders in the norm group. The score 3.2 is equivalent to the average score of third-graders in November. One limitation of GEs is in interpreting these in-between scores, 5.6, 2.3, and so on, since they are calculated as approximate, not

Grade equivalent: Norm-referenced grade-level performance.

exact, scores. Estimates are also made for grade levels beyond the norming group, although GEs are generally not used beyond the ninth grade because not all students take all subjects. Perhaps the most serious misinterpretation is the belief that a student who scores, say, 6.0, should be in the sixth grade, or knows as much as a sixth-grader. Grade determination is based on local school policy and the level of achievement of students in a particular school, whereas the GE is based on a national norm. Thus, although seemingly easy to understand, GEs have to be carefully interpreted.

PERSONALITY ASSESSMENT

Personality assessment can be thought of as consisting of two traditions, one closely tied to psychology and concerned with measures used by trained counselors and clinicians, and a second in which separate aspects of personality are assessed by teachers and researchers who may not have extensive psychological training.

Psychologists have been concerned with measuring personality for many years. Although there are many definitions of personality, a common theme is that it involves the total individual—noncognitive, affective traits as well as cognitive characteristics. This wholistic emphasis is evident in personality instruments that assess general adjustment, such as the Minnesota Multiphasic Personality Inventory (MMPI). The MMPI is a self-report instrument for adults aged 16 and above. Fourteen scales are reported, including paranoia, hysteria, social introversion, schizophrenia, and depression. The objective is to identify thinking and behavior that are not "normal," that may be psychopathic. Interpretation of the results of the MMPI, which is difficult and complex to understand, requires a highly trained, skilled clinician. Other self-report personality instruments are the Adjustment Inventory, California Psychological Inventory, and Psychological Inventory. Unstructured, or projective, tests, such as the Rorschach Inkblot Test and the Thematic Apperception Test, assess personality structure on the basis of an individual's response to an ambiguous picture or other stimulus. All of these instruments require a trained clinician for proper interpretation and application of the results. These instruments are not used very much in educational research.

Commonly used are less comprehensive instruments that assess a part of personality. These are not intended to identify psychopathology. They measure such traits as self-concept, cognitive style, and locus of control, important individual traits related to learning and motivation. The instruments are designed so that educators without clinical training can understand and use the results. We will briefly consider the most commonly used type, measures of self-concept.

Self-concept, or self-image, can be defined as the way an individual characterizes oneself. It is a description formed by self-perceptions and beliefs. Although it is possible to measure a single, global self-concept, most instruments are designed to assess many different self-concepts, such as descriptions about the physical, social, academic, moral, and personal self. The items in the instruments require self-report perceptions.

Typically, short statements are presented that describe various aspects of self-concept. The subjects answer each item by indicating whether it is true for them, or whether they agree or disagree with whether the statement is like them. For example, subjects would be directed to answer "yes" or "no" or "true" or "false" to the following statements:

1. I have few friends.
2. I have happy parents.
3. I have a nice looking body.
4. I am good at schoolwork.
5. I make friends easily.
6. I get good grades.
7. I am happy in school.
8. I like my teachers.
9. I am confident of my athletic ability.

Often the scoring of the instruments indicates a positive or negative self-concept, an interpretation that has an evaluative component termed self-esteem. It has to do with how we feel about our self-concept. In the literature *self-concept* and *self-esteem* may be used interchangeably, so it is necessary to examine the nature of the items to understand what is being measured.

ATTITUDE, VALUE, AND INTEREST INVENTORIES

Attitudes, values, and interests are generally thought of as noncognitive or affective traits that indicate some degree of preference toward something. Preferences are important in education since they influence motivation and goals, which in turn affect achievement. The most common measure of these preferences in educational research is through self-report inventories, in which students answer questions to indicate how they feel about something or what their beliefs are. We will discuss several types of inventories, with examples from actual studies. As you will note when reading educational research, such inventories are used extensively.

Types of Inventories

Attitudes are defined as predispositions to respond favorably or unfavorably to an object, group, or place. They reflect likes and dislikes and generally predict behavior. A common approach to measuring attitudes is through scaled items. A **scale** is a series of gradations that describes something. Scales are used frequently to measure attitudes as "more than" and "less than" or ranging between very positive to very negative. The most typical format for a scaled item is following a question or statement with a scale of potential responses. The subjects indicate their attitudes by checking the place on the scale that best reflects their feelings and beliefs about the statement. The **Likert scale** is the most widely used example. In a true Likert scale the statement includes a value or positive or negative direction, and the subject indicates agreement or disagreement of the statement.

Scale: Series of gradations.

Likert scale: Measures level of agreement to a statement.

EXAMPLE: LIKERT SCALE

It is very important to go to college.

| strongly agree | agree | neither agree nor disagree | disagree | strongly disagree |

Likert-type scales, which have a different form, begin with a neutral statement, and the direction or gradation is provided in the response options.

EXAMPLE: LIKERT-TYPE SCALE

Mrs. Stadler's classroom management is:

outstanding   excellent   good   fair   poor

It should also be pointed out that Likert-type scales are useful for measuring traits other than attitudes. Such measures are usually referred to as rating scales. Statements and response options can be selected for a wide variety of needs, as indicated in the following examples.

EXAMPLES: RATING SCALES

How often does your principal visit your classroom?

| every day | two or three days a week | once a week | once every two weeks | once a month |

How often does your teacher give praise?

| always | most of time | sometimes | rarely | never |

How did you feel about your performance on the exam?

| very satisfied | somewhat satisfied | somewhat dissatisfied | very dissatisfied |

Note that there is not always the same number of possible responses on a Likert-type scale. There is usually a minimum of 4 options, and there can be as many as 11. Some questions will have a middle option, and others will have an even number of options to "force" the subject to one side of the scale or the other. However if a neutral or middle choice is not provided and this is the real attitude or belief of the subject, the subject will be forced to give an inaccurate response (or may choose not to respond at all).

A good example of a Likert-type attitude scale for research can be seen in a study of the relationship between parent involvement and several qualities of school settings, such as socioeconomic status, teachers' degree level, grade level, class size, and principals' perceptions. In this investigation the opinions of teachers and principals were assessed by Likert-type questionnaires. Following are some examples of items, each with a five-point response scale ranging from strongly agree to strongly disagree or from almost always to almost never.

EXAMPLES: LIKERT ITEMS

"I feel that I am making a significant difference in the lives of my students."

"I have to follow rules at this school that conflict with my best professional judgment."

"I believe that student learning is linked directly to teachers' efforts and skills."

"I know exactly what is covered by teachers in the grade level above me and below me."

(Hoover-Dempsey, Bassler, & Brissie, 1987, p. 425)

Each of these items was scored separately in different subscales.

   Another commonly used measure of attitudes is the **Semantic Differential**, which has adjective pairs that provide a series of scales. Each adjective acts as an end anchor, and the subject checks a point between each end anchor of each scale to indicate attitudes toward some person, concept, or idea. Original research with the Semantic Differential found three clusters or types of adjectives: evaluative, such as good/bad and valuable/worthless; potency, such as heavy/light and strong/weak; and activity, such as slow/fast and active/passive. Although the true Semantic Differential uses the same set of adjective pairs in the three clusters, changing the object or concept that is being studied and changing the adjective pairs to be appropriate are common in educational research.

Semantic Differential: Seven-point scale with adjective pairs.

EXAMPLES: SEMANTIC DIFFERENTIAL-TYPE ITEMS

Science Test

Fair ____ ____ ____ ____ ____ ____ ____ Unfair
Hard ____ ____ ____ ____ ____ ____ ____ Easy

Eskimos

Bad ____ ____ ____ ____ ____ ____ ____ Good
Active ____ ____ ____ ____ ____ ____ ____ Passive
Honest ____ ____ ____ ____ ____ ____ ____ Dishonest
Helpful ____ ____ ____ ____ ____ ____ ____ Unhelpful
Shallow ____ ____ ____ ____ ____ ____ ____ Deep

The Minnesota School Attitude Survey uses a Semantic Differential approach to measure a number of attitudes quickly, for example,

Famous Plays

important ____ ____ ____ ____ ____ unimportant
pleasant ____ ____ ____ ____ ____ unpleasant

Art

important ____ ____ ____ ____ ____ unimportant
pleasant ____ ____ ____ ____ ____ unpleasant

Being Liked by Other Students

important ____ ____ ____ ____ ____ unimportant
pleasant ____ ____ ____ ____ ____ unpleasant

Other approaches to measuring attitudes may be encountered in the literature, such as a Thurstone or Guttman scale. Almost all rely on the self-reports of the subjects, and most are easy to administer and score. The major limitation of attitude measurement is obtaining reliable and valid results. Reliability for attitude scales is generally around .75; evidence for validity is difficult to obtain because an attitude is an unobservable construct, and construct-related evidence is needed for validity. We also know that attitudes are subject to change and do not always predict behavior well since they are only one of many influences. Nevertheless, attitudes are essential aspects of both inputs and results of schooling, and research has found important relationships between attitudes and achievement.

Like attitudes, interests are concerned with preferences. Both are related to favorable or unfavorable responses toward something. Interests, however, are feelings and beliefs about an activity rather than an object, concept, or person. Many interest inventories assess likes and dislikes toward various occupations, such as the Kuder Occupational Interest Survey, the Strong-Campbell Interest Inventory, and the Vocational Preference Inventory, so that the examinee, with the help of a trained counselor, can plan future vocational and educational goals. These instruments are used primarily for individual counseling and are not found much in research. Other, nonstandardized interest inventories are sometimes used in research to indicate specific types of attitudes. Often the terms *attitude* and *interest* are used interchangeably in the research literature.

Values refer to the worth that is attached to an object, activity, or belief. Like attitudes and interests, values can be defined in a number of ways, so it is necessary to examine items in a value survey to know what is being measured. Established instruments that measure values, such as Rokeach's Value Survey, Study of Values, and Gordon's Surveys of Values, tend to assess personal and social values that may not relate well to educational outcomes. The Study of Values, for instance, assesses the relative strength of values in six categories: theoretical, economic, aesthetic, social, political, and religious. Rokeach's Value Survey measures the importance of traits like freedom, pleasure, wisdom, beauty, helpfulness, ambition, independence, lovingness, and politeness.

Problems in Measuring Noncognitive Traits

Compared to cognitive measures, such as achievement and aptitude tests, noncognitive instruments generally have lower reliability and validity. One difficulty with noncognitive measurement is clearly defining what is being assessed. There are different definitions of terms like *attitude, belief, value,* and *personality.* Thus, the same labels can be used, but what is being measured can be different. An "attitude" toward mathematics can mean one thing in one study and something different in another study. Consequently, when reading research that uses noncognitive instruments it is important to examine the operational definition of the trait that is being measured, which is best accomplished by reading the actual items in the scale. The results are meaningful only in regard to the way in which the attitude or personality trait is measured, not by how the researcher labels or communicates the findings in titles or conclusions.

Most noncognitive measures are susceptible to two sources of error: response set and faking. **Response set** is the tendency of the subject to respond in the same way, regardless of the content of the items, for example, always selecting the neutral category or the "strongly agree" category in a Likert scale or marking the favorable adjectives on a Semantic Differential. An especially troublesome type of response set is social desirability. This is the tendency to respond to the items in a way that is socially acceptable or desirable, regardless of the true or real attitudes or beliefs of the individual. For example, if a question asks students about their alcohol consumption, the responses may be influenced by what the students think is socially accepted. Or students may indicate an interest in attending college because that is more desirable socially than not attending college. Response set tends to be more prevalent on Likert-type inventories, with ambiguous items, and in situations in which the subjects are not motivated to give honest answers. In evaluating noncognitive instrumentation it is best to look for techniques that lessen response set, such as forced-choice responses, short inventories, an approximately equal number of positively and negatively worded items, alternation of positive and negative adjectives in the same column on a Semantic Differential, ensurance of anonymity, and motivation of subjects.

Response set: Tendency to respond in the same way.

Faking occurs when the subjects give a deliberately inaccurate indication of their attitudes, personality, or interests. Faking is usually dependent on the purpose of the test and the consequences of the results. Sometimes it occurs if the researcher indicates that certain results will have positive consequences; sometimes subjects fake responses simply to please the researcher (which is why someone other than the researcher probably should administer the instrument). In other situations faking occurs because the results have important consequences for the individual, for example, to determine admission to college or selection for a management training program. Occasionally subjects will fake to provide a more negative picture. Faking can be controlled by establishing good rapport with the subjects and proper motivation, by disguising the purpose of the instrument and research, and using a forced-choice format. There are also techniques to detect faking. Whatever the approach, it is best for the instrument to be pilot-tested with similar subjects to ensure that problems like response set and faking are controlled as much as possible. If little or no attention is given to these problems, it is more likely that the responses will be invalid.

OBSERVATIONS

Tests and other types of instruments already discussed are similar in relying on subjects' self-reports. Although self-reports are relatively economical and easy to obtain, they have limitations, such as response set, subject motivation, and faking, that may bias the results. A second major type of data collection, which does not rely on self-reports, is the observational method. Observational techniques, although also containing limitations, are more direct than self-reports. The observation of behavior as it occurs yields first-hand data without the contamination that may arise from tests, inventories, or other self-report instruments. Moreover, observation allows the description of behavior as it occurs naturally. Any kind of self-report introduces artificiality into the research. Observation of behavior in natural settings also allows the researcher to take into account important contextual factors that may influence the interpretation and use of the results.

There are several types of observational data-gathering techniques. Some observations are made in natural settings and others in controlled, laboratory settings. Observations may be guided by a very general problem and complete flexibility about what and who to observe, whereas other observations are very specific and highly structured. Observers may be detached, even unknown, from the subjects, or they may essentially become subjects themselves. The different types of observations range from qualitative to quantitative in approach. Quantitative observations are more controlled and more systematic and rely on numbers to summarize what has been observed. Qualitative approaches are much less controlled, allowing observers' hunches and judgments to determine the content and sequence of what is recorded. In this chapter we will focus on the more controlled, quantitative types of observation. Qualitative observations will be discussed in Chapter 11.

Inference

A major factor in observational research is the extent to which the person who is recording observed behavior makes inferences, or judgments, about what is seen or heard. Although there will always be some degree of inference, the amount can vary considerably. At one extreme, the observer may record specific, easily identified behaviors, such as "asks a question" or "wrote objectives on the board." These are called **low-inference observations** because the observer does not have to interpret what is seen. Either it is present or not, and the observer makes no judgment about its meaning. The recorded behaviors are then summarized and interpreted by someone else; the inference is made after all the data have been gathered. At the other extreme are observations that require the observer to make and record a judgment or interpretation. This approach, referred to as **high-inference observation,** requires the observer both to see relevant behaviors and to make inferences about their meaning. A common example of high-inference observation is that of the principal, who on the basis of a few visits to a classroom, rates a teacher as excellent, good, adequate, or poor on dimensions of teaching, such as "classroom management" or "asking questions."

Low-inference observation: Little interpretation or judgment.

High-inference observation: Record interpretations or judgments.

EXAMPLE: HIGH-INFERENCE OBSERVATIONS

"Observers also filled out a high-inference rating form designed to measure global aspects of the physical class environment, the teacher's instruction and management skills, and teacher-student interpersonal relations . . . all items were in the form of 5-point rating scales, with higher scores designating the more desirable pole." (Mitman, 1985, p. 151)

With low-inference observation the reliability is usually high, but you need to understand clearly how the recorded behavior is translated to a "result." This can be a complex process and will involve some degree of arbitrary judgment, for example, how many times a teacher needs to give praise to be judged competent in praising students or how many student questions during a class period indicates acceptable student involvement. Critics of low-inference systems also point out that teaching and learning may not be understood by recording specific behaviors without putting them into context.

In high-inference observations the competency of the observer in making correct judgments is critical. Training high-inference observers is more difficult, and reliability is often lower, as compared to low-inference observation. With high-inference results greater trust in the observer is needed. Thus you should look for any factors that may bias a high-inference observer, such as the researcher also acting as the observer or observers knowing about the expected results of the study.

Some observations are in between the low- and high-inference extremes. One such approach is to make high-inference ratings and indicate the specific behaviors and contextual factors that led to the inference implied in the judgment.

Laboratory Observation

The most controlled observational techniques are found in laboratory studies. A specified environment is created by the researcher and the observations are recorded during the study. A well-structured form or procedure is used to record specific behaviors that have been identified before the study begins. Low-inference observations are made, and methods of summarizing and analyzing the observations are specified in advance. The emphasis is on objectivity and standardization; usually the study is an experiment.

Subjects in laboratory observation may give biased responses because they know they are in an experiment and know they are being observed. They may respond according to their interpretation of how they "should" respond, given the treatment they experience, or they may give answers they believe the researcher wants. These are called "demand" characteristics. Deception, in which the subjects are not told the real purpose of the study, is commonly used to reduce the effects of demand characteristics, but there are serious ethical problems with lying to subjects, even if they are debriefed after the study.

Structured Field Observations

Most observational studies in education take place in the field, in schools and classrooms where behavior occurs naturally. The typical approach is to define the behaviors to be observed, identify a systematic system of coding and recording them, train observers to use the system, and go to the school or other setting and make the observations. The intent is to measure the frequency and/or duration of predetermined behaviors.

The behaviors can be recorded in several ways. The most common approach is to indicate the number of times a behavior occurs during a specified time period. The observer has a list of behaviors that may be observed, and every time a behavior is seen a tally is placed next to that behavior. Sometimes the observer will observe for a short time, such as one to three minutes, then record all the behaviors seen in that time; and sometimes the recording is done continuously. With high-inference structured instruments, the observer may not record anything for an hour or more.

A recent example of structured field observations concerned the effect of specified instructional methods on the academic achievement and classroom behavior of seventh-graders. Teachers were observed to determine if they were using the assigned instructional methods.

EXAMPLE: STRUCTURED FIELD OBSERVATIONS

"Each teacher was observed by trained observers for one class period on 3 successive days in the fall, winter, and spring. Separate observations were made and recorded each 60 seconds . . . according to 11 predefined categories. . . . During the first 10 seconds of the minute-long coding period, the observers recorded the behavior of students. . . . During the remainder of the minute, they coded the category of teacher behavior." (Hawkins, Doueck, and Lishner, 1988, p. 36)

Observer Effects

The observer is the key to observational research, and the quality of the results depends to a great extent on how the observer and the procedures for observing affect the subjects. In reading observational research you should be aware of the following potential limitations.

Observer Bias   Bias is a type of error that occurs in a single direction, in this case because of the background, expectations, or perceptions of the observer. For example, if an observer of classroom management techniques has a predetermined idea that a particular approach is best, and the teacher who is observed does not show this style, the observer may have a tendency to bias the observations in a negative direction. On the other hand, bias in a positive direction may occur when observers record the behavior of a style of management they believe to be most effective.

You should look for one of several procedures to reduce potential observer bias. First there should be evidence that the observer has been trained and will provide reliable results. The evidence for training should be based on research done before the actual study is implemented. Second, if possible, two or more observers should independently observe the same behavior. The average of these observers reduces the bias that may result from having only one observer. Third, bias can also result because of prejudice toward certain races; toward one gender or the other; and toward other characteristics such as physical attractiveness, social class, and exceptionalities. Thus, it is best if the observers do not know about the characteristics of the subjects, or at least know as little as possible.

Contamination   Contamination occurs when the observer has knowledge of one or more aspects of the study and this knowledge affects subsequent observations. One type of contamination results from knowledge of the hypothesis of the study. If the observer knows which group is "expected" to do best, for example, he or she may unconsciously favor that group. Contamination also occurs if the observer is assigned to more than one type of group. For example, if an observer begins with a group of "expert" teachers and then observes "poor" teachers, the second group will probably receive ratings lower than it deserves because of the comparison. It would be much better to have several observers assigned to "expert" teachers and different observers assigned to "poor" teachers. Contamination is less likely to occur with specific targeted behaviors, trained observers, and ignorance of the observers concerning expected outcomes and which groups are experimental or control.

Contamination: Knowledge of the study influences observer or interviewer.

Halo Effect   The **halo effect** occurs when an observer allows an initial impression about one aspect of a person or group to influence observations on other aspects. For example, an initial positive impression about a teacher, based on the way the teacher begins a class, may create an overall positive "halo" so that ratings of subsequent behaviors, such as questioning or monitoring of classroom activities, are higher than they should be. The halo effect is an inappropriate generalization about all aspects of the observation. It is suspected in ratings of different behaviors that are all about the same, showing a positive relationship between unrelated scales. The halo effect, like other sources of errors in observation, is reduced with adequate training.

Halo effect: Specific ratings affected by general impression.

INTERVIEWS

The **interview** is a form of data collection in which questions are asked orally and the subjects' responses are recorded. There is direct verbal interaction between the interviewer and the respondent, which has both advantages and disadvantages compared to self-report tests, inventories, and questionnaires. A skilled interviewer, by establishing a proper rapport with the subject, can enhance motivation and obtain information that might not otherwise have been

Interview: Oral questions and answers.

offered. More accurate responses are obtained as the interviewer clarifies questions that the subject may have and follows up leads (probing). The interview allows for greater depth and richness. In face-to-face interviews, the interviewer can observe nonverbal responses and behaviors, which may indicate the need for further questioning to clarify verbal answers. The interview can be used with many different types of persons, such as those who are illiterate or too young to read or write. The presence of an interviewer tends to reduce the number of "no answers" or "neutral" responses, and the interviewer can press for more complete answers when necessary. In comparison to questionnaires, interviews usually achieve higher return rates; often as many as 90 or 95 percent of the subjects will agree to be interviewed.

One disadvantage of interviews is that because they are expensive and time-consuming compared to other methods of data collection, the sample size is often small. With small samples a high response rate is needed to avoid bias in the nature of the sample. The number of refusals to be interviewed, if greater than 10 or 15 percent, may seriously bias the results. The advantages of flexibility and the opportunity for probing and clarification allow for a certain degree of subjectivity. Depending on the training and experience of the interviewer, this subjectivity may lead to biased responses or the biased recording and interpretation of responses. These effects will be discussed in greater detail following a brief summary of different types of interview questions.

Types of Interview Questions

For most quantitative investigations an interview schedule is constructed that contains the questions that will be asked. In most cases the questions on the interview schedule are precisely what the interviewer will ask the subjects. There are three types of interview questions: structured, semistructured, and unstructured. **Structured questions** give the subject choices from which an answer is selected. For example, in a study of student attitudes, there may be four possible answers to the question "How important is it to you to obtain high grades in school? Is it critical, very important, important, or not very important?" Structured questions are often used in telephone interviews, which for some purposes can provide data comparable to those obtained through personal interviews at about half the cost.

Semistructured questions do not have predetermined, structured choices. Rather, the question is open-ended yet specific in intent, allowing individual responses. For instance, an interviewer may ask, "What are some things that teachers you like do best?"

Structured questions: Subject chooses from responses provided.

Semistructured questions: Specific questions without preexisting response options.

The question is reasonably objective, yet it allows for probing, follow-up, and clarification. It is the most common type of interview question in educational research.

Unstructured questions are open-ended and broad. The interviewer has a general goal in mind and asks questions relevant to this goal. Thus there is some latitude in what is asked, and often somewhat different questions are used with each subject. The unstructured interview is difficult to conduct. It is highly subjective and requires considerable training and experience. Thus, in research that has employed unstructured questions look carefully for evidence that the interviewer has the appropriate expertise to conduct the interview and then interpret the results.

Unstructured questions: Open-ended, general questions.

Regardless of the type of interview, it is important that the questions are worded so that the subject is not led to a particular answer. A **leading question** biases the results by encouraging one answer from all the subjects. For example, if the interviewer asks, "Wouldn't you agree that Mrs. Jones is an excellent teacher?" the subjects are led toward a yes response.

Leading question: Encourages a certain answer.

Interviewer Effects

The ideal role of the interviewer is to act as a neutral medium through which information is transmitted. The interviewer should not have an effect on the results, except to make it possible for the subject to reveal information that otherwise would not have been known. However, because of the one-on-one nature of the interview there are several potential sources of error. Like observers, interviewers must be careful that preexisting bias does not influence what they hear or record, a possibility if they harbor stereotypes about certain types of subjects. Contamination can also occur if the interviewers have knowledge of facets of the study. They should not be aware of which subjects are receiving special treatments or how certain results will have positive benefits. The halo effect can also occur with interviewers. Obviously, they need to be trained so that many of these potential sources of error will not arise. Interviewers also need to be trained to establish positive rapport with the subjects.

There is some evidence that certain characteristics of the interviewer may influence the results. For example, matching interviewers and subjects on demographic variables such as age, socioeconomic status, race, and gender may provide more valid results. Generally, most inhibition in responding occurs with persons of the same age but different gender. Interviewers should dress according to existing norms or in a fashion familiar to that of the respondents, not in such a way that the subjects sense that particular responses are desirable.

Additional error may occur from the way the interview is conducted. It is important for the interviewer to be pleasant, friendly, and relaxed in establishing a relationship with the subject that is conducive to honest interchange and little inhibition. This result is often accomplished by beginning the interview with "small talk." Probing should be anticipated and planned for in the training of the interviewers, and specific types of probes should be identified for certain situations. Consider a recent study that interviewed children to ascertain their causal explanations following success and failure in schoolwork.

EXAMPLE: INTERVIEW PROBING

"The first probe was always a simple repetition of the child's response, in the child's own words. . . . If the repetition probe was ineffective, the interviewer would ask, 'Did he always try or just try sometimes?' " (Frieze and Snyder, 1980, p. 190)

The manner in which the interviewer records responses may affect the results. At one extreme, a tape recorder can provide a verbatim record of the answers. The tapes can then be analyzed by several judges to increase validity. This method is most useful with unstructured questions, which lend themselves to greater subjectivity on the part of the interviewer. However, the mere presence of a tape recorder may inhibit some subjects. Consequently if a tape recorder was used in research, you need to look for assurance that subjects were not affected by its presence. At the other extreme, the interviewer can wait until the interview is over and then write notes that summarize the results. This procedure is more prone to error because it is easier for interview bias to affect what is remembered and recorded. To reduce this source of error most interviewers take some notes during the interview. Rarely can interviewers record the exact response of the subject. More typically, they write brief notes for each question during the interview that can be expanded after the interview is over. One way to increase reliability is to send a copy of the interviewer's notes to each subject, giving them an opportunity to add or revise as necessary.

LOCATING AND EVALUATING EDUCATIONAL MEASURES

Literally thousands of instruments have been used in educational research over the past 50 years. When you read research you will encounter many different measures. How will you know if they are providing valid and reliable information? As pointed out earlier, research is only as good as the measurement on which it is based. Consequently, it is best to be able to evaluate the instruments that were used by studying the information provided by the researchers in a report or article. Often, however, there is insufficient information in the article to make an informed judgment. In that case, a number of sources can be used to both identify and evaluate existing educational measures. Some of the sources summarize the instruments and others provide a critique.

The Educator's Desk Reference: A Sourcebook of Educational Information and Research (Freed, Hess, & Ryan, 1989): Describes the uses and limitations of leading standardized tests.

Index to Tests Used in Educational Dissertations (Fabiano, 1989): Describes tests and test populations used in dissertations from 1938 to 1980; keyed by title and selected descriptors.

The ETS Test Collection: The Educational Testing Service (ETS) has developed several sources that describe thousands of tests and instruments. The *Test Collection Bibliographies* cover published and unpublished measures in several areas, including achievement, attitudes and interests, personality, special populations, and vocation/occupation. Each of over 200 separate bibliographies describes instruments and appropriate uses and can be ordered from ETS. *Tests in Microfiche* lists unpublished research instruments, also in a wide variety of areas. *The ETS Test Collection Catalog* includes five volumes: *Volume 1: Achievement Tests and Measurement Devices* (1986), *Volume 2: Vocational Tests and Measurement Devices* (1988), *Volume 3: Tests for Special Populations* (1989), *Volume 4: Cognitive Aptitude and Intelligence Tests* (1990), and *Volume 5: Attitude Tests* (1991). Each volume contains full descriptions of the instruments, with author, title, and subject indexes.

Tests: A Comprehensive Reference for Assessments in Psychology, Education, and Business, 2nd ed. (Sweetland & Keyser, 1986): Provides a description of over 3,100 published tests, including purpose, cost, scoring, and publisher.

Test Critiques, Vols. 1–7 (Keyser & Sweetland, 1984–1988): Gives in-depth evaluations for widely used, newly published, and recently revised instruments in psychology, education, and business. Contains "user-oriented" information, including practical applications and uses, as well as technical aspects and a critique by a measurement specialist. The companion, *Test Critiques Compendium*, reviews 60 major tests from *Test Critiques* in one volume.

The Tenth Mental Measurements Yearbook (Conoley & Kramer,

1989): Provides 569 reviews of 396 commercially available tests in several different areas, including character and personality, achievement, and intelligence. References for most of the tests facilitate further research. (Earlier editions were published by Oscar Buros and J. V. Mitchell.) Reviews of tests newly published or revised since 1989 are contained in the Supplement to the Tenth Mental Measurements Yearbook (Kramer, Conoley, & Murphy, 1990).

Tests and Measurements in Child Development: Handbook I and II (Johnson, 1976): Two volumes describe about 900 unpublished tests and instruments for children through age 18.

Evaluating Classroom Instruction: A Sourcebook of Instruments (Borich & Madden, 1977): Reviews instruments that can be used in the classroom to evaluate teacher and student behavior. Observation schedules are included.

A Sourcebook of Mental Health Measures (Comrey, Backer, & Glaser, 1973): This reference describes about 1,100 instruments related to mental health, including juvenile delinquency, personality, and alcoholism.

Measures for Psychological Assessment: A Guide to 3,000 Original Sources and Their Applications (Chun, Cobb, & French, 1974): A list of tests used in research reported in 26 different psychological journals.

Measures of Social Psychological Attitudes (Robinson & Shaver, 1973): Describes hundreds of attitude instruments used in psychological and sociological research.

Mirrors for Behavior III: An Anthology of Observation Instruments (Simon & Boyer, 1974): About 100 observation instruments are described in various fields, including medicine, business, and anthropology, as well as education.

Socioemotional Measures for Pre-School and Kindergarten Children: A Handbook (Walker, 1973): Describes instruments to measure attitudes, personality, self-concept, and social skills of young children.

Handbook for Measurement and Evaluation in Early Childhood Education (Goodwin & Driscoll, 1980): A comprehensive review of affective, cognitive, and psychomotor measures for young children.

In addition to these sources, an excellent way to obtain information about an instrument is to contact its developer. The developer may have a technical manual to send to you and may know about other researchers who have used the instrument. Technical manuals are almost always available for published tests.

Finally, you may want to try a computer search of journal articles that have up-to-date information on critical evaluations of an instrument's validity and reliability and other studies that have used it. In the ERIC data base a proximity search is one alternative. In a proximity search terms that make up the name of the instrument, or related terms, are used to locate relevant articles. The data base for *Psychological Abstracts*, PsycINFO, indexes major instruments by name.

CONSUMER TIPS
Criteria for Evaluating Instrumentation

1. **Evidence for validity should be stated clearly.** The researchers should address validity by explicitly indicating the type of evidence that is presented (content-related, criterion-related, or construct-related), the results of analyses that establish validity, and how the evidence supports the inferences that are made. For evidence that does not match well with the subjects or situation of the investigation, the researcher should indicate why it is reasonable to believe that the results are appropriate and useful. References should cite previous research that supports the validity of the inferences. It is best to collect evidence for validity in a pretest or pilot test.

2. **Evidence for reliability should be stated clearly.** The researchers should clearly indicate the reliability of all measures. The type of reliability estimate used should be indicated, and it should be consistent with the use of the results. Reliability should be established in a pretest or pilot test with subjects similar to those used in the research. High reliability is especially important for results that show no difference or no relationship.

3. **A clear description of the instruments should be indicated.** Sufficient information about the instrument should be given to enable the reader to understand how the subjects gave their responses. This information includes some idea of the type of item, which is often accomplished by providing examples. It is also necessary to indicate how the instrument is scored.

4. **A clear description of the procedures for administering the instrument should be indicated.** The reader needs to know when the instrument was given and the conditions of its administration. Who gave the instrument to the subjects? What did they know about the study? What were the subjects told before they answered the questions? Did anything unusual happen during the administration? Did the subjects understand the directions for completing the

instrument? These questions are especially critical for standardized tests.

5. Norms should be specified for norm-referenced tests. The norms used to determine the results need to be clearly indicated. What is the nature of the norm group? Is it appropriate to the type of inferences that are made?

6. Procedures for setting standards should be indicated for criterion-referenced tests. It is necessary to know how the standards used to judge the results are set. Were experts consulted to verify the credibility of the standard? What is the difficulty level of the items in relation to the standard?

7. The scores used in reporting results should be meaningful. Often standard scores or some type of derived scores are used in reporting the results. Whatever the scores, they should not distort the actual differences or relationships, either by inflating or deflating the apparent differences or relationships.

8. Measures of noncognitive traits must avoid problems of response set and faking. Researchers need to indicate how response set and faking are controlled when measuring personality, attitudes, values, and interests. Special attention should be given to the manner in which the subjects are motivated.

9. Observers and interviewers should be trained. It is important to show that the observers and interviewers in studies have been trained to avoid such problems as bias, contamination, and halo effect. Interviewers need to know how not to ask leading questions and how to probe effectively. Interobserver reliability should be indicated.

10. In high-inference observations the qualifications of the observers to make sound professional judgments should be indicated. With low-inference observations reliability is usually high, but if high-inference observations are used the characteristics and training of the observer are more important and should be specified.

11. The effect of the interviewer or observer should be minimal. Examine the characteristics of the interviewers. Could these traits create any error in the nature of the responses obtained? Were appropriate steps taken to establish a proper rapport with the subjects? Any possible effects of the observer on the subjects should be noted. Observers should be as inconspicuous as possible.

OUTLINE SUMMARY

1. Educational measures.
   A. Cognitive/noncognitive.
   B. Off-the-shelf/commercially prepared.
   C. Self-report/indirect.

2. Tests.
   A. Norm-referenced.
      (1) Differentiates between individuals.
      (2) High variability.
      (3) Nature of the norm group is critical.
   B. Criterion-referenced.
      (1) Low variability.
      (2) Setting of a standard is critical.
   C. Standardized tests.
      (1) Standard procedures for administration and scoring.
      (2) Technically sound.
      (3) Achievement tests.
      (4) Aptitude tests.
   D. Standard scores.
      (1) May exaggerate raw score differences.
      (2) Useful for statistical purposes.
      (3) Grade equivalents often misinterpreted.
3. Personality instruments.
   A. Comprehensive assessments require a highly trained clinician.
   B. Measures of self-concept frequently used.
4. Attitude, interest, and value inventories.
   A. Scales provide a gradation of responses.
   B. Reliability and validity may be weak.
   C. Two major sources of error.
      (1) Response set.
      (2) Faking.
5. Observation.
   A. The degree of inference: high or low.
   B. Effect of setting.
      (1) Laboratory.
      (2) Field.
   C. Observer effects.
      (1) Observer bias.
      (2) Contamination.
      (3) Halo effect.
6. Interviews.
   A. Advantages.
      (1) Enhance subject motivation.
      (2) Clarify subject questions.
      (3) Probe for clarification.
      (4) Record nonverbal as well as verbal responses.
      (5) Useful for all types of subjects.
      (6) Increase responses.
      (7) High return rate.

   B. Disadvantages.
 (1) Expensive.
 (2) Time-consuming.
 (3) Small sample.
 (4) Lack of training and expertise.
 (5) Loss of anonymity.
   C. Interview questions.
 (1) Structured.
 (2) Semistructured.
 (3) Unstructured.
   D. Interviewer effects.
 (1) Ask leading questions.
 (2) Bias.
 (3) Contamination.
 (4) Halo effect.
 (5) Demographic characteristics.
 (6) How responses are recorded.
7. Secondary sources identify and evaluate existing instruments.
8. Criteria for evaluating instrumentation.
   A. Clearly stated validity.
   B. Clearly stated reliability.
   C. Clearly described instruments.
   D. Clearly described procedures.
   E. Norms and procedures for setting standards should be indicated.
   F. Scores should be meaningful.
   G. Response set and faking avoided.
   H. Observers and interviewers trained.
   I. Observers qualified for high-inference judgments.
   J. Effects of observers and interviewers controlled.

STUDY QUESTIONS

1. What are some ways of classifying educational measures?

2. What is the difference between off-the-shelf and locally developed tests?

3. What is the difference between criterion-referenced and norm-referenced tests?

4. Why are changes in scores difficult to obtain with many standardized tests?

5. What is the difference between standardized achievement tests and standardized aptitude tests?

6. Why are standard scores difficult to interpret?

7. Give some examples of different ways of measuring self-concept and attitudes.

8. What is the difference between Likert and Semantic Differential scales.

9. Identify factors that affect the measurement of noncognitive traits. How does each one affect the results?

10. What are the advantages of observations rather than self-reports?

11. Under what circumstances would it be better to involve high-inference rather than low-inference observation?

12. In what ways are observer and interviewer effects the same?

13. Compare the interview with the questionnaire. What are the advantages and disadvantages of both?

14. Identify criteria for evaluating instrumentation. What would you look for when reading the instrumentation section of a research article?

Chapter
7

Descriptive, Correlational, and Causal-Comparative Research

We now turn our attention to research designs commonly employed to obtain data. **Research design** refers to the way information is gathered from subjects and, in the case of experimental research, the nature of the treatments that are controlled by the investigator. In this chapter we will consider three types of nonexperimental research designs, and in Chapter 8 we will review various types of experimental designs. It is important to understand design to be able to identify possible extraneous variables that may affect the interpretation of the results.

Research design: How information is obtained.

THE PURPOSE OF NONEXPERIMENTAL RESEARCH

In Chapter 1 a distinction was made between experimental and nonexperimental research. While experimental research is used to understand causal relationships by manipulating an independent variable, nonexperimental research essentially describes existing phenomena without changing some condition to affect subjects' responses. You may find that some educators use the terms *nonexperimental* and *descriptive* interchangeably. To understand research design, though, it is better to think about different types of nonexperimental research, with descriptive being one type. Other types are correlational, relationship, survey, historical, case study, and even qualitative designs. In each case there is no manipulation of an independent variable. In this sense, a nonexperimental design investigates the current status of something. It is a report of the way things are, what is, or what has been.

DESCRIPTIVE STUDIES

Characteristics of Descriptive Studies

A descriptive study simply describes a phenomenon. The description is usually in the form of statistics such as frequencies or percentages, averages, and sometimes variability. Often graphs and other visual images of the results are used. Descriptive research is particularly valuable when an area is first investigated. For example, there has been much research on the nature of classroom climate and its relationship to student attitudes and learning. A first step in this research is to describe adequately what is meant by "classroom climate," initially by a clear constitutive definition, then operationally with measures. Climate surveys, which assess such characteristics as how students talk and act toward one another; how they feel about the teacher and learning; and feelings of openness, acceptance, trust, respect, rejection, hostility, and cooperation, are used to understand classroom atmosphere. Once this understanding is achieved, various dimensions of climate can be related to student learning and teacher satisfaction, and ultimately climate can be controlled to examine the causal relationship between them. For many teachers, instruments that assess climate can be very useful in describing the nature of their class.

Suppose you read a study on the relationship between principals' leadership styles and teachers' attitudes. You should first look for an adequate description of leadership styles of principals and attitudes of teachers since the usefulness of the results depends on credible descriptions. Much of the current emphasis on accountability in our schools is based on descriptive research, examining such student "outcomes" as current levels of achievement or drop-out rates. The questions in the box on top of the next page are investigated with descriptive research designs.

A good example of a descriptive study investigated the reasons children give for their successes and failures in school (Cauley & Murray, 1982). The procedure was to ask a sample of second- and third-graders to read and define words and then ask them some questions about how well they did. The results were summarized by showing the percentage of children who made various attributions (reasons).

EXAMPLES: DESCRIPTIVE RESEARCH DESIGN QUESTIONS

What do teachers think about magnet schools?

How often do students write papers?

What is the nature of the papers students are required to write?

What percentage of students score above 1100 on the SAT?

What forms of communication are used in the school district?

How often are higher-order questions used in the classroom?

What type of reinforcement does the teacher use?

EXAMPLE: DESCRIPTIVE RESEARCH

"Their initial attributions were primarily task attributions (46% to 58% said the words were easy). Their own effort was the next most common cause of their success (40% of the responses). When asked for a second response, the subjects evenly divided their answers among the four types of attributions." (Cauley and Murray, 1982, p. 476)

Another example of descriptive research is illustrated by a study of how teachers use homework in high schools (Murphy & Decker, 1988/1989). In this study 2,986 high school teachers were asked to answer 37 questions about 5 components of homework (policies, purpose, amount, review and feedback, and parental and school support). The results are described by the frequency and percentage of answers to each question.

EXAMPLE: DESCRIPTIVE RESEARCH

"The majority of the teachers (51%) reported that students finished between 81% and 100% of their homework, whereas another one third (30%) declared that the completion rate was between 61% and 80%. Teachers also noted that there was a group of about one fifth of the students (19%) who completed less than 60% of their work. Whereas these numbers are better than those reported by certain students, they reveal that many homework assignments are being ignored by high school students." (p. 266)

CONSUMER TIPS
Criteria for Evaluating Descriptive Studies

1. Conclusions about relationships and causal relationships should not be made. An important limitation of descriptive studies is that such conclusions are not warranted. It is easy to make assumptions from simple descriptions about how two or more variables are related, but you should not do so. For instance, suppose a study describes the types of questions students and teachers ask in a classroom, reporting that teachers ask "low-level" questions and students do not ask questions at all. It would be tempting to conclude that there is a relationship between these phenomena. However, such a conclusion is not warranted. To address the question of relationship, teachers who ask "high-level" questions would also have to be included.

2. Subjects and instrumentation should be well described. When evaluating descriptive research you should pay particular attention to the subjects and the instrumentation. You should know whether the sample is volunteer and whether the results would have been different if other subjects had been included. The instrumentation section should have documentation of validity and reliability, and the procedures for gathering the data need to be specified. You should know when the data were collected, by whom, and under what circumstances. For example, a description of what is occurring in a class may differ, depending on whether the observer is a teacher, principal, or parent.

3. Graphic presentations should not distort the results. Since graphs are used frequently to present descriptive results, you need to be careful in interpreting the resulting "picture." Graphs, whether a histogram, pie chart, or frequency polygon, show an image of the results, and we are more likely to remember the image rather than the numbers that correspond to it. This is fine when the image is a reasonable representation of the numbers, but numbers can be manipulated in a graph to present different images. One type of distortion to look for is in the vertical dimensions of the graph. The size of the interval between different scores is set by the researcher, and this size greatly affects the resulting image. In fact, a crafty researcher can make fairly substantial differences appear quite small by decreasing the size of the intervals between scores or other measurement units, or the researcher can make small differences look large. For example, look at the two graphic presentations in Figure 7.1. Although each graph has summarized the same information about expenditures per pupil, the visual results are different because the size of the interval between each amount is much smaller in one graph than in the other.

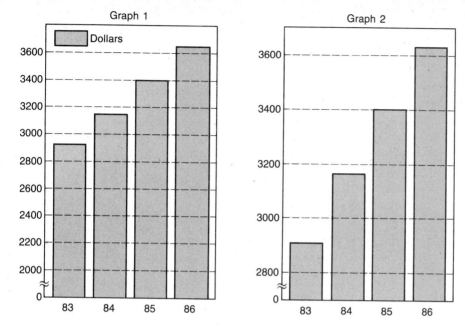

Figure 7.1 Current expenditures per pupil in the United States. (*Source:* Statistical Abstract of the United States, 1987, p. 123.)

RELATIONSHIP STUDIES

Relationship studies investigate the degree to which variations or differences in one variable are related to variations or differences in another variable. Relationships are important in our understanding of teaching and learning and schooling for several reasons. First, relationships allow us to make a preliminary identification of possible causes of students' achievement, teachers' performance, principals' leadership, and other important educational outcomes. Second, relationships help us identify variables that may have to be investigated further. Third, relationships allow us to predict the value of one variable from the value of a second variable. Because of these very useful purposes, it is not surprising that the language of research is dominated by the term *relationship.* As a consumer of research you need to be fully informed about what relationship studies can and cannot tell us.

In some studies, relationship is conceptualized and researched as a difference between different groups of subjects. In other studies it is thought of as a correlation among two or more variables. Correlation may refer in a generic sense to relationship or to the specific statistical technique of correlation coefficient. A "difference" relationship is obtained by comparing two or more groups on a variable. A simple example is a study of the relationship between gender and school grades. A sample of female students' grades could be compared to the grades of a sample of male students. The question is answered by comparing males to females on, say, grade point average for the same courses. The results show how differences in one variable, sex, relate to differences on another variable, grade point average. If the results indicate that females have a higher grade point average, there is a relationship between the two variables. Notice, however, that this is not a causal relationship. We can predict, to a certain extent, whether females or males have a higher grade point average, but we do not know how being male or female affects or causes grade point average.

Another example is a study of the relationship between learning style and achievement. Suppose there are four types or categories of learning style and a measure of reading achievement. A sample of students representing each type of learning style can be obtained, and the average reading achievement of the students in each group (each learning style) can be compared. This method also provides a measure of the differences among the groups, which represent a relationship between learning style and achievement. In this case we must be careful not to conclude that the learning styles *caused* differences in achievement. The best we have is a prediction that students with a particular type of learning style will have higher or lower achievement. Learning style may affect or influence achievement, but our relationship study does not give us a good measure of cause and effect.

A published example of a relationship study that uses differences between groups investigates the relationship among locus of control, academic level, and gender of ninth-grade students (Boss & Taylor, 1989). In this study, a measure of locus of control was administered to 267 ninth-graders. The results were presented by showing the scores of six groups of students: males and females in basic, general, and advanced academic programs. Conclusions were made about relationships by examining the differences among the six groups on locus of control. (See box on next page.)

Simple Correlational Studies

Used in a specific sense as a correlation coefficient, correlational studies indicate relationships by obtaining two scores from each subject. The pairs of scores are used to produce a scattergram and to calculate a correlation coefficient. Each score represents a variable in the study. For example, variables such as self-concept, cog-

EXAMPLE: RELATIONSHIP STUDY OF DIFFERENCES AMONG GROUPS

"Advanced level students were more internally responsible for their intellectual-academic failures than general level students. Surprisingly, neither general nor advanced level students were more internally responsible for their intellectual-academic failures than the basic level students." (p. 320)

nitive style, previous achievement, time on task, and amount of homework completed can be related to achievement, attitudes, self-concept, and motivation. Grades in student teaching can be related to principals' ratings of effective teaching. In each case a correlation coefficient expresses the nature of the relationship between the variables.

Often more than two variables are investigated in a single study, resulting in several correlations. In a study of the relationship between dimensions of the school and parental involvement (Hoover-Dempsey, Bassler, & Brissie, 1987), teachers and principals of 66 schools reported perceptions of efficacy, organizational rigidity, and instructional coordination. These measures, along with the school's socioeconomic status, were related to parental involvement. The study showed that the teachers' sense of efficacy and the school's socioeconomic status are related positively with the percentage of parent conferences, parent volunteers, parental home tutoring, parental involvement in home instruction, and teachers' perception of parental support.

When reading correlational research you should examine carefully the selection of instruments and subjects since the results depend to a great extent on the nature of the instruments and the answers given by a sample of subjects. The first aspect of instrumentation to examine is reliability. If the instrument is not reliable, it is more difficult to obtain a significant correlation coefficient. Consequently, the researcher should demonstrate evidence of reliability for the types of persons in the study. It is also important for the instrument to provide a range of responses from a sufficient number of subjects. That is, the scores on the measures must have wide variability and good dispersion, and there must be enough subjects to obtain a significant correlation. If the scores are about the same on a variable, it is difficult to relate the variable to anything else. For example, if a study examines the relationship between ratings of effectiveness and teaching style and all the teachers in the sample are rated as excellent, there would be no chance of finding a relationship. Similarly, it is difficult to find relationships between achievement of gifted students and other variables because of the lack of variability of achievement among these students. Most correlational studies need to have at least 30 subjects, and more than 30 are needed for studies in which the relationship may be small.

The lack of variability can be the result of an instrument that fails to differentiate along a continuum, or the subjects may be too homogeneous on the trait being measured. In either case, you will need to be careful in your interpretation of relationship studies that fail to find significant relationships. If there is a lack of variability, you will not know whether there really is no relationship or, because of a small range of responses, a particular study was unable to show the relationship. In other words, just because the study did not report a relationship does not mean that it does not exist. A study may fail to show a relationship for many reasons, only one of which is that, in reality, a relationship does not exist.

There is also a limitation on finding "significant" relationships in a study that has a very large number of subjects and/or variables. Some researchers, using what is called the "shotgun" approach, measure a large number of variables, selected without a reasonable rationale for their inclusion, with the hope that some of the many correlations that are calculated will be significant. However, in such studies some of the correlations will be significant by chance alone, and without a theoretical or practical reason for inclusion, the results will be difficult to interpret. When thousands of subjects are used it is also possible to calculate statistically "significant" correlations that are actually quite small. Consequently, the "relationship" that is reported may be very small and of little value. We will discuss this limitation later in this chapter.

Prediction Studies

In a prediction study, correlation coefficients show how one variable can predict another. Whereas in a simple relationship study, both variables are measured at about the same time, a predictive study shows how one variable can predict what the value will be on a second variable at a later time. Predictions are made constantly in education. Teachers predict students' behavior. Principals predict teachers' behavior. Students are selected to special programs because they are expected to do well or to do better than others. Coaches predict the performance of their players. Students are counseled to attend particular colleges or to pursue certain occupations.

The results of these studies make a more accurate estimate of prediction possible. Suppose you are director of admissions at a selective university. You must choose a small number of students from the large pool of applicants. How should you select the students to be admitted? One approach would be simply to select applicants randomly from all who apply, but in all probability some of the admitted students would fail and others who would thrive at the university would be rejected. So you decide to use some criteria to predict which students are most likely to succeed. Because one predictor is probably previous achievement, you look at the high school grade point average (GPA) of each applicant. If it turns out that it is correlated with college GPA, you have identified a variable that can be used to predict success in college. High school students with a high GPA are likely to have a higher college GPA than high school students with a low GPA. High school GPA precedes college GPA and would therefore be called a **predictor variable.** College GPA would be termed the **criterion variable.**

Predictor variable: Predicts the criterion variable.

Criterion variable: The predicted dependent variable.

In a prediction study it is necessary to collect data on a group of subjects over a length of time. Data collection can be longitudinal, that is, first collecting predictor variable data, waiting a specified amount of time, and then obtaining criterion variable data. This approach for the preceding example would involve recording the GPA of high school students before they started college, then waiting, say, for a year and recording their first-year college GPA. Another approach is to study retrospectively the performance of subjects on predictor variables. With either approach, once a predictive relationship is established, it needs to be "tested" with another sample of subjects. The "tested" prediction, which will be lower than the original one, is the relationship that most closely indicates how well the predictor variable will predict the criterion variable with future groups of subjects. Thus in evaluating prediction research you need to look for the "tested" predictive relationship. In a recent predictive study of student success in a gifted program (Lustberg, Motta, & Naccari, 1990), the WISC-R, teachers' recommendations, grades, and achievement test scores were used as predictors, and the criterion variable was the degree of success in a gifted program. Notice in the method section how the authors indicate that one group of students is used to establish the predictive relationship and another group of students is used to "test" it.

The accuracy of predictions will be influenced by several factors. One is the reliability of the measures of the predictor and criterion variables. If the measures are not highly reliable, the prediction will be lower than it would be with more reliable measures. Another factor is the length of time between the predictor and criterion variables. In most cases, predictions involving a short time span are more accurate than those involving a long time span because of the general principle that the correlation between two vari-

EXAMPLE: PREDICTIVE RESEARCH

"This study was conducted in two phases. The initial phase of the study involved 120 elementary school students aged 6 through 11 years. These students had different degrees of success in a gifted program. . . .

The second phase of the investigation involved random selection of an additional 41 subjects from the same gifted program. . . . In phase two, an attempt was made, using the results of phase one data, to predict those students who were known to have been either marginally or highly successful in the program." (p. 127)

ables decreases as the amount of time between the variables increases; also, with more time there is a greater opportunity for other variables to influence the criterion variable, which would lower the prediction. Finally, criterion variables that are affected by many factors, such as success in college, leadership, a successful marriage, and effective teaching, are more difficult to predict than relatively simple criterion variables such as success in the next mathematics class or being admitted to at least one college.

In many situations predictions are most accurate if more than one predictor variable is used. For example, in predicting college GPA, several variables may be predictive, and by combining them we can make more accurate decisions about who should be admitted. In studies in which several predictor variables are combined, a statistical procedure called **regression analysis** provides a single index of the predictive power of all the predictor variables together. A **coefficient of multiple correlation,** symbolized by R, is the correlation of all the independent variables (predictor variables) to the dependent variable (criterion variable). In interpreting regression analysis it is important to know about the correlations of the independent variables with one another. It is most desirable to have independent variables that are not correlated with one another but are correlated with the dependent variable. If the independent variables are correlated with one another, the predictive power of some of the variables may be masked.

A recent study investigated organizational work characteristics that predict teachers' career dissatisfaction (Conley, Bacharach, & Bauer, 1989). The predicted dependent variable was measured by asking teachers in 47 schools to rate the degree to which they were satisfied with career goals and expectations. The predictive independent variables were organizational factors in each school, such as role ambiguity, absence of authority, communication, supervi-

Regression analysis: Combines several predictor variables.

Coefficient of multiple correlation: The combined correlation of several predictor variables.

EXAMPLE: PREDICTIVE RESEARCH

"Our final three hypotheses dealt with classroom environment factors
. . . In elementary schools we find that where teachers perceive class
size as manageable, the reported level of career dissatisfaction is lower
than in elementary schools in which teachers perceive class size as
less manageable. . . . In secondary schools, only the perceived absence of student learning problems . . . and the perceived absence of
student behavior problems . . . emerged as predictors of teacher career
dissatisfaction." (p. 72)

---

sory behavior, promotion, and classroom environment. The results
showed that career dissatisfaction is predicted differently for elementary and secondary schools.

CONSUMER TIPS
Criteria for Evaluating Correlational Studies

The following criteria are useful in interpreting and evaluating correlational research, including both simple correlational and predictive studies.

   1. **Causation should not be inferred from correlation.** The most
important principle in evaluating correlational research is not to
infer causation. This is not as easy as it sounds, for many relationships sound as if they do infer causation. For example, if you find
a positive relationship between time-on-task and achievement, it
is easy to think that by increasing time-on-task there will be an
increase in achievement. Although it may be true, it cannot be concluded from a correlational finding for two reasons. First, the direction of possible causation is not clear. That is, it may be that
higher achievement causes students to be more on-task. Second,
other variables associated with time-on-task that are not included
in the study may affect the relationship and may, in fact, be causally
related. For instance, perhaps students who spend more time-on-
task have a higher aptitude for learning, better motivation for learning, and more parental support than students who spend less time-
on-task. Perhaps teachers interact differently with students who are
on-task compared to students who tend to be off-task. This principle
is illustrated more clearly in a relationship between student
achievement and per-pupil expenditures. Although a positive re-

lationship exists, it would be a mistake to think that achievement can be affected simply by spending more money because many other variables also related to per-pupil expenditure, such as family background, are the actual causes of student achievement.

Take as a final example of this principle the following "true" statement: There is a positive relationship between students' weight and reading achievement. Unbelievable, you think? Examine the explanation in Figure 7.2. There is a positive relationship between the two factors because a third variable, age, is related to weight. Obviously, there is a positive relationship between age and reading achievement. If you were puzzled by the first conclusion, you were implying causation, probably thinking something about how weight may cause achievement. The conclusion that would follow is that achievement could be improved by fattening up the students!

2. The reported correlation should not be higher or lower than the actual correlation. You need to be aware of factors that may increase or decrease a correlation. One factor is the nature of the sample from which the correlation is calculated. If the sample is more homogeneous on one of the variables than is the population, the correlation will be lower than that for the population as a whole. Conversely, if a sample is more heterogeneous on the variable than the population, the correlation will be higher than that for the population as a whole. Thus, it is important to examine the nature of the sample and the conclusions that may be made for the population.

A second factor is the range of scores on the variables that are correlated. If the variability of scores on one variable is small, the correlation will be low. This is sometimes referred to as **restriction in range.** If the range is restricted, the variability is reduced, and without adequate variability the correlation will be low. Thus in some research in which the range is restricted, the actual relationship is higher than that which is reported. This principle explains the modest relationships found between admissions criteria and subsequent performance. Typically, only a portion of the students are admitted, which restricts the range on the variables used for admissions.

Restriction in range: A small range.

A third factor relates to the reliability of the measures of the correlated variables. As already noted, correlations are directly related to reliability—the lower the reliability the lower the correlation. A lowering of the correlation because of unreliability is called **attenuation** and is sometimes "corrected" statistically to show what the correlation would be if the measures were more reliable.

Attenuation: Lowering of correlation because of unreliable measures.

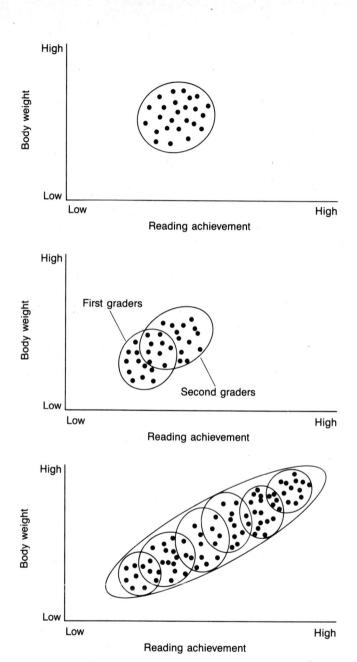

Figure 7.2 Relationship between weight and reading achievement. (*Source:* McMillan and Schumacher, 1989, pp. 289–290.)

3. **Practical significance should not be confused with "statistical" significance.** Researchers use the word *significant* in two ways. In one sense it refers to a statistical inference, which means the coefficient that is calculated is probably different from zero, that is, no relationship (Chapter 9 discusses this concept in greater detail). Thus a researcher may report that "a correlation of .30 is significant." This type of phrase is associated with the statistical meaning of significance. Another meaning of significance implies importance or meaningfulness of the practical value of the correlation. This is a more subjective judgment, one that should be made by the reader of the research as well as by the researcher. One important principle of correlation needs to be considered in making this judgment. Because correlations are expressed as decimals, it is easy to confuse the coefficient with percentages. However, the correlation coefficient is not an indication of the percentage of "sameness" between two variables. The extent to which the variables share common properties or characteristics is actually indicated by the square of the correlation coefficient. This is called the **coefficient of determination,** and it is a much better indicator of practical or meaningful significance than is the correlation coefficient. For example, a correlation of .50, squared, indicates that the variables have 25 percent in common, or 25 percent "explained" of what can be accounted for, which leaves 75 percent unexplained. Thus if the correlation between achievement and some other variable is .70, which is regarded as a "high" correlation, about 50 percent of what can vary with respect to achievement is not predicted or accounted for by the correlation.

Coefficient of determination: The square of the correlation coefficient.

4. **The size of the correlation should be sufficient for the use of the results.** Much larger correlations are needed for predictions with individuals than for groups. Crude group predictions can be made with correlations as low as .40 to .60, whereas correlations above .75 are usually needed to make predictions for individuals. In exploratory studies low correlations (e.g., .25 to .40) may indicate a need for further study, but higher correlations are needed for research to confirm theories or test hypotheses. In many studies using regression analysis, correlations between .20 and .40 are common and usually indicate some practical significance.

5. **Prediction studies should report accuracy of prediction for new subjects.** To use the results of prediction research, it is necessary to know the accuracy of the predicted relationship. This figure is found by testing a presumed predictive relationship with a new, different group of persons.

6. **Procedures for collecting data should be clearly indicated.** It is important to indicate, in detail, the procedures used to collect the data used in calculating the correlations because the procedures

affect reliability. Correlation coefficients are directly related to the reliability of the measures and the sampling of subjects.

USING SURVEYS IN DESCRIPTIVE AND RELATIONSHIP STUDIES

Survey research has evolved over the years to become a popular methodology of the social sciences. It is especially frequent in sociology, which is the field most closely associated with surveys. In a survey, the investigator selects a group of respondents, collects information, and then analyzes the information to answer the research questions. The group of subjects is usually selected from a larger population through some type of probability sampling, which allows accurate information to be collected about a large population from a small sample. In other surveys an entire population is included. Most surveys describe the incidence, frequency, and distribution of the characteristics of the population, such as people's attitudes, voting intentions, television viewing habits, food preferences, and demographic facts.

Surveys are used frequently in business, government, public health, politics, psychology, sociology, and transportation, as well as in education. In addition to being descriptive, surveys are also used to investigate relationships between variables. They are not used, except in rare circumstances, to investigate cause-and-effect relationships. Surveys are either given to one or more samples or populations at one time or are given more than once to the same subjects over a specified length of time. These differences have important implications for interpreting results and are discussed next as cross-sectional and longitudinal methods.

Cross-Sectional Surveys

In a **cross-sectional survey**, information is collected from one or more samples or populations at one time. There are two types of cross-sectional surveys. One type simply studies a phenomenon as it occurs at one time, for example, political surveys and surveys that study an attitude or characteristic of a group. A good illustration is "The 21st Annual Gallup Poll of the Public's Attitudes Toward the Public Schools" (Elam & Gallup, 1989), which in recent years has been published in *Phi Delta Kappan*. The purpose of this poll is to estimate the attitudes of the adult civilian population in the United States toward many different aspects of schooling, including the perceived "biggest problems with which the public schools . . . must deal," inner-city schools, part-time work by high school stu-

Cross-sectional survey: Given at one time.

dents, length of the school year and day, and parental choice. The sample consists of 1,584 adults, representing all areas of the country and all income levels. Each adult was interviewed in his or her home in May or June 1989. This survey is also considered to be descriptive research.

Another type of cross-sectional survey is intended to compare different age categories of subjects to investigate possible developmental differences or relationships. For example, if researchers are interested in changes in students' self-concepts between sixth and twelfth grades and factors that may affect self-concept at various ages, a cross-sectional survey could be designed in which samples of current sixth- through twelfth-grade students are selected and questioned. It should be emphasized that all subjects are asked the questions at about the same time (e.g., October 1990).

Cross-sectional surveys are convenient and allow some tentative conclusions about how individuals may change over time. However, caution is advised for two primary reasons. First, there may be important differences between the subjects who are sampled in each grade or in each age category. For instance, if the sampling is done within a school, an assumption is that the type of students attending the school has not changed. If current sixth-graders are different in important ways, besides age, from twelfth-graders, conclusions about changes over time are affected. Second, because the data are obtained at one time, what may show as a "difference" from sixth to twelfth grade may not represent a change. It could be that twelfth-graders did not, when in sixth grade, have the same characteristics of current sixth-graders.

Longitudinal Surveys

In a **longitudinal survey** the same group of subjects is studied over a specified length of time. Thus, a longitudinal study of self-concept might begin in 1990 with sixth-graders and continue until 2002 for the same subjects. Data are collected at different times, usually over several years. There are variations of longitudinal surveys, depending on the subjects who are sampled or used to make up the "same group." In what is called a trend study, a general population is studied over time, although the subjects are sampled from the population each year or time of data collection. In a cohort longitudinal study a specific population, such as the entering college class of 1990, is studied, and in a panel study the same individuals are surveyed at each data-collection time.

The advantage of a longitudinal survey is that the limitations of cross-sectional designs are avoided. However, a serious disadvantage may be loss of subjects, which occurs with studies that

Longitudinal survey: Same subjects surveyed over time.

extend over a long period of time and with populations that are difficult to track (e.g., following high school or college graduates). Not only will the sample size sometimes become too small for adequate generalizations, but also there may be a systematic loss of certain types of subjects. For example, a longitudinal study of attitudes of high school students should consider the fact that some of the sample will drop out, leaving mainly those who in all probability have more positive attitudes.

It should be noted that the terms *longitudinal* and *cross-sectional* are used to describe research that would not be thought of as a survey. You may read in an article that a cross-sectional or longitudinal design was used. However, the study may or may not be considered a survey, probably depending on whether a sample was selected from a larger population.

CAUSAL-COMPARATIVE STUDIES

We have seen how correlations and differences between groups can be analyzed to examine relationships between variables. Although most nonexperimental, quantitative research designs explore simple relationships or predictive relationships, some nonexperimental designs do investigate cause-and-effect relationships. These designs can be called causal-comparative. We will look at two types of causal-comparative designs, *ex post facto* and correlational.

Ex Post Facto Research

In many situations in educational research the main question of interest is a causal one, but the circumstances of conducting the research do not allow an experiment. In these situations an independent variable is identified and studied to see its effect on a dependent variable. For example, what is the effect of attending prekindergarten (independent variable) on academic performance at the end of the first grade (dependent variable)? What is the effect of single-father homes on student achievement? What is the effect of class size on achievement? In each of these questions the effect of the independent variable is of primary interest, yet it is difficult, if not impossible, to experimentally control it. It is possible, however, to identify subjects who have experienced each type of "treatment" in the past and see if they are different on the dependent variable. The name of the design to conduct this type of study is **ex post facto.** In *ex post facto* research the investigators decide

Ex post facto: Presumed cause that occurred in the past.

whether one or more preexisting conditions have caused subsequent differences between subjects who experienced different types of conditions (the phrase *ex post facto* means "after the fact").

Ex post facto designs have some similarities with both experimental and correlational designs. Like an experiment, there is typically a "treatment" and/or "comparison" group, and the results are analyzed with the same statistical procedures. Of course in *ex post facto* research there is no manipulation of the independent variable because it has already occurred, but the comparison of group differences on the dependent variable is the same. Like correlation studies, there is no manipulation of the independent variable, so that technically the study is nonexperimental. However, in a correlation two or more measures are taken from each subject, whereas in *ex post facto* research each subject is measured on the dependent variable.

In conducting an *ex post facto* study the researcher selects subjects who are as similar as possible except for the independent variable that is being investigated. For example, in a study of the effect of class size on achievement, the researcher needs to locate groups of subjects who are similar in all respects except whether they attended large or small classes. In making the final selection of the groups of subjects, the researcher must be aware of possible extraneous variables that make causal conclusions problematic. Thus in a study of class size the only difference between students who attend small classes and those who attend large classes should be the size of the class, not such factors as socioeconomic status, quality of teachers, teaching methods, curriculum, student ability, and student motivation. That is, if the students in all the small classes had more ability, better teachers, or higher motivation, these factors could affect achievement in addition to, or in spite of, class size.

A recently published example of *ex post facto* research illustrates the potential as well as the limitations of this design. Mounts and Roopnarine (1987) investigated the effect of same-age and mixed-age preschool classrooms on social-cognitive play patterns. To conduct the study, the researchers located four preschool classrooms of same-age children, two three-year old classes and two four-year old classes, and two classes that had both three- and four-year-olds. The classrooms were carefully selected so that the percentage of each sex as well as the physical layout, play and instructional materials, and teacher-child ratios were the same. The children were enrolled about the same amount of time prior to the observations of their behavior, and all children were from middle-class backgrounds. It is important to indicate that these factors were not different for the same-age as compared to the mixed-age classrooms since these could be extraneous variables that could affect the nature of the children's play. However, with only six classrooms it is possible for other factors that are not accounted for to affect play, such as differences in teachers, characteristics of aides, and unique factors in one or two classes. Thus, although the researchers were careful to select classes that would be the same in most respects, except whether each was same-age or mixed-age, with so few classrooms there was the chance that other factors would affect the results. Also, the results would be limited in generalizability. What may have been true for these few classrooms may or may not be true for other preschool programs.

Correlational Causal-Comparative Research

Although the vast majority of correlational research is concerned only with relationships, some statistical techniques use correlations and investigate cause-and-effect questions. One technique, called path analysis, uses the correlations of several variables to study causal patterns. A causal "model" is established, based on theory, which shows by arrows the causal sequence that is expected. The correlations between the variables in the model provide empirical evidence for the proposed causal links. A relatively new technique, structural equation modeling, is more powerful than path analysis because the measures tend to be more reliable and the inferences more valid. Structural equation modeling is often called LISREL and is sometimes referred to as latent variable causal modeling. Although both of these techniques are useful for examining causal questions, they are sophisticated statistically and difficult to use. Also, they have the same fundamental limitations as all correlational data. Unmeasured variables related to both the independent and dependent variables are always a source of potential alternative causal explanations. These techniques sound, and in fact are, complicated, but interpretation is still based on understanding the meaning of simple correlations.

CONSUMER TIPS
Criteria for Evaluating Causal-Comparative Research

1. The primary purpose of the research should be to investigate causal relationships when an experiment is not possible. The experiment is the best method for studying cause-and-effect relationships, so causal-comparative studies should be used when it is not possible or feasible to conduct an experiment. There should be sufficient evidence in prior research to indicate that relationships exist between the variables and that it is appropriate to study causal relationships. Without existing empirical evidence of relationships, a strong theoretical rationale is needed.

2. The presumed causal condition should have already occurred. It is essential for the condition represented by the independent variable to have occurred before data are collected on the dependent variable. The "treatment" must have already taken place for a study to be causal-comparative.

3. Potential extraneous variables should be recognized and considered. It is crucial for the researcher to show the reader that all potential extraneous variables have been considered. Because existing groups are usually used in the comparison, these variables are usually differences in characteristics of the subjects, but other factors may also be related. It is incumbent on the researcher to present evidence that the groups being compared differ only on the dependent variable. Failure to do so suggests that the groups have not been carefully selected to avoid the influence of extraneous variables.

4. Differences between groups being compared should be controlled. When it is clear that there are measurable differences between groups being compared, it is necessary to use appropriate procedures to control their effect. Matching subjects is one procedure, and statistical techniques can also be used.

5. Causal conclusions should be made with caution. Even when all potential extraneous variables have been controlled, which is rare, it is best to accept with caution results that seem to suggest a causal relationship. Researchers should indicate possible limitations and frame the finding as "suggesting" a causal relationship. In almost all causal-comparative studies, there will be sufficient reason to be tentative in concluding cause-and-effect relationships.

OUTLINE SUMMARY

1. Descriptive studies.
   A. Describe a phenomenon, usually with simple descriptive statistics.
   B. Provide an understanding of a phenomenon.
   C. Relationships and causal relationships are not studied.
   D. Subjects and instruments are key criteria.
   E. Graphic presentations of data should not distort results.
      (1) Graphs provide effective images of results

   (2) Changes in the distance of the interval between scores can distort results.
2. Relationship studies.
   A. Allow prediction and identification of important variables.
   B. Difference relationships.
   C. Correlational relationships.
      (1) Subjects and instruments need to provide a range of responses.
      (2) Lack of variability leads to small relationships.
      (3) Large samples may lead to small but statistically "significant" relationships.
3. Prediction studies.
   A. Contain predictor (independent) and criterion (dependent) variables.
   B. Predictions are more accurate with reliable measures.
   C. Predictions are less accurate as the time between measures increases.
   D. Regression analysis examines several predictors.
   E. Prediction does not imply causation.
   F. Practical significance is related to the coefficient of determination.
   G. New subjects are needed for accurate predictions.
   H. Correlations for predicting individuals need to be higher than correlations for predicting groups.
4. Surveys.
   A. Describe the characteristics of a population.
   B. Cross-sectional.
      (1) Study one phenomenon at one time.
      (2) Study different groups at the same time.
      (3) Convenient.
      (4) Differences in characteristics of subjects may affect the results.
   C. Longitudinal.
      (1) Same subjects are surveyed over time.
      (2) May lose subjects over time.
5. Causal-comparative studies.
   A. Nonexperimental with causal implications.
   B. *Ex post facto.*
      (1) Similar groups are compared on differences in the past.
      (2) Differences between subjects in compared groups may affect results.
   C. Correlational.

STUDY QUESTIONS

1. What do researchers accomplish with nonexperimental studies?
2. In what ways can the characteristics of subjects affect the interpretation of descriptive and correlational studies?
3. How can graphs be used appropriately and inappropriately to summarize descriptive data?
4. Why should causation not be inferred from correlation?
5. Why is it important to examine the size of correlations as well as narrative conclusions about relationships?
6. What criteria would support a credible prediction study?
7. What is the difference between cross-sectional and longitudinal surveys?
8. What are the advantages and disadvantages of using a cross-sectional rather than a longitudinal survey?
9. Give some examples of studies that would be classified as *ex post facto*. What are some possible limitations in the design?

Chapter
8

Experimental and Single-Subject Research

In descriptive, correlational, and causal-comparative designs, the researcher has no control over what has happened or what will happen to the subjects that may affect their responses to the dependent variable. We now turn to different types of designs in which the researcher does have such control. These designs, experimental and single-subject, provide the best approach to investigating cause-and-effect relationships. However, experiments are rather difficult to carry out in educational settings in ways that permit definitive conclusions. Many limitations, because of the applied nature of most educational experiments, often affect the credibility of the research. You will need to be aware of these limitations to judge the usefulness of findings from such studies.

CHARACTERISTICS OF EXPERIMENTAL RESEARCH

There are two essential characteristics of all experimental research: direct manipulation of the independent variable and control of extraneous variables. Direct manipulation of the independent variable means that the investigator has direct control of when the subjects receive the independent variable and how much of it each subject receives. In an experiment, subjects who have received different amounts of the independent variable are compared. Thus, there must be some type of difference or variation in the independent variable, and the researcher must be able to manipulate, or control, the time during which these different amounts are received by or experienced by the subjects. One simple way to provide such manipulation, for instance, is to give a medicine to one group of subjects and compare their progress with subjects who received no medicine. The difference in the independent variable is receiving some or no medicine, and the researcher determines when some of the subjects take it. In educational research, the method of instruction, type of feedback given to students, curricula, type of grouping, amount of learning time, and assignments are common independent variables manipulated in experiments.

A second characteristic is control of extraneous variables. In an experiment the researcher seeks to keep constant for all subjects all variables, conditions, events, and procedures except the independent variable. Such factors are kept constant to eliminate them as possible explanations for the cause-and-effect relationship. In other words, the effect, which is measured by differences on the dependent variable, should be produced only by variations in the independent variable. Control of extraneous variables is necessary to conclude that the independent variable is causally related to the dependent variable. Such control, relatively easy in contrived laboratory experiments, is a continuing concern in educational research.

Control is established by either eliminating a possible extraneous variable or keeping the effect of a possible extraneous variable constant for all groups. Some extraneous variables can be eliminated. For example, in an experiment to investigate which of two methods of instruction is most effective, teachers may be assigned to a particular method. To eliminate experimenter bias, a potential extraneous variable, the teachers should not be told about the experiment, or at least not informed of the research hypothesis. Control is more commonly achieved by keeping the effect of an extraneous variable constant for all groups of subjects. For instance, in a study of teaching methods, student aptitude will be related to the dependent variable, achievement, and this factor can be controlled by having the same overall level of aptitude in each group of subjects. This will control any differential influence of aptitude.

EXPERIMENTAL VALIDITY

The purpose of a research design is to provide answers to research questions that are credible, that reflect reality. In the language and jargon of experimental research, two concepts are used to describe the level of credibility that results from the studies. The first, **internal validity,** refers to the extent to which the independent variable, and not other extraneous variables, produced the observed effect. A study is said to be "strong" in internal validity if most plausible extraneous variables have been controlled, and "weak" if one or more extraneous variables have differentially affected the dependent variable. As we will see, there are many ways to design experiments, and each design controls for different extraneous variables. Therefore, some designs are relatively strong in internal validity, whereas other designs are relatively weak.

Internal validity: Control of extraneous variables.

The second concept, **external validity,** refers to the extent to which the results can be generalized to other subjects, measures, treatments, procedures, and settings. A list of factors to consider in making appropriate generalizations is included in Chapter 1. To be able to make appropriate generalizations, you will need to attend carefully to the specific procedures for implementing a treatment, just as you need to know about the subjects' age, gender, socioeconomic status, and other characteristics to generalize appropriately to other individuals or groups. External validity is also described as "weak" or "strong," depending on the specifics of the study's design. It is quite possible for a study to be strong in internal validity and weak in external validity. In fact since the primary purpose of an experiment is to control extraneous variables, external validity is often weak.

External validity: Generalizability of results.

Several major categories summarize most possible extraneous variables. These categories, often referred to as "threats" to internal validity, constitute factors that may weaken the argument that the independent variable was solely responsible for the observed effects. We will discuss these threats briefly and then consider them in the context of different experimental designs. These factors represent the most important aspects of an experiment in interpreting the overall credibility of the research. When you read an experiment you should keep each threat in mind and ask, Is this a plausible threat to the internal validity of the study?

History

In an experiment some amount of time elapses between the onset of the independent variable and the measurement of the dependent variable. Although this time is necessary for the independent variable to take effect and influence the subjects, it allows for other events to occur that may also affect the dependent variable. **History** is the category of uncontrolled events that influence the dependent variable. If some event does occur during the study that is plausibly related to the dependent variable, you do not know if the inde-

History: Extraneous events that affect the dependent variable.

pendent variable, the event, or some combination of the two produced the result. In this sense the event is confounded with the independent variable; the two cannot be separated.

History can occur in or out of the experimental setting. Suppose that during a study of the influence of a unit on the Far East on multicultural attitudes of students, a major crisis occurs in China. If the students are affected by the crisis, which in turn influences the way they respond to a multicultural attitude questionnaire, this event, external to the experimental setting, constitutes a history threat to the internal validity of the study. History threats can also occur within an experimental setting. For example, a series of unexpected announcements that distracted a class that was receiving one method of instruction could adversely affect the influence of the lesson. Students in this class might score lower than other classes, but you do not know if this result is caused by the distraction or the method of instruction.

Selection

In most experiments two or more groups of subjects are compared. One group receives one level of the independent variable, and the other groups receive other levels of the independent variable. In some experiments the subjects are randomly assigned to levels of the independent variable. This procedure ensures that the different groups of subjects are comparable on such characteristics as ability, socioeconomic status, motivation, attitudes, and interests. However, in some experiments the subjects are not randomly assigned, and sometimes only a few subjects are randomly assigned. In these circumstances it is probable that there will be systematic differences between the groups on characteristics of the subjects. If these differences are related to the dependent variable, we would say that there is a threat of **selection** to internal validity. For example, suppose one class is assigned to receive the blue health curriculum and another class receives the red health curriculum. The students are not randomly assigned to the classes; in fact the students who have the blue curriculum are more capable academically than the students in the other class. At the end of the experiment the students who had the blue curriculum did better on a test of health concepts than the other class. Surprised? Obviously the result is related to the initial differences between the classes, and the study would be judged to have very weak internal validity.

Selection: Threat from the characteristics of subjects.

Selection is also a threat when the subjects are selected in a way that affects the results. As previously discussed, volunteers may respond in ways that nonvolunteers would not. Or suppose one group of subjects had a choice in the "treatment" experienced and another group had no choice. It is likely in such circumstances that the selection process will affect the findings.

Maturation

It has been pointed out that there is some passage of time in an experiment. Just as events extraneous to the subjects may affect the results (history), changes that may occur within the subjects over time may also alter the results. These changes are called threats of **maturation.** People develop in naturally occurring ways that over a sufficient period of time can influence the dependent variable independent of a treatment condition. This can include physical, social, and mental development. For example, in an experiment of the effect of a new orientation course on the adjustment of college freshmen, the researcher may measure adjustment before college begins and then again at the end of the first year, after an orientation class. Although it would be desirable to attribute positive changes in adjustment to the orientation course, the researcher needs to consider the natural maturation process of 18- and 19-year-olds and how much adjustment will be influenced by this process.

Maturation: Threat from changes in subjects over time.

Maturation also includes relatively short-term changes in people as they become tired, bored, hungry, or discouraged. Imagine that a researcher, who needs to measure the attitudes of third-graders toward science, mathematics, reading, and art, asks the children to answer questions for an hour to complete the questionnaire. What do you suppose the children are doing after the first 20 minutes or so?

Pretesting

A pretest is a measure of the dependent variable given before the treatment begins. When it is used in an experiment it is possible for the subjects to act differently because they took the pretest. For example, if two groups are given a pretest measuring their self-concept, the subjects may be sensitized to issues concerning the development of self-concept because they took the pretest. While one group may receive a treatment to improve self-concept, subjects in another group may become motivated to do some outside reading that they otherwise would not have done; this reading would probably affect changes in their self-concept and the results of the study. This threat is termed **pretesting.** Pretesting is also a threat when one group of subjects is given a pretest that improves performance on the posttest. This effect is most likely in short studies of a single group on measures of factual material.

Pretesting: Threat from the effect of taking the pretest.

Instrumentation

The nature of the measurement used for the dependent variable can affect the results of research in several ways. **Instrumentation** refers to threats to internal validity because of changes or unreliability in measurement. If the measures are not reliable, the results are not valid. Instrumentation also refers to changes in the measures or procedures for obtaining data. For example, if a researcher in an observational study has one set of observers for one group of subjects and a second set of observers for another group, any differences between the groups may be due to the different sets of observers. Observers or interviewers can also become bored or tired or change in other ways that affect the results.

One additional aspect of instrumentation important for experiments is that the measures used must be able to be affected, or show change, as a result of the independent variable. Some standardized instruments of general skills or knowledge may not be able to be changed very much, such as measures of intelligence, critical thinking, or verbal aptitude.

Instrumentation: Threat from unreliability and changes in measurement.

Treatment Replications

In an experiment the treatment is supposed to be repeated so that all the members of one group receive the treatment separately and independently of the other members of the group. Thus if the researcher is testing a new method of instruction with a class of subjects, there is really only one replication of the treatment; that is, the treatment is conducted once. Each class is like one subject, and hence several classes are needed to do the experiment properly. **Treatment replications** is a threat to internal validity to the extent that the reported number of subjects in the study is not the same as the number of replications of the treatment.

Treatment replications: Number of replications of treatments.

Subject Attrition

Subject attrition (some researchers will refer to this threat as mortality) occurs when subjects systematically drop out or are lost and their absence affects the results. This is most likely to be a problem in longitudinal research that extends over a long period of time, but it can also be a threat to short experiments if one of the treatments causes subjects to drop out. For example, if a study indicates that college seniors as a group are better critical thinkers than college freshmen, subject attrition is a possible extraneous variable since it is likely that students who are not good critical thinkers have dropped out of college and are not included in the senior sample.

Subject attrition: Loss of subjects.

You should consider this threat in an experiment if a substantial number of subjects are lost in the groups that are compared.

Statistical Regression

Statistical regression refers to the tendency of subjects who score extremely high or low on a pretest to score closer to the mean of both groups on the posttest, regardless of the effects of the treatments. That is, very low pretest scores will be higher on the posttest and very high pretest scores will be lower on the posttest. Statistical regression is a result of measurement error and is a function of mathematical probability. It is a problem when subjects are selected for research *because* they have high or low scores. For example, in studies of programs to help low achievers or students with low self-concepts, the subjects are initially selected on the basis of low pretest scores. It would be expected that mathematically, without any influence of a treatment, the posttest scores of these students will be higher because of statistical regression.

Statistical regression: Change of extreme scores to those closer to the mean.

Diffusion of Treatment

In experiments with two or more groups that receive different treatments it is best if the groups do not know about one another. If a control or comparison group does come into contact with a treatment group or knows what is happening to that group, the effects of the treatment could spread to both groups. **Diffusion of treatment** is the threat of any likelihood that a treatment given to one group affects other groups that do not receive the treatment. Suppose a researcher tests the effect of preschool on children by randomly assigning one twin from each family to a preschool. One twin attends preschool and the other twin stays home. Diffusion of treatment is a threat because it is probable that any influence of the preschool is "diffused" to the other child when they are home together.

Diffusion of treatment: Treatment effect on one group affecting other groups.

Experimenter Effects

Experimenter effects refer to attributes or expectations of the researcher that influence the results. In an ideal experiment, the investigators would have no effect on the subjects; they would be detached and uninvolved. Attributes of the experimenter include such characteristics as age, sex, race, status, hostility, authoritarianism, and physical appearance. Subjects may respond differently to certain characteristics. For example, studies suggest that female

Experimenter effects: Characteristics or expectations of experimenter.

counselors are more likely than male counselors to elicit more self-disclosure from the client.

Experimenter expectancies refer to deliberate and unintentional effects of bias on the part of the experimenter, which is reflected in differential treatment of the subjects, such as being more reassuring to the group the experimenter "wants" to do better. If the experimenter is involved in the research as an observer, as an interviewer, or in implementing a treatment, there must be procedures for assuring the reader that bias has not influenced the results. For example, if the experimenter is observing beginning teachers who have been assigned a mentor teacher, a step that is hypothesized to result in more effective teaching compared to beginning teachers who do not have a mentor teacher, the expectation of the experimenter may influence what he or she observes and records. In fact this potential source of error is true for all observers and interviewers, whether or not they are the researchers who are conducting the study. Observers and interviewers should be unaware of the specifics of the research. They should not know the hypothesis of the study or which subjects are the "experimental" ones.

Subject Effects

In an ideal experiment the subjects behave and respond naturally and honestly. However, when people become involved in a study they often change their behavior simply because they understand they are "subjects," and sometimes these changes affect the results. **Subject effects** refer to subject changes in behavior, initiated by the subjects themselves, in response to the experimental situation. If subjects have some idea of the purpose of the study or the motivation for doing "well," they may alter their behavior to respond more favorably. Subjects will pick up cues from the experimental setting and instructions, which will motivate them in specific ways (these cues are called demand characteristics). Subjects in most studies will also want to present themselves in the most positive manner. Thus there may be positive self-presentation or social desirability, which may affect the results. For instance, most people want to appear intelligent, competent, and emotionally stable, and they may resist treatments that they perceive as manipulating them in negative ways or they may fake responses to appear more positive. Some subjects may increase positive or desirable behavior simply because they know they are receiving special treatment (this is termed the Hawthorne effect). Control group subjects may try harder because they see themselves in competition with a treatment

Subject effects: Effects from awareness of being a subject.

group or may be motivated because they did *not* get the treatment (this may be termed the John Henry effect or compensatory rivalry). Other subjects, when they realize that they were not selected for what they believe is a preferred treatment, may become demotivated (resentful demoralization). Finally, many individuals will react positively, with increased motivation or participation, because they are doing something new and different (this is termed the novelty effect). As you can see, there are many possible subject effects.

Whenever you read experimental research you should keep these possible extraneous variables in mind. As we review some of the most frequently used experimental designs you will see that some of these threats are of greater concern in some designs than in others. Other potential threats are related more to how contrived the study is, rather than to the design itself, and some threats are never completely controlled. Some of the extraneous variables influence generalizability by being confounded with the treatment. For example, if a study shows a change in a morning class that received one method of instruction and no change in an afternoon class that received a different method, time of day is confounded with the effectiveness of the treatment. There is a causal relationship, but it may be generalized only to morning classes.

TYPES OF EXPERIMENTAL DESIGNS

We now turn our attention to experimental designs used to investigate cause-and-effect relationships. We will consider six types of designs, although there are many others. These six designs will illustrate how some threats to internal validity are controlled by specific features of the design and how other threats are not controlled.

Aspects of experimental designs include treatments manipulated by the researcher, pretests and posttests, the number of groups in the study, and the presence or absence of random assignment. These aspects of the study will be represented in this chapter through the following notation system:

R Random assignment
X Treatment condition (subscripts indicating different treatments)
O Observation (pretest or posttest)
A, B, C, D   Groups of subjects

Single-Group Posttest-Only Design

This and the next two designs are often called preexperimental because they usually have inadequate control of extraneous variables. In some circumstances one of these three designs can provide good information, but as we will see, few threats to internal validity are controlled.

In the single-group posttest-only design, the researcher identifies a group of subjects, gives the group a treatment, and then makes a posttest observation of the dependent variable. It can be represented as follows:

Single-group   Group   Treatment   Posttest
posttest-only   A   →   X   →   O
design:

This is the weakest experimental design because without a pretest or another group of subjects, there is no way to compare the posttest result with anything else; and without a comparison, there is no way to know if the treatment effected a change in the subjects. This design is useful only when the researcher can be sure of the knowledge, skill, or attitude that will be changed before the treatment is implemented, and when there are no extraneous events occurring at the same time as the treatment that could affect the results.

Single-Group Pretest-Posttest Design

This design differs from the single-group posttest-only design by the addition of a pretest.

Single-group   Group   Pretest   Treatment   Posttest
pretest-   A   →   O   →   X   →   O
posttest
design:

A single group of subjects is given a pretest, then the treatment, then the posttest. The results are determined by comparing the pretest score to the posttest score. Although a change from pretest to posttest can be due to the treatment, there are also many possible extraneous factors to be considered. Suppose an experiment is conducted to examine the effect of an in-service workshop on the attitudes of teachers toward gifted education. An instrument measuring these attitudes is given to all teachers in a school division before two-day workshops are conducted and again after the workshops (one workshop for each school). What are some possible threats to the internal validity of this study?

First, because there are no control or comparison subjects, we cannot be certain that extraneous events have not occurred, in addition to the workshop, that would change attitudes. Perhaps an article that appeared in the local paper during the two days of the workshop changed some attitudes, or maybe some of the teachers in some groups gave moving testimonials. Second, if the teachers begin with negative attitudes for some reason, regression would be a threat. Third, pretesting is a significant threat in this study because taking the pretest questionnaire may affect attitudes. Fourth, attrition would be a problem if a significant number of teachers who do not like the workshop fail to show up for the posttest. Fifth, maturation is a potential threat if the teachers are tired at the end of the second day. Finally, experimenter and subject effects are definitely threats in this type of study since it is probable that the teachers would want to "please" the person conducting the workshop.

This design will have more potential threats to internal validity as the time between the pretest and posttest increases and as the experimental situation becomes less controlled and contrived. The design can be good for studies in which subject effects will not influence the results, such as achievement tests, and when history threats can be reasonably dismissed. The design is strengthened if several pretest observations are possible, thereby providing an indication of the stability of the trait. If there are a sufficient number of both pretests and posttests, the study may be called a *time series* design. In this design it is necessary to use the same instrumentation with the same subjects, or similar subjects, over an extended period of time. It is a good design for frequently occurring measures of the dependent variable at regular intervals.

Nonequivalent-Groups Posttest-Only Design

The third preexperimental design has a comparison or control group but no pretest:

Nonequivalent-groups posttest-only design:	Group	Treatment	Posttest
	A $\rightarrow$	X $\rightarrow$	O
	B	$\longrightarrow$	O

One group of subjects receives the treatment (group A), while the other group (B) acts as a control, receiving no treatment at all in this diagram. In some nonequivalent-groups posttest-only designs two or more groups receive different treatments:

Group   Treatment   Posttest
$$
\begin{array}{ccc}
A & \rightarrow & X_1 & \rightarrow & O \\
B & \rightarrow & X_2 & \rightarrow & O \\
C & \rightarrow & X_3 & \rightarrow & O \\
\end{array}
$$

The crucial feature of this design is that the subjects in each group may be different in ways that will differentially affect the dependent variable. That is, one group may be brighter, more motivated, better prepared, or in some other way different from the other groups. Thus, selection is the most serious threat to the internal validity of this design. Without a pretest it is difficult to control for such selection differences. For example, if teachers in one school received one type of form that will be used to evaluate their teaching during the year, and teachers in another school used a different type of evaluation form, you might conclude that if teachers in the first school were judged to be more effective, the forms were causally related to this difference in effectiveness. However, it may be that the teachers in the first school were already more effective. It is also possible that there will be extraneous events in one school that will affect the results. Other threats are also possible with this type of experiment, depending on the specifics of the design. It is best employed when groups of subjects are comparable and can be assumed to be about the same on the trait being measured before the treatment is given to the subjects.

Nonequivalent-Groups Pretest-Posttest Design

This design, which is often referred to as a quasi-experimental design because it closely approximates the most desirable experimental designs, is commonly used in educational research. It is the same as the nonequivalent-groups posttest-only design, with the addition of a pretest:

Nonequivalent-   Group   Pretest   Treatment   Posttest
groups pretest-
posttest-design:
$$
\begin{array}{ccccc}
A & \rightarrow & O & \rightarrow & X & \rightarrow & O \\
B & \rightarrow & O & \xrightarrow{\hspace{3cm}} & O \\
\end{array}
$$

In this diagram there are two groups of subjects (A and B). One group (A) takes the pretest (O), receives the treatment (X), and then takes the posttest (O); the other group (B) takes the pretest, receives no treatment at all, and takes the posttest. In this diagram group B is considered to be a "control" group because it does not receive any type of treatment. In other nonequivalent designs two or more different treatments may be compared, as indicated in the following diagram:

Groups   Pretest   Treatment   Posttest

$$A \rightarrow O \rightarrow X_1 \rightarrow O$$
$$B \rightarrow O \rightarrow X_2 \rightarrow O$$

As a hypothetical illustration of this design, suppose Mr. Jones, a social studies teacher, wants to see if a new way to give praise to students is more effective than the method presently being used in the school. Because it would be awkward to use different approaches in the same classroom, Mr. Jones decides to give the new type of praise to his morning class and to use an afternoon class as a comparison group. At the beginning of the same new unit on the Civil War, Mr. Jones gives his students a pretest of their knowledge. He then uses the new approach to giving praise with students in the morning class and continues to use the same approach he has been using with his afternoon class. Both classes take the unit posttest at the same time.

The most serious threat to the internal validity of this design is selection. For example, Mr. Jones may find that students do better with the new type of praise, but that may be because the students in the morning class are brighter or more motivated than those in the afternoon class. Even though there is a pretest, which helps to reduce the threat of selection, differences in the subjects must be addressed. Often researchers will use measures of other characteristics of the subjects to show that even though the groups are not "equal," there are probably no significant differences between them. For example, in a study comparing three teaching methods, each method was used in a different year with college students taking the same sociology class.

EXAMPLE: COMPARING SUBJECTS IN DIFFERENT GROUPS

"In order to determine comparability of students in each condition, several checks were made: the students' overall GPAs, major GPAs, and Missouri standardized IQ scores. No significant differences were found across the treatments on these three measures, lending credence to comparability of groups at the start of each study. These measures, then, give relatively confident information that differential selection of subjects can be ruled out as a significant alternate explanation to study results." (H. W. Smith, 1987, p. 151)

The nonequivalent-groups pretest-posttest design is often used when subjects are available in existing, or "intact," groups such as classes. In the example, Mr. Jones used two intact classes; in the Smith study, three different college classes were used. This procedure, using intact groups, creates problems other than selection. If the classes meet at different times of the day, as did Mr. Jones's classes, time of day is also an extraneous variable. In Smith's study, the classes met in different years, so the year of the class, an extraneous variable, is confounded with the treatments. In both of these examples the same teacher conducted all the treatments. Although in one respect this is a good method—because if different teachers were in each class, teachers would be an extraneous variable—it also increases the potential for experimenter effects. Perhaps the most serious limitation is that the "treatment" is given only once to each class. In effect there is only one replication of the treatment, so that other extraneous events associated with that one replication may affect the results. Thus, treatment replication is a potential threat to internal validity. Even though a pretest is used in this design, pretesting is not likely to be an extraneous variable since its effect is probably the same for both groups.

Randomized-Groups Posttest-Only Design

This design and the one that follows are often termed "true" experimental designs because they include comparison groups that have been randomly assigned to different treatments or to a treatment and control condition. In the randomized-groups posttest-only design, subjects are first randomly assigned to the different treatment or control conditions, given the treatment (or no treatment if control), and then given the posttest. The design, with a control group, is represented by the following diagram:

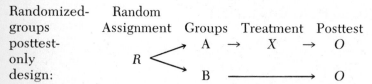

Randomized-groups posttest-only design:

Random Assignment   Groups   Treatment   Posttest

$$R \Big< \begin{array}{ccccc} A & \to & X & \to & O \\ B & \xrightarrow{\hspace{3cm}} & & & O \end{array}$$

If a comparison group, rather than a control group, is included, the design would look like this:

Random Assignment   Groups   Treatment   Posttest

$$R \Big< \begin{array}{ccccc} A & \to & X_1 & \to & O \\ B & \to & X_2 & \to & O \end{array}$$

In most educational experiments there is a comparison group rather than a control group because in education there are limited resources and limited time to work with students; thus it is more a matter of how to use time rather than adding to an already full day of instruction. In reading studies, therefore, you will usually find methods or approaches compared to one another.

Random assignment means that each subject has the same probability of being in either the treatment or comparison or control group. The purpose of random assignment is to equalize the characteristics of the subjects in each group. This equalization can be assumed when a sufficient number of subjects is randomly assigned to each group (generally ten or more). The obvious strength of random assignment is the control of selection as a threat to internal validity. It is assumed that the subjects in each group are essentially "equal" on any characteristics that may affect the dependent variable. Other threats, however, need to be considered that are not controlled by random assignment, including diffusion of treatment, experimenter effects, subject effects, treatment replication, and extraneous events within a group of subjects.

An example of a study with a randomized posttest-only design investigated the effect of four imagery and pictorial strategies on oral prose-learning performance (Guttman, Levin, and Pressley, 1977). Three experimental treatments and one control condition were compared. The subjects were told to listen to a story. Subjects in one group were told to use imagery, subjects in another group to focus on the pictures, and subjects in the third treatment to use imagery and look at the pictures. The subjects then listened to the story and were asked to respond to posttest questions. There was no pretest; and "subjects were randomly assigned to one of four experimental conditions: control, imagery, partial, and complete" (p. 475). This study could be diagrammed as follows:

Random
Assignment   Groups   Treatment   Posttest
                A   →X_1 (imagery) →   O
                B   →X_2 (partial) →   O
    R   C   →X_3 (complete)→   O
                D   (control)   →   O

Randomized-Groups Pretest-Posttest Design

This "true" experiment has both a pretest and a posttest. Otherwise it is the same as the randomized posttest-only design. A pretest is used to equalize the groups statistically, in addition to what random assignment provides. Researchers use a pretest with random assignment when there may be small, subtle effects of different treatments, when differential subject attrition is possible, and when there is a need to analyze subgroups who differ on the pretest. Subjects can be randomly assigned before or after the pretest. In some studies the pretest scores are used to match subjects, and then one subject from each pair is randomly assigned to each group. The following describes a randomized two-group pretest-posttest experiment:

EXAMPLE: RANDOMIZED-GROUPS PRETEST-POSTTEST DESIGN

"The purpose of this study was to assess the effects of an activity-centered health education program on the general health beliefs and self-reported behavior of fourth, fifth, and sixth graders using classrooms as the units of analysis. Ten schools . . . were randomly selected to receive the newly developed health curriculum, compared to 10 schools . . . that continued to use a science textbook. Both treatment groups were pretested and posttested with a 28-item questionnaire." (Brooks, 1988, p. 149)

The study can be diagrammed as follows:

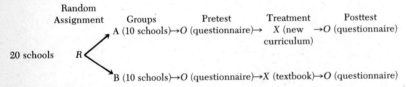

Table 8.1 summarizes the six designs concerning threats to internal validity. Although the "scorecard" will give you a good start in evaluating the credibility of an experiment, each study must be judged individually. Overall credibility is determined not so much by the particular design but by how well the researcher understands and controls for possible threats.

Factorial Experimental Designs

All of the designs we have considered in this chapter have one independent variable. Many experiments, as well as nonexperimental studies, will have two or more independent variables and are called **factorial designs.** Factorial experimental designs are extensions of the designs summarized in this chapter that study more than one independent variable, or factor, and the interaction be-

Factorial designs: Containing two or more independent variables.

Table 8.1 INTERNAL VALIDITY SCOREBOARD

Design	History	Selection	Maturation	Pretesting	Instrumentation	Treatment replications	Subject attrition	Statistical regression	Diffusion of treatment	Experimenter effects	Subject effects
Single-Group Posttest-Only	−	−	−	NA	?	?	?	−	NA	?	?
Single-Group Pretest-Posttest	?	?	−	−	?	?	?	−	NA	?	?
Nonequivalent-Groups Posttest-Only	?	−	?	NA	?	?	?	?	?	?	?
Nonequivalent-Groups Pretest-Posttest	?	?	?	?	?	?	?	+	?	?	?
Randomized-Groups Posttest-Only	?	+	+	NA	?	?	?	+	?	?	?
Randomized-Groups Pretest-Posttest	?	+	+	?	?	?	?	+	?	?	?

In this table a minus sign indicates a definite weakness, a plus sign means that the threat is controlled, a question mark indicates a possible source of invalidity, and NA means that the threat is not applicable to the design.

tween independent variables. There are two primary purposes for
using factorial designs. One is to see if the effects of a treatment
are consistent across different characteristics, such as age, gender,
or aptitude. The second is to examine interactions, which are relationships that can only be investigated with factorial designs. If
a study is testing the effect of two methods of instruction, for example, computerized compared to traditional, it might be desirable
to know if the effectiveness of the methods was the same for males
as for females. Thus, in such a study we would have two independent variables, each with two levels. The design, described as a 2
× 2 design, may be diagrammed in different ways, as illustrated in
Figure 8.1. (If a study has one independent variable with two levels
and a second independent variable with four levels, it would be

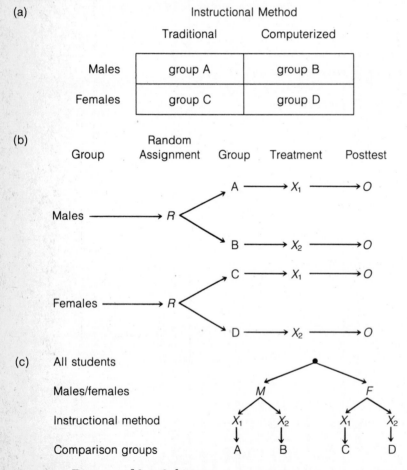

Figure 8.1 Diagram of 2 × 2 design.

called a 2 × 4 design.) Figure 8.1b and c show that the students were first divided into groups of males and females and then randomly assigned to the two instructional methods.

Interactions are very important since much of what we do in education is based on the assumption that we should match student characteristics with appropriate teacher feedback or instructional methods. What may work well for one student may not work well for other students. Factorial designs allow us to test these assumptions. **Interactions** occur when the effect of one variable differs across the levels of the other variable. In other words, the impact of a variable is not consistent across all levels of the other variable. Applying this definition to the example in Figure 8.1, we would have an interaction if the difference between males and females for computerized instruction was not the same as the difference between males and females for traditional instruction. This result would show that the effect of the method of instruction depends on whether we are studying males or females. In a sense method and sex are operating together. An important aspect in interpreting results is that because of possible interactions, what may not be true for a total group may be true for certain subjects in the population. That is, if a study shows that for all fourth-graders, together, it makes no difference whether they have homework assignments or not, an interaction might show that some low-ability students benefit greatly from homework compared to other low-ability students who receive no homework.

Interaction: Effect of independent variables together.

CONSUMER TIPS
Criteria for Evaluating Experimental Research

1. **The primary purpose is to test causal hypotheses.** Experimental research should be designed to investigate cause-and-effect relationships that are anticipated with clear research hypotheses. There should almost always be a research hypothesis in an experiment. If there is no research hypothesis there may be insufficient descriptive or relationship evidence to justify conducting an experiment, or the researcher may be uninformed about the need for a hypothesis.

2. **There should be direct manipulation of the independent variable.** An essential aspect of an experiment is that the researcher has direct control, manipulation of, the treatment that subjects will receive. If it is not clear that such manipulation has occurred, the capability to make causal interpretations will be limited.

3. **The experimental design should be clearly identified.** Although it is not necessary for the researcher to use the specific

language in this chapter to identify a design (e.g., randomized-group posttest-only), it is important that there are sufficient details about the design to enable you to understand what was done to which subjects and the sequence of measurement and treatments. In fact there should be enough detail so that you could replicate the study. As we have noted, the threats you need to focus on to evaluate the study depends to a certain extent on the design. If you cannot understand the design, it is a clue that the researcher may not have understood it either.

4. The design should provide maximum control of extraneous variables. The essence of a good experiment is that the effect of all variables except one, the independent variable, are controlled through the design and procedures of the study. The researcher should indicate how specific aspects of the design control possible extraneous variables. Obvious threats, such as selection in the nonequivalent-groups designs, need to be addressed. If obvious threats are not controlled by the design, the researcher should present a rationale for why a particular threat is not a plausible alternative explanation for the results. Failure to provide such a rationale may indicate that the researcher does not fully understand how extraneous variables can influence results.

5. The treatments should be sufficiently different from one another. One of the major reasons of an experiment's failure to show the hypothesized relationship is that the treatments are not strong enough to affect the dependent variable, or different treatments are so much alike that they do not differentiate on the basis of the dependent variable. For example, a comparison of cooperative and small-group instruction is less likely to show a difference in achievement than a comparison of cooperative and individualized instruction. At the same time, you should be careful when interpreting an experiment in which a treatment is compared to a control group. In education, *any* additional treatment is likely to have some positive effect as compared to no additional treatment.

6. The determination of "subjects" depends on independent replications of the treatments. A critical aspect of an experiment is that each "subject" receives the treatment independently from all other subjects. In a classic experiment, each subject is randomly assigned to treatments and experiences each treatment independently. In some studies, subjects are randomly assigned to groups and then all the subjects in each group receives one treatment "together." Technically, each group in this situation is one "subject." If each person experiences the treatment separately from the others, each person is considered to be one subject. However, if only one treatment is given to a group of people, the group should be identified as one subject. In reading an experimental study, you should look for the number of times the treatment is replicated, which should be the same as the number of subjects in the study. As we will see in the next chapter, the statistical results of research are highly dependent on the number of subjects.

SINGLE-SUBJECT RESEARCH

In the designs we have considered in this chapter subjects are studied in groups. By conducting experiments with groups of subjects, individual differences are pooled together and the results can be generalized to other persons who are like the subjects. However, there are circumstances in which it may not be possible or ethical to administer a treatment to a group of subjects. In these situations, researchers focus their experiments with individual subjects through **single-subject designs,** which use one subject to study the influence of an experimental treatment. The approach of the design is to repeat measures of the dependent variable before and after a treatment is implemented. The basis of comparison is the difference in behavior prior to receiving the treatment and behavior during the treatment. Single-subject designs are used extensively in research with exceptional children and in counseling, where the focus of change is on individuals rather than on groups.

Single-subject design: Individual behavior recorded before and after a treatment.

Characteristics of Single-Subject Research

McMillan and Schumacher (1989) summarize five characteristics of single-subject research:

   1. Reliable measurement: Since these designs involve multiple measures of behavior, it is important for the instrumentation to be reliable. Conditions for data collection, such as time of day and location, should be standardized, and observers need to be trained. Consistency in measurement is especially crucial in the transition before and after the treatment.
   2. Repeated measurement: The same behavior is measured over and over again. This step is different from most experiments, in which the dependent variable is measured only once. Repeated measures are needed to obtain a clear pattern or constancy in the behavior over time. They control for the normal variation of behavior that is expected within short time intervals. This aspect of single-subject designs is similar to time-series studies, which investigate groups rather than individuals and do not provide for a "return" to conditions that were present before the treatment was implemented.

3. Description of conditions: A clear, detailed description of the conditions of measurement and the nature of the treatment is needed to strengthen internal and external validity.

4. Baseline and treatment conditions: Each single-subject study involves at least one baseline and one treatment condition. The **baseline** refers to a period of time in which the target behavior (dependent variable) is observed and recorded as it occurs without a special or new intervention. The baseline behavior provides the frame of reference against which future behavior is compared. The treatment condition is a period of time during which the experimental manipulation is introduced and the target behavior continues to be observed and recorded. Both the baseline and treatment phases of the study need to be long enough to achieve stability in the target behavior.

Baseline: Behavior before and/or after the treatment.

5. Single-variable rule: During a single-subject study, only one variable should be changed from baseline to treatment conditions. In some studies two variables are changed together during the same treatment condition. This is an interaction in single-subject research.

Types of Single-Subject Designs

Although some single-subject designs can be rather complex and may seem complicated, most are easily recognized variations of an A–B–A or multiple-baseline design.

A–B–A Design   Single-subject designs use a notation system in which A refers to a baseline condition and B to a treatment condition. The order of the letters indicates the sequence of procedures in the study. Thus, in an A–B design there is one baseline and one treatment condition. In an A–B–A design the treatment condition is followed by another baseline, as indicated in the following diagram:

A–B–A   Baseline   Treatment   *Baseline*
Single-   *X X X X X X X X*
subject   *O O O O O O O O O O O O O O O O O O O O O O O O*
design:

If the treatment is removed, the design is called an A–B–A **withdrawal design.** The treatment is introduced after a number of baseline observations and is stopped to return to the same condition that was present during the baseline. The design allows a strong causal inference if the pattern of behavior changes with the addition and withdrawal of the treatment. Without the second baseline phase (some single-subject studies will use only an A–B design), extraneous events that occur at the same time as the treatment may in-

Withdrawal design: Treatment removed after implementation.

fluence the behavior. Extraneous events are well controlled when the pattern of behavior changes twice, or even more often in some designs (e.g., A–B–A–B). For example, suppose a teacher is interested in trying a new procedure to reinforce a student, Mary, to increase Mary's time-on-task (time actually engaged in studying and learning). The dependent variable is time-on-task. The teacher would observe the percentage of time Mary is on-task for several days to establish a baseline. Then the teacher would introduce the new reinforcement technique, which is the treatment, and continue to record the percentage of Mary's time-on-task. After a few days of the new treatment (when the behavior is stable), the teacher withdraws the new technique of reinforcing Mary's behavior and records the percentage of time-on-task for this second baseline period. Figure 8.2 shows how the results would be graphed and indicates evidence that the new technique is affecting Mary's time-on-task. Given the positive benefits of the new type of reinforcement, the teacher would want to reinstitute it.

One limitation of the A–B–A design is the difficulty in interpreting a positive change that does not change during the second baseline. In this situation the treatment may be so strong that its effect lasts a long time, or something else may have occurred with the treatment that affected the behavior and did not stop when the treatment did.

Multiple-Baseline Designs   In a single-subject **multiple-baseline design,** observations are made on several subjects, different target behaviors of one or more subjects, or different situations. Thus,

Multiple-baseline design: More than one subject, behavior, or setting.

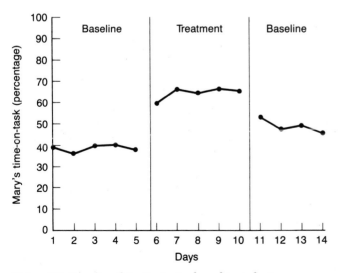

Figure 8.2 Results of A–B–A single-subject design.

multiple-baselines are conducted across subjects, behaviors, or settings. A design that has more than one subject may implement the treatment with each subject or use one or more subjects as a control condition. Different behaviors are studied when a treatment is applied to more than one target behavior. For example, the effectiveness of using time-out for institutionalized retarded individuals can be observed for several types of behavior, including taking food from others and hitting others. If a study examined the effect of the same treatment on behaviors in several different settings or situations, such as different classes, a multiple-baseline across-settings design is employed. For instance, an investigator may be interested in whether a particular type of praise is as effective with an individual in math class as it is in science class.

Multiple-baseline designs provide better evidence for internal validity and also extend the generalizability of the results. For example, a recently published study used an *A–B–A–B* multiple-baseline design, across subjects, to test the effectiveness of reprimands in lessening disruptive behavior. In this study the treatment was implemented with one subject, and the effect was recorded for the person receiving the treatment and for her friend.

EXAMPLE: MULTIPLE-BASELINE SINGLE-SUBJECT DESIGN

"After stable baseline performance was obtained for both Jeanette and Natalie, reprimands were made contingent upon Jeanette's disruptive behavior. . . . During this condition, Natalie's disruptive behavior was not reprimanded. After a return to baseline conditions, reprimands were again made contingent upon Jeanette's disruptive behavior." (Van Houton, Nau, Mackenzie, Sameoto, and Colavecchia, 1982, p. 78)

CONSUMER TIPS
Criteria for Evaluating Single-Subject Research

1. **There should be reliable measurement of the target behavior.** It is important for the measurement to be standardized and consistent. Evidence for reliability should be presented in the procedures section of the study. If more than one observer is used, interobserver reliability should be reported.

2. **The target behavior should be clearly defined operationally.** There should be a detailed definition of the dependent variable, described operationally in terms of how it is measured.

3. **Sufficient measures are needed to provide stability in behavior.** There should be enough measures to establish stability in

the behavior that is measured. Typically a minimum or three or four observations is needed in each phase of the study to provide measures that do not show more than a small degree of variability. This step is especially important for the baseline condition since this is the level of behavior against which behaviors occurring during the treatment are compared, but it is also necessary for the treatment condition. Usually there is the same number of measures during each phase of the study.

4. Procedures, subjects, and settings should be fully described. Since the external validity of single-subject designs is relatively weak, the usefulness of the results depends to a great extent on the match between the procedures, characteristics of the subjects, and settings in the study with other subjects and settings. The best judgments of the extent of this match are made when there is a detailed description of what was done, to whom, and where.

5. A single, standardized treatment should be used. The procedures for administering the treatment should be standardized so that precisely the same treatment is given each time. Only one treatment, or one combination of treatments, should be changed from the baseline to treatment phases of the study.

6. Experimenter or observer effects should be controlled. Because of the heavy reliance on a single observer, who in many cases is the same person as the experimenter, it is important to indicate how bias is controlled, that is, how bias is not a potential threat to internal validity. Judging the credibility of the researcher may not be easy, although you will find hints of bias in many parts of the research report or article.

7. Results should be practically significant. The results of most single-subject studies are analyzed by inspecting their graphic presentation and judging whether the patterns of behavior in different phases of the study appear to be different. This judgment should be based on graphs that do not distort differences by artificially increasing the intervals used to describe the behaviors. Clear differences should be evident, and they should be significant in practical terms, showing enough of a difference clearly to affect the behavior of the subject. Some single-subject studies use a statistical analysis of the results, but a "statistically significant" difference still needs to be practically significant.

OUTLINE SUMMARY

1. Experimental research.
   A. Investigates cause-and-effect relationships.
   B. Manipulates the independent variable.
   C. Controls extraneous variables.

(1) Eliminates possible extraneous variables.

(2) Holds constant extraneous variables.

D. Experimental validity includes internal and external validity.

E. Threats to internal validity.

    (1) History.

    (2) Selection.

    (3) Maturation.

    (4) Pretesting.

    (5) Instrumentation.

    (6) Treatment replications.

    (7) Subject attrition.

    (8) Statistical regression.

    (9) Diffusion of treatment.

   (10) Experimenter effects.

   (11) Subject effects.

2. Experimental designs.

A. Single-group posttest-only.

    (1) No comparison.

    (2) History threats significant.

B. Single-group pretest-posttest.

    (1) Most threatened by history.

    (2) Weak in pretesting, maturation, and experimenter and subject effects.

C. Nonequivalent-groups posttest-only—most threatened by selection.

D. Nonequivalent-groups pretest-posttest.

    (1) Subject to selection threats.

    (2) Stronger than preceding designs.

E. Randomized-groups posttest-only.

    (1) Control for many threats.

    (2) Random assignment of subjects.

F. Randomized-groups pretest-posttest—increases the likelihood of finding significant differences between groups.

G. Factorial experiments.

    (1) Test for interactions.

    (2) Two or more independent variables, one of which is manipulated.

3. Evaluation of experiments.

A. The study should include a hypothesis, manipulation of the independent variable, and indication of design.

B. It should control or address possible extraneous variables.

C. Treatments should be as different as possible.

D. Each replication of the treatment is one "subject."

4. Single-subject research.
    A. Individual behavior is observed and recorded.
    B. Standardized, repeated measurement before the treatment (baseline) and during the treatment establishes stability of behavior.
    C. A single variable is changed from baseline to treatment.
    D. Single-subject designs are $A-B-A$; $A-B-A-B$; or multiple baseline across subjects, settings, or behavior.
    E. Generalizability depends on descriptions of subjects, settings, and behaviors.
    F. Experimenter and observer effects need to be controlled.
    G. Practical significance is needed in interpreting the results.

STUDY QUESTIONS

1. What are the essential characteristics of experiments with groups of subjects? How are experiments different from relationship studies?

2. Why is internal validity important in interpreting experiments?

3. Give an example of how extraneous events (history) can threaten the internal validity of an experiment.

4. In what experimental designs is selection a serious threat to internal validity? Why?

5. How is selection "controlled" in the nonequivalent-groups pretest-posttest designs?

6. Under what circumstances are so-called "preexperimental" designs valid?

7. What are potential threats to the internal validity of any type of experimental design? Why?

8. What does it mean to say that the number of "subjects" in a study is equal to the number of replications of the treatment?

9. Give an example of a factorial design.

10. Why is an "interaction" important in research?

11. What are the characteristics you would look for in a good single-subject design?

12. What are the advantages of a multiple-baseline single-subject design?

13. How are the results of a single-subject design analyzed? What does it mean to have "practical" significance?

Chapter
9

Analyzing Statistical Inferences

It may not be much of an understatement to say that you probably are not particularly eager to get to this chapter. There is usually a perception that complex mathematics are involved in understanding statistical principles and that the strange symbols and letters encountered are of little practical value. Although it is true that most statistical procedures require complex calculations, the computer handles these very efficiently. We will focus on the logic and meaning of the procedures, which will not require sophisticated mathematics, and on understanding and evaluating the use of the procedures in research reports and articles. There are no statistical formulas or calculations.

THE PURPOSE AND NATURE OF INFERENTIAL STATISTICS

As indicated in Chapter 5, statistics are mathematical procedures used to summarize and analyze numerical data. Fundamental descriptive statistics were reviewed in Chapter 5. In this chapter we will concentrate on procedures that use descriptive statistics to estimate from a sample what is true for a population, or what is true given the inexact nature of measurement. These procedures, called **inferential statistics,** are necessary to provide a better understand-

Inferential statistics: Infers characteristics of a population.

192

ing of the precise nature of descriptions, relationships, and differences on the basis of data collected in a study.

Degree of Certainty

It would be pleasant (and profitable) if we could be certain in our predictions. How certain is a principal that a particular kind of evaluation procedure will provide credible information on which to base merit salary increases? Are you confident in your ability to predict who will win a race or an election? If we know that a sample of sixth-graders will pass a minimum competency test, how certain can we be that all sixth-graders will pass it? The degree to which we can be "certain" in each of these circumstances, as well as in other questions, will vary. In some cases we can be relatively certain, whereas in other situations we are not very sure at all. There is some degree of uncertainty in the questions addressed in educational research, and inferential statistics indicate in a precise way what it is we can, for the most part, be certain about. In research the degree of certainty depends on the amount of error in sampling and measurement.

Estimating Errors in Sampling and Measurement

Sampling was discussed in Chapter 4 as a procedure for studying a portion of a larger population. Subjects in the sample are measured to derive results *for the sample.* Inferential statistics are then used to *infer* to the entire population. Suppose a researcher is interested in the attitudes of seventh-graders toward learning and school. The population is large, say 1,000 seventh-graders, so a sample of 100 seventh-graders is selected randomly and these students respond to the attitude questionnaire. Then the researcher uses the results from the sample to infer the attitudes of all 1,000 seventh-graders. Since there is some degree of error in the sample, it must be taken into account in making the inference to the population. That is, even with a random sample, the mean attitude of the sample drawn is not exactly the same as that for the entire population. A second or third random sample of 100 students would result in a somewhat different mean.

If a researcher did take three random samples, which one is most correct? Which one can we be most certain will provide the most accurate estimation of the population? The answer is that we do not know because we have not measured the entire population. But we can estimate, on the basis of one sample, the error that should be considered in inferring the attitudes of the population.

So if the attitude of the sample was 25, on a scale from 10 to 35, and there was little error, we might estimate the population attitude to be somewhere between 23 and 27. If there was a large error, the estimate might be between 21 and 29. We use inferential statistics to indicate the precise range in which the actual mean attitude for the 1,000 students lies. Thus, we would conclude that the attitude of the population is probably between two values. This is what is indicated in national polls when the results are summarized as a number plus or minus some value (e.g., for 46 percent ± 3 percent, the value for the total population is probably between 43 and 49 percent).

Suppose a researcher uses the entire population. Would the measure be the "real" or "actual" value of the trait for the population? Although in this circumstance there is no sampling error, there is measurement error, which also needs to be taken into consideration. We infer a real or true value on a trait from imperfect measurement. Just as in sampling error, each time you measure a group the result will be somewhat different, depending on the reliability of the instrument. If the instrument is highly reliable, there will be little error, but if the reliability is low, the results could vary considerably each time. Thus, we take this error into account with inferential statistics by indicating the range in which true scores are likely to lie. The estimates of the true values of the population are then used to compare two or more values to see if "significant" differences exist between the groups that are being compared.

The Null Hypothesis

In a study that compares two groups on a measure of achievement the question that is investigated is whether, in truth or in reality, there is a difference between the groups. Since we know there is error, it is more accurate to conclude that there probably is or is not a real difference. The procedure for making the decision about whether there is or is not a difference begins with a **null hypothesis.** As indicated in Chapter 2, the null hypothesis is a statement that no difference exists between the populations that are being compared. In a relationship study, the null hypothesis would indicate that there is no relationship. The researcher uses inferential statistics to determine the probability that the null hypothesis is untrue, or false. If the null is untrue, the researcher concludes that there probably *is* a difference between the groups. Thus, if we can reject the null hypothesis, the chances are good that we are not wrong in saying that there is a difference.

Null hypothesis: Statement of no difference or relationship.

Inferential statistics tell us the probability of being wrong in rejecting the null hypothesis. This probability is called the **level of significance,** which is indicated with the small letter p and is reported as $p = x$. The value of p indicates how often the results would be obtained because of chance (rather than a "real" difference). Thus, if $p = .20$, there is a 20 percent probability that the difference is due to a chance variation, that is, error in sampling and measurement. This is too great a chance to accept in research. Typically, researchers will not conclude that there is an actual difference in the populations unless the probability of obtaining the difference by chance is less than 5 percent ($p < .05$). This is a convention that is translated to mean a "statistically significant" difference. If the level of significance is .001, there is only 1 chance out of 1,000 that the difference obtained is due to chance. This would be a stronger result than a p value of .01 (1 chance out of 100). If the decision is to reject the null hypothesis when it is in fact true (no difference in the populations), the researcher has made what is called a **Type I error.** The probability of making this type of error is equal to the level of significance. It is also possible to fail to reject the null hypothesis when it is in fact not true and should have been rejected. This is called a **Type II error.**

Level of significance: Probability of being wrong in rejecting the null.

Type I error: Rejecting the null when it is true.

Type II error: Not rejecting the null when it is not true.

In most studies the researcher will indicate the level of significance of rejecting each null hypothesis. Since there is no absolute rule in what constitutes "statistical" significance, it is necessary to interpret summary narrative statements in the context of the actual p values. Sometimes a p value between .10 and .05 is called "marginally" significant. In exploratory studies a p value of .10 may be judged sufficient to conclude that a "significant" difference exists. In medicine, where the probability of being wrong has serious consequences, a "significant" difference may require a p value of .0001. Usually researchers will report the lowest level of probability. That is, $p < .03$ means the actual p value is between .02 and .03.

The level of significance is affected by three factors. The first is the difference between the groups being compared. The greater the difference, the lower the p value. The second is the degree of sampling and measurement error. The lower the error, the lower the p value. The third factor is the size of the sample. If a very large sample is used, the p value will be lower than if the sample size is small. In fact in some studies a seemingly small difference may be reported as "significant," usually because of the large number of subjects. If there is some kind of systematic error or bias in the sampling or measurement, the results may be "significant" statistically but weak in internal validity.

The level of significance helps us make a statistical decision related to the null hypothesis. When the null hypothesis is rejected, we examine the design of the study to see if there are extraneous variables that may explain the results. If the null hypothesis is not rejected, we are tempted to conclude that there is, in reality, no difference or no relationship. In a very well-designed study, failure to reject the null hypothesis is just as important, scientifically, as rejecting it. The problem is that in many studies that find "no significant differences," there are usually factors in the design that may have contributed to the finding, for example, low reliability, sampling error, low number of subjects, diffusion of treatment, and other threats to internal validity. We simply do not know if there is really no difference or if the study as designed fails to show the difference that in fact exists.

In Chapter 7 it was pointed out that there is an important difference between "statistical" significance and "practical" significance. Practical significance is related to the importance and usefulness of the results. The null hypothesis and level of significance refer *only* to statistical significance. It is up to each consumer to judge the practical importance of what may be in a scientific sense "statistically" significant. This judgment is made by examining the actual differences or relationships that are called statistically significant and considering the context in which the results are used. A very small but statistically significant difference in the reading achievement of students may not justify changing the instruction if teachers' attitudes are negative toward the new approach. In the end, only the reader can determine what is practical and meaningful in using the results. Your conclusions are more important than those stated by the researchers.

INTERPRETING RESULTS OF INFERENTIAL TESTS

Inferential statistics are procedures used to obtain a level of significance for rejecting a null hypothesis. There are many different inferential procedures. Each is used to analyze the results of particular research designs. Thus, depending on the design, a specific statistical formula is used to obtain a level of significance appropriate to the null hypothesis. Most of the procedures you will read about are **parametric** statistics. These statistics are used when certain assumptions can be made about the data, such as having a population that is normally distributed, equal variances of each group, and interval-level measures. If these assumptions cannot be met, researchers use **nonparametric** statistics. The interpretation of

Parametric: Statistical procedures based on certain assumptions.

Nonparametric: Assumptions for parametric tests are not met.

the results is the same with both types of statistics, but parametric statistics have greater power to detect significant differences. The computational equations are different, but both test a null hypothesis and report a level of significance. Parametric tests are used even when all needed assumptions are not clearly met. We will consider commonly used parametric and nonparametric procedures.

The *t*-test

The **t-test,** a parametric statistical equation, is most often used to test the null hypothesis that the means of two groups are the same. The *t*-test is also used to see if a correlation coefficient is significantly different from zero (no correlation) and to compare a mean to a set value. In comparing two means, the researcher uses the two sample means, the group variances, and the sample size with a formula that generates a number, called the *t* value or *t* statistic. This *t* value is then used to obtain a level of significance for rejecting the null hypothesis that the population means are the same. In most studies the researcher will report the *t* value for each *t*-test, with corresponding *p* values. The *t* values may be in a table or in the narrative of the results section. Often there will be a table of the means of each group, with accompanying *t* values.

t-test: Compares two means.

There are two different forms of the *t*-test. One, the independent-samples *t*-test, is used in designs in which there are different subjects in each group, for example, two randomly assigned groups on a posttest of achievement. If the subjects in the groups are paired or matched in some way, a second form of the *t*-test is used. This may be called a dependent-samples, correlated, or matched *t*-test. It is most commonly used in the single-group pretest-posttest design when the same group of subjects is given both the pretest and posttest. Following are some examples of the *t*-test in published studies:

EXAMPLES: *t*-TEST

"Significant differences were found between experimental and control teachers in the use of the experimental instructional practices . . . the mean combined valence score for the 15 observed experimental teachers was 1.03 (*SD* = 12.99) while the mean valence score for the 17 observed control teachers was −13.11 (*SD* = 13.74). This difference was significant (*t* = 3.02, df = 31, *p* < .05)." (Hawkins, Doueck, and Lishner, 1988, p. 40)

"All three predictions were statistically supported. For the free-recall measure, the mean performance of students in both picture conditions surpassed that of students in the no-picture control condition, *t*s = 3.66 and 3.18 for mnemonic and nonmnemonic, with no significant difference between the two picture variations, *t* < 1." (Mastropieri, Scruggs, and Levin, 1987, p. 512)

"For the matched groups' *t* tests the mean differences showed relatively greater GPA achievement for the high extrinsic motivation-low intrinsic motivation group, mean differences being: most challenging, .04; least challenging, .30. The *t* test for correlated samples yielded a *t* of 2.19, *p* < .05, for the least challenging difference, establishing a statistically significant superiority of extrinsic motivation over intrinsic motivation subjects on GPA in least challenging courses." (Kahoe and McFarland, 1975, p. 434)

The *df* in the first example refers to "degrees of freedom." This number is used to calculate the level of significance and is approximately equal to the number of subjects in the study. It may be indicated in parentheses after the *t* without the letters *df*. In other articles the degrees of freedom may be implied or indicated in a table of results and not in the narrative.

Simple Analysis of Variance

Simple **analysis of variance** (abbreviated **ANOVA**) is a parametric procedure that has the same basic purpose of the *t*-test: to compare group means to determine the probability of being wrong in rejecting the null hypothesis. Whereas the *t*-test compares two means, ANOVA can compare two or more means. In effect, ANOVA is an extension of the *t*-test that allows the researcher to test the differences between more than two group means. In *simple* ANOVA (also called one-way ANOVA) a single independent variable is analyzed with a single dependent variable. For instance, if a researcher compares three types of students, high, medium, and low socioeconomic status (SES), on a measure of locus of control, there are three levels of the independent variable. ANOVA would test the null hypothesis that there is no difference among the means of all three groups. It would be referred to as a 1 × 3 ANOVA (one independent variable with three levels). The ANOVA equation uses the variances of the groups to calculate a value, called the *F* statistic (or *F* ratio). The *F*, analogous to the *t* value, is a three- or four-digit number em-

Analysis of variance (ANOVA): Compares two or more means.

ployed to obtain the level of significance that the researcher uses to reject or fail to reject the null hypothesis. If the F value is large enough, the null hypothesis can be rejected with confidence that at least two of the population means are not the same.

In the preceding example, let us assume that the locus of control means for each group are as follows: high SES, 30; medium SES, 23; low SES, 22. The null hypothesis that is tested is that $30 = 23 = 22$. If the F statistic calculated with ANOVA is 4.76 and the p value is .01, the null would be rejected. However, this analysis does not indicate *which* pair or pairs of means are different. In some studies the results are such that the different pairs are obvious (such as in this example), but in most studies there is a need for further statistical tests to indicate those means that are significantly different from other means. These tests are called **multiple comparison procedures** (or post hoc comparisons). There are several types of multiple comparison procedures, including Fisher's LSD, Duncan's new multiple range test, the Newman-Keuls, Tukey's HSD, and Scheffe's test.

Multiple comparison procedures: Indicate which pairs of means are different.

The results of a simple 1×3 ANOVA are summarized in the following example.

EXAMPLE: ONE-WAY ANOVA AND MULTIPLE COMPARISON TEST

"The number of trials each subject required to reach criterion was used to calculate the mean number of trials for each training group. A one-way analysis of variance was performed that revealed a statistically significant effect for Group, $F(2, 21) = 5.97$, $p < .01$. . . . To determine the order of acquisition of each of the concepts Duncan's multiple range test was performed. The results of this analysis indicated that the ICT and ECT training groups were significantly different from each other, as were the ICT and TIT groups ($p < .05$). The only comparison that failed to reach significance was between ECT and TIT." (Abramson, Cooney, and Vincent, 1980, p. 194)

The numbers in parentheses after the F are degrees of freedom. The first is the number of groups compared minus one, and the second is the approximate number of subjects in the study. Both of these numbers are used with the F ratio to obtain the level of significance.

Factorial Analysis of Variance

As stated in Chapter 8, factorial designs have more than one independent variable and enable the investigation of interactions among the independent variables. The statistical analysis of such designs requires the use of **factorial analysis of variance.** The most common factorial ANOVA has two independent variables and is therefore referred to as a *two-way* ANOVA. In a two-way ANOVA three null hypotheses are tested: one for each independent variable and one for the interaction among them. Consequently, there are three *F* ratios, one for each null hypothesis. The test for each independent variable, sometimes called a *main effect*, is similar to a one-way ANOVA for that variable by itself. Thus, there will be an *F* ratio and corresponding *p* value for each independent variable. If one variable in a factorial design has two levels and another variable has three levels, the analysis would be a 2 × 3 ANOVA. A 3 × 3 × 4 ANOVA would mean that there are three independent variables, two with three levels and one with four levels.

In interpreting factorial ANOVA studies, you will find that significant interactions are often presented in a graph. The graph is constructed to show how the means of all the groups compare. The values of the dependent variable are placed along the vertical axis of the graph, and levels of one of the independent variables are on the horizontal axis. The means of all the groups are then indicated in the graph by reference to the second independent variable. For example, in Figure 9.1 there is an illustration of a significant in-

Factorial analysis of variance: Two or more independent variables analyzed together.

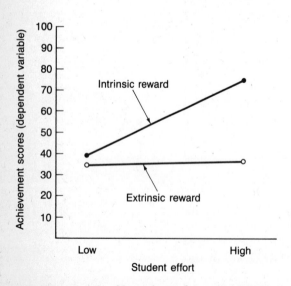

Figure 9.1 Graph of hypothetical 2 × 2 ANOVA and interaction.

teraction. The two independent variables are student effort (high or low) and type of reward (intrinsic or extrinsic). The results of the 2 × 2 ANOVA indicate that overall high-effort students did better on achievement, a main effect for effort, and that there was a significant interaction—high-effort students who received an intrinsic reward did better than high-effort students who received an extrinsic reward. For low-effort students it did not matter if they received intrinsic or extrinsic rewards.

There are many variations of factorial designs and many different terms are used to describe specific types of analyses. You may read such terms as *split plot, randomized block, within subjects,* or *repeated measures* in the results sections of articles. Regardless of the language, the results are interpreted in basically the same manner. There is some type of null hypothesis that needs to be tested, and the *F* ratios indicate whether statistically significant differences are present.

Analysis of Covariance

Analysis of covariance (ANCOVA) is a variation of ANOVA. It is used to adjust for pretest differences that may exist between two or more groups. For instance, suppose in an experiment that one group has a mean value on the pretest of 15 and the other group has a pretest mean of 18. ANCOVA is used to adjust the posttest scores statistically to compensate for the three-point difference between the groups. This adjustment results in more accurate posttest comparisons. The pretest used for the adjustment is called the covariate. Several other types of covariates can also be used in a study, such as socioeconomic status, aptitude, attitudes, and previous achievement. Sometimes a covariate other than the pretest is used with the pretest covariate, and sometimes covariates are used when there is no pretest in the design of the study. Covariates are helpful only if they are related to the dependent variable. ANCOVA is used with both one-way and factorial designs.

Analysis of covariance (ANCOVA): Adjusts for differences between groups.

Multivariate Statistics

Each of the preceding parametric statistical procedures represents what is termed a **univariate** analysis because a single dependent variable is used. However, in many complex social situations, such as schools, there is often a need to study simultaneously two or more dependent variables. For example, a teacher may be inter-

Univariate: One dependent variable analyzed.

ested in comparing two teaching methods on attitudes toward learning and school. A principal may want to determine the effect of a new homework policy on parent involvement, student confidence, and achievement in each of several different subject areas. In such situations it would be a mistake to analyze each dependent variable separately, with a different ANOVA or *t*-test. The correct approach is to use a **multivariate** statistical procedure. Multivariate statistics analyze all the dependent variables in a single procedure, which is important in accounting for the relationships between the dependent variables. For each of the univariate statistical procedures, there is a multivariate analog (e.g., Hotelling's T for the *t*-test, and MANCOVA for ANCOVA).

Multivariate: Two or more dependent variables analyzed together.

Multivariate procedures are being reported in the literature more and more each year. Although the computations and interpretation of multivariate tests are complex, they employ the same basic principles for rejecting the null hypotheses. It should also be pointed out that some researchers have a somewhat different definition of the term *multivariate*, which may refer to any study that has more than one variable, either independent or dependent. In this definition, multiple correlation would be considered to be a multivariate procedure.

Chi-Square

When researchers are interested in the number of responses or cases in different categories, they use a procedure called **chi-square** to analyze the results. The null hypothesis is that there is no difference between an observed number and an expected number of responses or cases that fall in each category. The expected number is usually that which would be expected by chance alone. Suppose an administrator wanted to see if there is a difference between the number of male and female students who take advanced placement courses. The expected number by chance alone would be an equal number of males and females in advanced placement courses. The administrator would use the chi-square test to determine if the actual number of male students taking advanced placement courses was significantly different from the number of female students taking advanced placement courses.

Chi-square: Tests frequency counts in different categories.

The chi-square test (represented by χ^2) can also examine questions of relationship between two independent variables that report frequencies of responses or cases. For example, a researcher may be interested in investigating the relationship between gender and choices of books for a book report. There may be several types of books, such as romantic, adventure, mystery, and biography. The researcher would count the number of males and females who choose each type of book and analyze the results with a chi-square to determine if the null hypothesis, that there is no relationship between gender and book choice, can be rejected. This type of chi-square may be referred to as a *contingency table*, in this example a 2 × 4 table. The result is often reported with a single measure of relationship called a *contingency coefficient,* which is interpreted in the same way as a correlation coefficient.

A recently published study investigated differences in the views of parents, teachers, and principals toward retention. The number of responses in each of five categories was examined for each of the three types of adults.

EXAMPLE: CHI-SQUARE TEST

"For the question on their general opinion of grade repetition, parents, teachers, and principals were asked to mark one of the following terms: 'never,' 'rarely,' 'occasionally,' 'usually,' or 'always' in response to the question, 'Children should be retained if they do not meet the requirements of the grade.' When responses of parents, teachers, and principals were examined by chi-square analysis, the contrasts attained the .0001 level of significance . . . the most obvious difference was in the tendency for parents to mark the extreme answers of 'never' and 'always' more frequently than teachers or principals." (Byrnes and Yamamoto, 1986, p. 15)

The results of a chi-square will usually be reported in a table that shows either the number or percentage of responses or cases in each category. If the number is less than five in any single category, the chi-square test needs to be "corrected" with what is called Yates's correction. This correction statistically adjusts the numbers to get a more valid result. Another approach when a small number of observations is observed is to use a procedure called the Fisher exact test. The results will indicate the value of the chi-square (χ^2) and the level of significance with the χ^2; for example, the result of the Byrnes and Yamamoto (1986) study was reported in the table as $\chi^2 = 35.474$; $p < .0001$.

The chi-square is a nonparametric statistical procedure because the data that are analyzed are nominal-level data, and assumptions of normal distribution and equal variances may not be met. There are nonparametric analyses that can be used instead of a particular parametric analysis. Some of these are summarized in Table 9.1.

Table 9.1   PARAMETRIC AND ANALOGOUS NONPARAMETRIC PROCEDURES

Parametric	Nonparametric
Pearson product-moment correlation coefficient	Spearman rank-order correlation coefficient
Independent samples *t*-test	Median test Mann-Whitney *U*-test
Dependent samples *t*-test	Sign test Wilcoxon test
One-way ANOVA	Median test Kruskal-Wallis ANOVA

CONSUMER TIPS
Criteria for Evaluating Inferential Statistics

1. Basic descriptive statistics are needed to evaluate the results of inferential statistics. Remember that the results of an inferential test rely on the descriptive data that were gathered—the means, variances, frequencies, and percentages. Although inferential statistics provide important information about the probability that conclusions about populations, or "true" values, are correct, the interpretation of the results depends on the descriptive statistical results. It may be misleading to rely solely on the conclusions of the inferential test results. You should always look at the more basic descriptive data to derive meaning from the results.

2. Inferential analyses refer to statistical, not practical, significance. Do not confuse statistical with practical significance. The results of inferential analyses should not be the sole criteria for conclusions about changing a practice or other decisions. It is easy to make too much of what appears to be a sophisticated procedure. The use of the inferential tests is not complicated and should be kept in balance with other considerations relative to the use of the results.

3. Inferential analyses do not indicate external validity. Although we use inferential statistics to infer population values from sample values, generalizability to other subjects and settings depends on whether the subjects were randomly selected, the characteristics of the subjects, and the specific design of the study.

4. Inferential analyses do not indicate internal validity. The extent to which a result shows a causal relationship depends on how the data were gathered and what happened to the subjects. The inferential test is used to conclude that there is a high probability that the null hypothesis is not true, that is, that there is a difference or relationship. This is the first and necessary step to conclude that one variable caused a change in another variable. Once the statistics show that there is a relationship or difference, you need to analyze the design and procedures to determine if there is adequate internal validity.

5. **The results of inferential tests depend on the number of subjects.** An important factor in determining the level of significance for a statistical test is the number of subjects. If there are many subjects, a very small difference or relationship can be "statistically significant"; if only a few subjects are used, what appears to be a large difference or relationship may not be "statistically significant." This phenomenon is especially important in experimental studies in which there is a difference between the number of subjects and replications of the treatment. If a researcher uses number of subjects when it is clear that the number of independent replications of the treatment is much smaller, the inferential test that leads to a conclusion to reject the null hypothesis may be invalid.

6. **The appropriate statistical test should be used.** It is important for researchers to use a statistical test that is appropriate to the design and questions of a study. Most journal reviewers and editors evaluate studies to be certain that the appropriate tests were employed. However, it is likely that many studies are published that use the wrong statistical test. The most likely mistakes are to use a parametric procedure when the assumptions for using such a test are not met and to use many univariate tests when a multivariate test would be more appropriate.

7. **The level of significance should be interpreted correctly.** Remember that the level of significance indicates the probability that the difference or relationship is not due to chance. It is not a definitive statement that there either is or is not a difference or relationship. A high level of significance (e.g., .20 or .40) does not necessarily mean that there is no difference or relationship in the population or in reality. Nonsignificant findings may result from inadequate design and measurement.

8. **Be wary of statistical tests with small numbers of subjects in one or more groups or categories.** Whenever there is a small number of subjects in a group, there is a good chance that the statistical test may provide spurious results. When only a few numbers are used to calculate a mean or variance, one atypical number may significantly affect the results. It is best to have at least 10 subjects in each comparison group and 30 subjects in calculating a correlation. The results of studies that use a small number of subjects also have less generalizability.

OUTLINE SUMMARY

1. Inferential statistics.
   A. Inferences from a sample to a population.
   B. Error in sampling and measurement.
   C. Null hypothesis.
      (1) Statement of no difference or no relationship.
      (2) Level of significance indicates probability that null is false.
      (3) Rejected with $p < .05$.
      (4) Probability of rejecting higher with large samples.
      (5) "Statistical" and "practical" significance are different (rejecting the null only addresses statistical significance).
      (6) Failure to reject.
2. Inferential tests.
   A. Parametric and nonparametric statistics.
   B. t-test.
      (1) Compares means of two groups.
      (2) Independent samples.
      (3) Dependent samples.
   C. Simple analysis of variance (ANOVA).
      (1) One independent variable.
      (2) Means of two or more groups.
      (3) Multiple comparisons.
   D. Factorial analysis of variance.
      (1) Two or more independent variables.
      (2) Two-way ANOVA.
   E. Analysis of covariance (ANCOVA).
      (1) Adjusts posttest scores.
      (2) Pretest or other variables as covariates.
   F. Multivariate statistics.
   G. Chi-square.
      (1) Nonparametric procedure.
      (2) Frequencies in different categories.
      (3) Relationships with contingency table.
   H. Results separate from internal and external validity.

STUDY QUESTIONS

1. Why is it necessary to use inferential statistics?
2. What is the relationship between inferential and descriptive statistics?
3. What is the difference between sampling error and measurement error?

4. How is the null hypothesis used in inferential statistics?

5. Why is it important to understand what "level of significance" means?

6. What is the difference between Type I and Type II error?

7. Does it matter whether or not the null hypothesis is rejected?

8. Why is it important to distinguish between "statistical" and "practical" significance?

9. Under what circumstances would it be appropriate to use nonparametric statistical tests?

10. Give an example of a study that would use an independent samples *t*-test.

11. Give an example of a study that would use simple ANOVA.

12. Give an example of a study that would use factorial ANOVA.

13. What does a factorial ANOVA tell us that a simple ANOVA does not?

14. Why would it be helpful to use ANCOVA rather than ANOVA?

15. Why are multivariate statistics used?

16. Give an example of a study that would use a chi-square statistical analysis.

Chapter
10

Historical and Qualitative Research

Educational research has been dominated by quantitative methods and designs. In recent years, however, a need for a greater variety of research methods, most notably more qualitative approaches, has been recognized. Although the vast majority of studies use quantitative techniques, it is more and more likely each year that you will also read research based on a different set of assumptions and methods. In this chapter we will review two approaches that have distinctive perspectives about how to gather and interpret data. It is important to remember that these methods are no less "scientific" than quantitative methods. One approach is not necessarily any better than another. Each has advantages and disadvantages, strengths and weaknesses. Most educational researchers would agree that problems are best investigated by using whatever methods are most appropriate, separately or in combination.

HISTORICAL RESEARCH

Historians are important to any field or discipline, providing insight to present practices by discovering, analyzing, and interpreting past events. **Historical research** is the systematic search for data related to past events and the interpretation of the data to arrive at conclusions. The conclusions increase our knowledge of why events occurred and the consequences of past events. This awareness in-

Historical research: The systematic study of past events.

208

creases our understanding of present events, practices, issues, and trends and helps us predict the future. This ability is especially relevant to education since so much of what we do seems to be something that has already been done. There seems to be a cyclical nature to educational practice. For instance, there is currently a great amount of emphasis on "critical thinking." Students need to be able to "think" and problem-solve, not simply have knowledge. In the early 1950s there was also an emphasis on good thinking skills, and much can be learned by examining what teaching methods and curriculum materials were most effective during that time.

Historical research may be undertaken for a variety of reasons. Some historical research is conducted simply to provide an accurate history of something that has not been previously documented. This work is similar to basic research since there may not be a specific use for the results. A more common reason is to clarify what has happened in the past so that inaccurate interpretations of past events can be avoided. For example, an administrator may base an idea about the effect of implementing a new policy on an inaccurate or incomplete understanding of what occurred in other schools in the past when a similar policy was implemented. Historical research reminds us that previous traditions, cultures, and values are valuable in understanding present-day problems and issues. Because so much educational practice is repetitive, historical research allows us to predict future behavior by documenting the similarities and differences between previous and present situations. A careful documentation of critical differences can prevent poor decisions.

The Historical Method

No single method of inquiry is used by historians, although the essential steps are the same as in other types of research: definition of a problem or topic, data identification and collection, data analysis, and synthesis of findings to formulate conclusions. The historical researcher has no control over treatments or data that may be available, so differences in methods are reflected in how the historian chooses to collect the data, ranging from interviews to sophisticated statistical analyses of census data.

Definition of a Problem or Topic   Good historical research problems are subject to the same criteria as in other methods of investigation. The problem needs to be clear, succinct, specific, and feasible. Since historians have no control over the amount of data that may be available, problems need to be considered in light of what data can be found and analyzed. If the problem is too broad and a great amount of data is available, it will be very difficult to conduct all of the necessary analyses and synthesize the findings. On the other hand, it is also possible for historians to choose a topic for which there are insufficient data, resulting in analyses that are tentative and shallow.

There are several predominant types of problems in historical research. One type is a history of an educational institution, movement, or person. Another type analyzes current educational issues. A third type reinterprets previous historical accounts or integrates separate histories that previously may not have been related. Much historical research in education has focused on questions that concern public schooling.

Following are some examples of problems from historical research articles. You will note that the writing style is less formal than that in most quantitative research reports.

EXAMPLES: HISTORICAL RESEARCH PROBLEMS

"As a start in addressing these issues, I have looked at changes in attitudes toward the intellectual development of infants and young children in the United States from 1900 to 1985. This study is based on a content analysis of 1,017 articles drawn from the popular literature directed toward parents. It is designed to offer a broad yet systematic view of changes in recommended child-rearing practices, with particular reference to changes in how young children's thinking and learning were viewed" (Wrigley, 1989, p. 43)

"Our purpose here is to assess the historiography of African American education in terms of its appraisal of the black struggle for learning and its ability to contribute to action for the emancipation of black America." (Butchart, 1988, pp. 333–334)

". . . I should like to turn to two questions about Dewey and his place in the history of educational research. I should like, first, to consider Dewey's approach to the systematic study of education, where it came from and what it involved; and then, I should like to investigate some, but certainly not all, of the reasons why Dewey's approach to educational inquiry did not take hold as widely or as enduringly as certain alternative approaches." (Lagemann, 1989, pp. 185–186)

Data Identification and Collection   For the historian, data comprise any object, written record, or recollection that may be related to the problem. Written records, or **documents,** are the most common source of data and are virtually anything written or printed, such as yearbooks, committee minutes, memos, newspapers, mag-

Documents: Written records of past events and people.

azines, diaries, and books. Records that are quantitative in nature, such as test scores, school budgets, family income, census data, school attendance, and dropout rates, are increasingly used by historians. Interviews provide data, and objects—called **relics**—such as furniture, art, buildings, machines, and cloths provide information through physical properties.

Relics: Historical data in the form of physical properties.

If the documents, relics, or reports provide original, firsthand information, they are primary sources. In a primary source the person writing the document or giving the interview was present when the event that is described occurred. It is as if primary sources reflect what a direct witness of the past event saw or heard. Secondary sources are secondhand documents or interviews. The individual giving the information was not a direct witness of the event but describes it from the accounts of others. Secondary sources include reviews of literature, reference books, textbooks, and most historical research articles. Historians rely as much as possible on primary sources. With secondary sources there are two levels of interpretation of the actual event, the person who wrote or provided the secondary source and the historian who is conducting the research. When reading historical research it is important to know whether the sources are primary or secondary. If there is excessive use of secondary sources, the investigator needs to assure you that they are accurate.

Data Analysis   In historical research, data analysis refers to the evaluation of the sources by the researcher to determine their worth and significance. Historians use two types of evaluation: external and internal criticism. **External criticism** refers to an analysis of a document to determine its authenticity. A document is authentic if it is genuine, that is, the original copy. For example, what evidence is presented to back up a claim that a letter was written by George Washington? Is the handwriting correct? What about the age of the paper? Is the style of writing the same as in other documents written by George Washington? Once authenticity is established, the researcher evaluates the document with **internal criticism,** which is a judgment about its accuracy. Accuracy refers to how closely the document reflects what actually occurred. For instance, minutes of a meeting can be authentic, but do they indicate what really occurred in the meeting? Do different accounts of the same event agree? An important part of internal criticism is an evaluation of the person who wrote the document or gave verbal accounts. Was the person competent and in a position to obtain accurate information? Would the person have any reason to be biased? Is the person thought to be truthful and accurate? Is there any discrepancy in different statements of the same event? Do different types of

External criticism: Judges authenticity of a document.

Internal criticism: Judges accuracy of a document.

evidence (e.g., different observers) provide the same information? How much time elapsed between the event and the recording of the event? Internal criticism is more difficult to establish than external criticism, especially in educational research, where authenticity is not usually a problem.

Synthesis of Findings to Form Conclusions   The final step in historical research is to organize and synthesize the data and formulate conclusions. This step involves the interpretation of the investigator, so it is best to look for evidence that the investigator is not biased. There is usually documentation of the evidence, which is then interpreted in a logical manner. Often this interpretation reflects particular interests and values. For example, many educational historians have interpreted past events within the framework that state-regulated public education was desirable. The interpretation is based on finding consistent information, patterns, and sequences of events. Often a causal inference is made when the historian shows that certain events were preceded by other events. Although any discovery about the antecedents of events is helpful, the historian is always limited in making causal inferences because of an inability to control or manipulate conditions that have already occurred. Like other researchers, historians generalize their conclusions on the basis of the evidence: the time period to which documents or other information pertain, the nature of a sample, and the settings.

CONSUMER TIPS
Criteria for Evaluating Historical Research

1. **Definitions of terms and concepts should be constant and specific.** Historical researchers should avoid using vague definitions of key terms and phrases. There is little analytical value in using terms that can be interpreted in different ways. For example, the phrase *educational reform* is too general because it can have different meanings. Also historians should note the meaning of terms in the context in which they were used. Present-day connotations of a term may be different than in the past. For example, the meaning of the term *public* has changed over time. In the eighteenth century *public* referred to educational institutions in which students learned together for the "public good," in contrast to tutorial education, which was considered "private." What we would refer to as a "private" college today would have been described as "public" in the eighteenth century. Quantitative terms, such as

teachers' salaries, length of the school day, student achievement, and *expenditures per pupil,* are defined differently in different periods of history. Thus, for historians to examine longitudinal patterns of change, the definitions of each period must be specified.

2. Historians should not confuse causation with correlation. As we have seen in quantitative studies it is easy to be tempted into a causal conclusion when the data are correlational. Historians can also confuse correlation with causation. Look for unwarranted causal inferences. Just because events occurred in a particular sequence does not mean that causative conclusions are justified. Most events are caused by multiple factors; very strong evidence is needed for the historian to be sure of the specific causes of an event.

3. Historians should not confuse facts with inferences. The historian should be careful to avoid making unwarranted inferences from established facts. For example, it may be a fact that there are laws making kindergarten mandatory, but that does not necessarily mean that the public values early education for its children, and it also may not mean that all children have, in fact, attended kindergarten. To make these inferences valid the historian needs to present evidence that is more directly related to the inferences themselves. Inferences of intent may not necessarily follow from a policy or the consequences of a policy. For instance, the fact that whites moved out of a city because of mandated busing of students does not mean that one of the intents of busing was to enhance segregation.

4. There should not be an excessive reliance on secondary sources. Historians need to be careful when most of their evidence is in the form of secondary sources. The best way to know how many secondary sources were used is to examine the nature of the sources carefully. Conclusions will not indicate the types of sources used.

5. External and internal criticism should be explicit and thorough. The historian's analysis of external and internal criticism should be clearly and thoroughly presented. You should not have any difficulty identifying both types of criticisms. The overall credibility of historical research depends heavily on credible external and internal criticism.

6. The findings of historical research should not be overgeneralized. As in other types of research, historians study a sample of persons, events, documents, and objects. Generalizations should be limited if there is a heavy reliance on secondary sources. The researcher needs to provide a good argument for generalizing beyond the specific evidence that is presented. Generalizability is enhanced when there is consistency of evidence from different sources or different times.

QUALITATIVE RESEARCH

In Chapter 1 qualitative research was described as a tradition of research techniques, as well as a philosophy of knowing, that is quite different from quantitative research. The term *qualitative* describes a number of different techniques that share some common characteristics, many of which can be traced to ethnography. **Ethnography** refers to an in-depth analytical description of naturally occurring behavior within a culture. Anthropologists engage in ethnographic research. In fact some researchers define ethnography as anthropological field study.

Other terms are also associated with qualitative research: *field research, naturalistic, participant observation, ecological,* and *case study.* The exact definition and use of these terms, as well as *qualitative,* vary. Educational researchers are likely to use *qualitative* in a more generic sense, as an approach that has some or all of the following characteristics.

Ethnography: In-depth involvement in a culture to describe naturally occurring behavior.

Characteristics of Qualitative Research

Studies that may be called qualitative will not necessarily exhibit each of these characteristics. It is more a matter of degree than of all or none.

Qualitative Research Is Carried Out in Natural Settings   A hallmark of qualitative research is that behavior is studied as it occurs naturally. There is no manipulation or control of behavior or settings. There are two reasons for this emphasis: the belief that behavior is best understood as it occurs without external constraints and control, and the belief that the situational context is very important in understanding the behavior. It is assumed that the setting influences human behavior, and therefore it is not possible to understand the behavior without taking into account the situational characteristics.

Qualitative Researchers Gather Data Directly   In qualitative studies the investigator will act as an observer in the setting that is being studied. Qualitative researchers spend considerable time in direct interaction with the participants they are studying. There is a reluctance to use other observers or to use quantitative measuring techniques.

Qualitative Research Provides Rich Narrative Descriptions Qualitative researchers approach a situation with the assumption that nothing is trivial or unimportant. Every detail is recorded and is thought to contribute to a better understanding of behavior. The descriptions are narrative rather than numerical, although some qualitative studies will have some simple numerical summaries. Nothing escapes scrutiny. The detailed approach to description is necessary to obtain a complete understanding of the setting and to accurately reflect the complexity of human behavior. To accomplish these goals the studies may extend over a long period of time and require intense involvement.

Qualitative Research Is Concerned with Process Qualitative researchers want to know how and why behavior occurs. In contrast with most quantitative studies, qualitative methods look for the process through which behavior occurs. For example, qualitative studies would be appropriate for understanding how teachers' expectations affect students' expectations and behavior.

Data Are Analyzed Inductively Qualitative researchers do not formulate hypotheses and gather data to prove or disprove them. Rather, the data are gathered first and then synthesized inductively to generate generalizations. Theory is developed from the "ground up," from the detailed particulars. The research questions are developed during the study. This approach is important because the qualitative researcher wants to be open to new ways of understanding. Predetermined hypotheses limit what will be collected and may cause bias.

Perspectives of Participants Are Important Qualitative researchers try to reconstruct reality as the participants they are studying see it. They do not apply predetermined definitions or ideas about how people will think or react. For example, a quantitative researcher may assume that a teacher's praise is interpreted in a certain way, whereas a qualitative researcher would be interested in how the participant interpreted the praise. The goal in qualitative research is to understand participants from their point of view.

Qualitative Research Problems

The research problem in a qualitative investigation is initially a general statement of the purpose of the study, referred to as a **foreshadowed problem.** It provides a focus for beginning the study, a broad framework that is refined as a result of the review of literature and the gathered data. Often the general purpose of the study includes an indication of the proposed methodology. The following examples of foreshadowed problems illustrate the broad framework from which the researcher begins.

Foreshadowed problem: A general framework for beginning a qualitative study.

EXAMPLES: FORESHADOWED PROBLEMS

"This study used ethnographic methodology to explore the academic world of regular and learning disabled high school students to determine what aspects of that world might relate to potential dropout behavior" (Miller, Leinhardt, and Zigmond, 1988, p. 465).

"This article focuses . . . upon how personal life factors are perceived by teachers as affecting professional role enactment." (Pajak and Blase, 1989, p. 284)

The foreshadowed problem is usually followed by more specific research questions, which may be presented at the beginning of the study or embedded in the data analysis. In the following example the researcher formulated a set of specific questions before collecting the data.

EXAMPLE: SPECIFIC QUESTIONS

"The overall purpose of this study was to determine the nature of the social organization of a low-track secondary English-reading classroom.

These research questions guided the data collection:

1. What is the nature of the social organization in the observed classroom?

2. What verbal and nonverbal actions/patterns of action does the teacher display as he interacts with students that have low-reading ability? How does the context of the learning situation/social organization influence the teacher's actions/patterns of action?

3. How does the teacher perceive and interpret his own actions in various contexts involving students that have low-reading ability? Does the teacher perceive his actions changing when working with students that have average or above average reading ability?

4. How do the students in the observed class and administrators of the school perceive and interpret the actions of the teacher during lesson interactions?" (Dillon, 1989, p. 230)

Qualitative researchers begin with a general idea of the purpose of the study to allow for changes as the data are collected. There is an interactive relationship between the problem and data, each influencing the other. The following statement of purpose illustrates how the problem can change during the study.

EXAMPLE: CHANGING RESEARCH PROBLEM

"The current study began as an investigation of teachers' diagnostic strategies as they tutored individual students in the skills of whole number addition . . . to see what kinds of diagnostic strategies they used and how they adjusted their instruction on the basis of their diagnoses. . . . As the study progressed, however, it became clear that detailed diagnosis was not an important goal. . . . The result was a shift in the study's focus from describing specific diagnostic strategies to examining how the teachers structured and sequenced subject-matter content for their students." (Putnam, 1987, pp. 14–15)

Selecting Participants

In qualitative studies the individuals who are investigated may be called participants rather than subjects. The participants are selected through purposeful sampling to provide an in-depth understanding of the phenomenon that is being studied. As indicated in Chapter 4, purposeful sampling is used to select individuals who will be most informative. It is not intended to be representative of a larger population. Often qualitative researchers will select individuals or cases that may be atypical, balanced by individuals who would be considered typical or represent the natural variation that exists on an important variable (quota sampling). You should look for the justification used in selecting participants. It should be clear to you how and why the participants were selected because the findings are highly dependent on the relatively low number of participants that characterizes qualitative research. A good example is provided by Putnam (1987) in his study of tutoring.

EXAMPLE: SELECTING PARTICIPANTS

"Four second-grade and two first-grade teachers . . . participated in the study. . . . Teachers were recruited to include as wide a range of backgrounds and approaches in the teaching of mathematics as possible. Some were recommended by their principals as being strong mathematics teachers. . . . Others agreed to participate in the study because they were interested but did not consider themselves to be particularly outstanding mathematics teachers." (pp. 17–18)

Obtaining Qualitative Information

Many methods are used to collect qualitative data, including observation, interviews, and analysis of documents. In all of these approaches the researcher takes an active role.

Qualitative Observations   In qualitative observations the researcher spends an extended period of time in a natural setting. By going directly to where behavior occurs naturally, to what is called a "field" setting, and being there for many hours or days, the researcher hopes to obtain a rich understanding of the phenomenon being studied. In reading the methods section of a qualitative article you should look for an indication of the time the researcher has spent in the setting. The quality of the results is directly related to the length of the observations. It is unlikely that valid and credible data will result from a few hours of observation.

An important aspect of the observation is the extent to which the researcher is an active participant with the subjects. If the researcher is a genuine participant in the activity being studied, he or she is called a **participant observer.** For example, to study the life of a college freshman, the participant observer would become a college freshman, directly experiencing everything other freshmen experience. This is essentially what an anthropologist would do in conducting ethnographic research on a culture. The anthropologist would virtually become a member of the group and live just as others in the group live.

In educational research it is rare for the investigator literally to adopt the same role as the individuals who are being studied. There may be some participation in some of the activities, but it is usually limited. The researcher interacts with the participants to establish a rapport and a relationship but not actually to become a participant. Researchers use several different terms to describe this type of observation, such as *limited observer, complete observer, observer-as-participant,* or *nonparticipant observer.* You can think of the degree of participation and involvement as a continuum, ranging from a participant observer on one end to a complete observer on the other end. A **complete observer** is totally detached from the behavior of the participants who are being studied. Of course the mere presence of an observer, whether involved or detached, may affect the behavior of those observed.

The more the researcher is actively involved with the participants the greater the chance that this involvement will significantly alter what occurs. Any degree of participant observation will affect what is observed. As a consumer you need to look for clues indicating that researcher participation may have been an important

Participant observer: Observer involved as a participant.

Complete observer: Observer detached from participants.

influence on the results, for example, emotional involvement or bias in the interpretation of what is recorded. The researcher should indicate a sensitivity for this effect and should take precautions so that the effect does not significantly distort the observations. Some researchers will indicate their biases and personal beliefs at the outset of the study to demonstrate an explicit concern to compensate for them.

Qualitative observers usually record observations as brief notes while they are observing. These brief notes are then expanded to become what are called **field notes.** Field notes are detailed written descriptions of what was observed and constitute the raw data that the researcher analyzes to address the research problem. The assumption is that nothing is trivial, so whatever is seen, heard, or experienced is recorded. Observers will also record their ideas, reflections, or hunches. It is critical for the field notes to be accurate and extensive. You will be able to judge the level of detail provided by the excerpts the researcher uses to illustrate conclusions, and the overall amount of data analyzed. Direct quotes from participants are used as much as possible, and the time frame, physical setting, and description of the researcher are also indicated.

The following example of field notes will give you some idea of the detail that is recorded. These field notes were collected as part of a study on mainstreaming learning-disabled high school students. What is reproduced here represents about one-tenth of the notes for an observation period of one and one-half hours.

Field notes: Detailed recordings of observed behavior.

EXAMPLE: FIELD NOTES

"I walked into Marge's class and she was standing in front of the room with more people than I had ever seen in the room save for her homeroom which is right after second period. She looked like she was talking to the class or was just about to start. She was dressed as she had been on my other visits—clean, neat, well-dressed but casual. Today she had on a striped blazer, a white blouse and dark slacks. She looked up at me, smiled and said: 'Oh, I have a lot more people here now than the last time.'

There were two women in their late twenties sitting in the room. There was only one chair left. Marge said to me something like: 'We have two visitors from the central office today. One is a vocational counselor and the other is a physical therapist,' but I don't remember if those were the words. I felt embarrassed coming in late. I sat down in the only chair available next to one of the women from the central office. They had on skirts and carried their pocketbooks, much more dressed up than the teachers I've seen. They sat there and observed. . . .

I looked around the room noting the dress of some of the students. Maxine had on a black t-shirt that had some iron-on lettering on it. It was a very well-done iron-on and the shirt looked expensive. She had on Levi jeans and Nike jogging sneakers. Mark is about 5'9" or 5'10". He had on a long sleeve jersey with an alligator on the front, very stylish but his pants were wrinkled and he had on old muddy black basketball sneakers with both laces broken, one in two places. Pam had on a lilac-colored velour sweater over a button-down striped shirt. Her hair looked very well-kept and looked like she had had it styled at an expensive hair place. Jeff sat next to her in his wheelchair. He had one foot up without a shoe on it as if it were sprained." (Bogdan and Biklen, 1982, pp. 76–77)

Qualitative Interviewing   In Chapter 6, structured, semistructured, and unstructured interview questions were summarized. Quantitative researchers will use all three types to gather data, but most interviews in a qualitative study are unstructured. The interviews can be unscheduled, consisting of informal conversations with participants, or can be scheduled with a specific purpose. Interviews are used to gather information that cannot be obtained from field observations, and to verify observations. Their purpose is to explain the participants' point of view, how they think and how they interpret and explain their behavior within a given setting.

Interviews can be held with individuals or groups. One type of formal, individual interview, the **key-informant interview**, is the most "ethnographic." It is based on the assumption that in-depth interviews with a few "key" participants, individuals who are particularly knowledgeable and articulate, will provide insights and understandings about the problem. However, the qualities that make key informants valuable also make them unrepresentative of the group. Thus, key informants should be carefully described, and the question of representativeness should be addressed by the researcher. Key informants should be selected after the researcher has become familiar with the setting to increase the probability that they will provide needed information truthfully. Informant bias may occur because of a person's position or values. Selecting key informants to represent the diversity of perspectives present in the setting lessens the potential for bias. As with all interviews, the skill of the interviewer is a critical ingredient to gathering valid data. As a general rule, skill is directly related to training and experience: The more training and experience, the greater the skill.

Key-informant interview: Interview of a few particularly knowledgeable participants.

In a second type of individual interview, the **life-history interview,** the researcher is interested in learning about the subject's life. The data from life histories are helpful in obtaining a historical perspective or a broad perspective on how an individual has developed. Life histories in educational research provide insights into career development. For example, life-history interviews of principals can examine factors that led them into administration and job satisfaction.

A group interview that has become popular in educational research is the **focus group interview.** A focus group is a one- to two-hour interview of 10 to 12 persons that is designed to promote interaction among the individuals and lead to a richer understanding of whatever is being studied. Focus groups have been used to evaluate products in marketing research for many years. A moderator guides the discussion, based on a topic guide that has been prepared in advance. The focus group technique is most useful for encouraging subjects, through their interaction with one another, to offer insights and ideas about a concept, idea, value, or other aspect of their lives about which they are knowledgeable.

Life-history interview: Information about what has occurred over an extended period of time.

Focus group interview: Group interview about a particular topic or problem.

Analyzing Qualitative Data

Observation and interview techniques result in a great amount of data that must be analyzed. Pages of field notes or interview transcripts must be critically examined, interpreted, and synthesized. The analysis is done during data collection as well as after all the data have been gathered. In many qualitative studies data collection and analysis are interwoven, influencing one another. The goal of the analysis is to discover patterns, ideas, explanations, and "understandings." Analysis requires the researcher to organize the data, separating it into workable units and looking for categories and concepts, topics, and themes. With often hundreds of pages of data, a qualitative analysis is quite a task.

The basic logic of qualitative analysis is inductive. Specific data elements have to be organized and then synthesized to derive the patterns and ideas that will form the basis of conclusions. There are many different approaches to this inductive analysis. It is important to understand the method of analysis used in a study because the quality of the research depends on a thorough and systematic analysis. The most common approach is to read through the data; look for words, phrases, or events that seem to stand out; and then create codes for these topics and patterns. The codes are then used as categories to organize the data.

"Families" of codes can be applied to most qualitative studies. The families include codes related to setting and context, subjects' definition of a setting, perspectives of subjects about other people and aspects of a setting, process changes over time, activities, events, techniques subjects use to accomplish things, and relationships and social structures. Once the data have been coded the researcher looks for relationships among the categories and patterns that may suggest generalizations. Note in the following example how the researcher explicitly indicates the process she used for coding and organizing the data.

EXAMPLE: CODING DATA

"I had previously made three copies of all field notes and interview transcripts to allow me to circle and code instances representing each category. At this point, I cut apart one copy of all field notes and interview transcripts, placing common incidents together on colored sheets of paper—a separate color for each category. This process helped me display the data in order to count the number of incidents under each category to see if saturation had occurred. I also continued to read the intact copies of the data to keep a wholistic picture in mind." (Dillon, 1989, p. 235)

Credibility of Qualitative Research

An important aspect of reading qualitative studies is to judge the overall credibility and usefulness of the results. In quantitative research the criteria for credibility are based primarily on the validity and reliability of instruments and internal validity. In qualitative research somewhat different criteria are necessary because its approach, design, and data are different and because it has a different history and tradition.

The primary criterion for evaluating qualitative studies is the credibility of the study. **Credibility** is defined as the extent to which the data, data analysis, and conclusions are believable and trustworthy. Are the themes and the patterns that emerge from the data plausible? Are they accurate, consistent, and meaningful? How much confidence do we have in the results and conclusions? Qualitative researchers judge the credibility of a study from a holistic perspective. Although it is difficult to identify single factors or design "flaws" in the overall judgment, the following principles relate to the credibility of any qualitative study.

Credibility: Believability and trustworthiness.

Triangulation   One of the most common analytical techniques to enhance the credibility of a qualitative study is **triangulation,** the use of different methods of gathering data—or collecting data with different samples, at different times, or in different places—to compare different approaches to the same thing. For example, a researcher might observe what appears to be a pattern and then see if the same pattern is repeated in interviews and in written documents or if the pattern was the same at different times. If the results of several methods of collecting data agree, the finding is judged to be credible.

Triangulation: Compares the findings of different techniques.

Reliability   The definition of *reliability* in qualitative research is somewhat different from the quantitative definition. Rather than looking for consistency of behavior, qualitative researchers are interested in the accuracy of their observations. Hence **reliability** is the extent to which what is recorded as data is what actually occurred in the setting that was studied. In other words, reliability is the fit between what occurs and what is recorded. Reliability is enhanced by detailed field notes, teams of researchers to ensure better comprehensiveness and accuracy, and the review of field notes for accuracy by participants.

Reliability: Extent to which what has been recorded is what actually occurred.

Internal Validity   Internal validity has already been introduced as a concept related to causal factors in an experiment. In qualitative research internal validity refers to a more general concept, the match between the researchers' categories and interpretations and what is actually true. That is, do the meanings, categories, and interpretations of the researcher reflect reality? Is a pattern actual or have limitations in the data gathering or situation distorted the findings?

Some of the same threats to internal validity in experiments can be applied to qualitative research: limitations related to maturation, history, selection, subject attrition, experimenter effects, and subject effects. Internal validity is strengthened if enough time is expended to obtain a valid judgment of what is being observed. A long and intense period of study allows triangulation and in-depth analyses of the data during data collection. Internal validity is also enhanced by abundant use of detail. For example, details of conversations and observations can illustrate patterns and interpretations. Finally, internal validity is strengthened by the search for negative or disconfirming evidence. The lack of findings that refute or disconfirm a pattern enhances internal validity.

Several of these principles are illustrated in the following example. Notice how triangulation and experimenter bias are addressed.

EXAMPLE: INTERNAL VALIDITY

"Because field notes cannot include everything that occurs in the class-room, there exists a potential bias in the selection of events to record. An attempt was made to overcome this and other possible sources of bias through several triangulation techniques. First, to counteract possible biases in data collection, multiple observers were employed. . . . Observations and interviews were conducted by the first author and three graduate assistants. Second, multiple data sources were used to compare the consistency of emerging trends. . . . As often as possible, a trend that was identified in one data source was corroborated by at least one other data source. Third, two analysts independently reviewed the data set and compared their findings. Finally, the data were thoroughly searched for disconfirming evidence . . ." (Miller, Leinhardt, and Zigmond, 1988, p. 471)

External Validity   External validity in qualitative studies is similar to that in quantitative studies, referring to the generalizability of the findings. Generalizability is often weak in qualitative studies because the purpose of the research is to increase an understanding of a phenomenon, not to represent a larger population, and the methods used in any single qualitative study are unique to that study. There is little or no emphasis on replications, a hallmark of quantitative research. Qualitative researchers will use terms such as *translatability* and *comparability* as concepts related to external validity. The emphasis is on how well the data, categories, analyses, and patterns are described and how well other researchers can understand the findings so that they can be used in other settings.

CONSUMER TIPS
Criteria for Evaluating Qualitative Research

1. **The researcher's background, interests, and possible bias should be clear.** Since a qualitative study is influenced greatly by the perspective of the researcher, it is necessary to know the researcher's background—previous experiences, motivations for the research, and characteristics that may affect the recording or interpretation of data. A common mistake of qualitative researchers is to allow expectations and preconceived ideas to affect what they observe, interpret, and conclude.

2. **The conceptual and theoretical frameworks for the study should be clear.** The frameworks selected by the researcher guide

the study and affect the results. You should look for an explanation of such frameworks early in the study, along with other thoughts and perceptions of the researcher.

3. The method of selecting participants should be clear. Qualitative studies research a few persons in depth rather than many subjects more superficially. Consequently, the choice of subjects is critical to the results of the study. The researcher should indicate how and why the participants were selected and the extent to which they are representative of others in the setting. It is best if the participants represent the diversity of persons in the setting.

4. The degree of researcher involvement in the setting should be indicated. You need to know how involved the researcher was in the setting that was studied. Although the researcher hopes to be as unobtrusive as possible, it is unrealistic to expect that he or she will not affect the setting and behaviors of the participants to some degree. Any distortion in the data can be more easily recognized if the researcher has had prolonged engagement with the participants. If the researcher is not very involved in the setting, it is more difficult to understand how his or her presence or other research procedures may have affected the participants.

5. Field notes should contain detailed objective descriptions of just about everything. This goal may seem impossible, but it is one to which qualitative researchers strive. They should give detailed descriptions of behaviors and indicate the place, time, date, and physical setting of the observations. The descriptions should avoid using interpretive words as *effective, positive attitude,* and *hostile.* Field notes that are not detailed suggest that the researcher may have missed important behaviors or may have biases that anticipated the results.

6. Researchers should be trained to conduct data collection. Since the researchers are directly involved in collecting data, either as observers, interviewers, or reviewers of documents, they should be trained in the procedures they use. Although adequate training is not easy to determine, you should look for some indication of previous experience that has been checked for adequacy. Untrained researchers are tempted to conduct qualitative research because it sounds so promising and interesting (and does not involve statistics). What happens is that there is usually a cursory level of involvement, without evidence for reliability.

7. The credibility of the research should be addressed. Researchers should summarize their procedures to enhance the credibility of the findings. They should analyze reliability, internal validity, and external validity and indicate limitations.

8. Descriptions should be separate from interpretations. In the core of the report you will find specific and general descriptions of what was observed or recorded and interpretations of the data. The descriptions are the basis for the researcher's analyses and interpretations. If these descriptions are not clearly separate from the analyses and interpretations, it is difficult for you to judge the reasonableness of the researcher's claims (e.g., if there was selective presentation of data or if inductive processes seem reasonable on the basis of the data presented). It is also difficult to know if the researcher was objective in recording or observing behavior.

9. **The researcher should use multiple methods of data collection.** The quality of qualitative research is greatly enhanced by multiple methods of collecting data. If only one method is used, the findings may be significantly influenced by the limitations of the technique. Multiple methods allow for triangulation, which is the strongest type of evidence for the credibility of the findings. If the study is limited to one method, its limitations should be addressed.

10. **The study must be long enough.** Accurate and credible qualitative research requires the researcher to become intimately involved with what is being studied, to know it completely. It usually takes a long time to achieve this intense level of involvement. It cannot be done in interviews of 20 minutes or observations that last a few hours. You need to know how much time the researcher spent with the participants. Sufficient time will be reflected in the detailed data and in the researcher's depth of understanding.

OUTLINE SUMMARY

1. Historical research.
   A. Investigates past events, persons, or institutions.
   B. Problems need to be chosen to allow in-depth analysis of available data.
   C. Documents—the most common source of data.
      (1) Include anything written.
      (2) Include test scores and other quantitative data.
      (3) Relics provide information through physical properties.
   D. Data analysis concerns the evaluation of sources.
      (1) External criticism determines authenticity.
      (2) Internal criticism determines accuracy.
   E. Findings are synthesized to form conclusions.
   F. Evaluating historical research.
      (1) Specific definitions of terms.
      (2) Correlation, not causation.
      (3) Facts need to be kept separate from inferences.
      (4) Most sources should be primary.

  (5) External and internal criticism.
  (6) Findings should not be overgeneralized.
2. Qualitative research.
  A. Ethnography.
    (1) Practiced by anthropologists.
    (2) Describes cultures.
  B. Characteristics.
    (1) Natural settings.
    (2) Researchers directly gather data.
    (3) Rich descriptions.
    (4) Concerned with process.
    (5) Data analyzed inductively.
    (6) Participant perspectives.
  C. Research problems.
    (1) Foreshadowed problems provide a general framework.
    (2) Specific questions follow foreshadowed problems.
    (3) Changes occur as data are collected.
  D. Purposeful sampling is used to select participants.
  E. Data collection.
    (1) Participant observations.
    (2) Limited-involvement observations.
    (3) Field notes provide detailed descriptions.
    (4) Key-informant interviews.
    (5) Life-history interviews.
    (6) Focus group interviews.
    (7) Descriptions should be separated from interpretations.
  F. Data analysis is inductive to discover patterns and understandings.
  G. Credibility.
    (1) Depends on the believability and trustworthiness of the data, data analysis, and conclusions.
    (2) Triangulation.
    (3) Reliability.
    (4) Internal validity.
    (5) External validity.
  H. Evaluating qualitative research.
    (1) Researcher perspectives.
    (2) Conceptual and theoretical frameworks.
    (3) The choice of participants.
    (4) Researcher involvement.
    (5) The extent of detailed descriptions.
    (6) Training of researchers.
    (7) Credibility.

(8) Descriptions separate from interpretations.
(9) Multiple methods.
(10) The length of the study.

STUDY QUESTIONS

1. Why is historical research conducted in education?
2. How can the findings of historical research be useful in solving today's educational problems?
3. How does the methodology of historical research compare to that of quantitative studies?
4. What is the difference between primary and secondary sources?
5. How are internal and external criticism used to enhance the credibility of historical research?
6. What are the major characteristics of qualitative research?
7. What is the difference between qualitative research and ethnography?
8. In what ways are qualitative research problems different from quantitative research problems?
9. How are participants usually selected for a qualitative study?
10. What types of roles may a qualitative observer assume in a study?
11. Why is it necessary to have very detailed field notes?
12. What are different ways to conduct qualitative interviews?
13. How are qualitative data analyzed?
14. What are some approaches for establishing the credibility of qualitative studies?
15. What is triangulation? How is it related to internal validity?

Chapter
11

Analyzing Discussion and Conclusions

We have come to the final section of research reports. Once the results of a study have been summarized, the researcher will present a nontechnical discussion of their meaning. This section of an article may be identified as "Conclusions," "Conclusions and Recommendations," "Findings," "Discussion," or "Discussion and Conclusions." Whatever the heading, this section is a critical part of the research.

PURPOSE AND NATURE OF THE DISCUSSION

The purpose of the discussion is to present an interpretation of the results, the conclusions, and recommendations for further study. Authors use the discussion to explain the meaning of the results and to speculate about their implications. The discussion is more than a summary of the study; it is an evaluation of the methodology and results to help readers understand what the results mean and how they can be used. It is essentially a synthesis of the study through the professional judgment of the researcher. The synthesis integrates the research problem and review of literature with the results. The professional judgment of the researcher is reflected in the nature of the synthesis and the implications suggested in the form of conclusions and recommendations.

You will find that discussion sections are the least structured parts of an article and that authors differ about their content and organization. Some authors begin the discussion with conclusions and then analyze the conclusions, whereas others will explain why they obtained the results, the limitations of the study, and then the conclusions. Some authors may even combine results with discussion and conclusions. We will consider each of the major aspects of the discussion section, even though the order in which these are found in articles will vary.

INTERPRETATION OF THE RESULTS

Once results are presented it is necessary to analyze and interpret them. This analysis is reasoned speculation to answer these kinds of questions: Why did the results turn out as they did? What may have affected the results? Are there any limitations that should be noted? To what extent were hypotheses supported? What is the meaning of the findings? How do the results relate to previous research findings? Interpretation of the results may be related to the research problem and/or hypothesis, the methodology of the study, and previous research on the problem.

Interpretation Related to the Problem and/or Hypothesis

Discussion sections often begin with a restatement of the problem or hypothesis, followed by some indication of the answer to the problem or degree of support for the hypothesis. There may be an evaluation that the findings provided a "strong" or "clear" answer or the hypothesis was "strongly" or "marginally" supported. Unexpected findings may be summarized as "surprising." In this type of interpretation the authors indicate their professional opinion about how well the data answer the questions. It is important when reading these interpretations to think about how experimenter bias may have influenced the opinions that are expressed. Your judgment about the relationship between the findings and the questions may be quite different from that of the researcher. Sometimes researchers will focus on findings that support their expectations and ignore findings that do not support their expectations.

Interpretation Related to Methodology

Throughout the book it has been stressed that the quality of research, its validity and credibility, is directly related to the extent to which plausible rival hypotheses can be ruled out as explanations of the results. The methodology of the research, the manner in which data are collected and treatments implemented, provides the basis for judging possible alternative hypotheses and explaining the results. Often, then, when researchers interpret the results, they refer to specific aspects of the methodology. Even if the researchers do not do so, you should. You may find significant weaknesses that are not addressed by the researcher in explaining the results. This finding would suggest that the researcher is unaware of the weakness or chooses to ignore its implications. In either case, your judgment of credibility is lessened.

For example, suppose a researcher uses a general measure of locus of control, Rotter's I-E (internal-external) scale, and expects to find that the locus of control as measured by Rotter's scale will be related to the reasons students give for cheating. The hypothesis may be that students who cheat believe that their performance is out of their control (external), whereas students who do not cheat believe that their performance is largely dependent on themselves (internal). If the results fail to show this relationship, a possible interpretation may be that the instrument, since it was a generalized measure, was not specific to the situation and therefore failed to show a relationship with cheating. If the researcher is unaware of the generalized nature of the measure, and also does not understand that locus of control is situation-specific, this lack of knowledge is reflected in the failure to mention these points in the discussion. If it seems that the researcher does not fully understand what is being studied, our overall judgment of the research is that it lacks credibility.

Interpretation Related to Selection of Subjects   One aspect of the methodology that may affect the results is the selection of subjects. As noted in Chapter 4, volunteer and available samples may give unique and limited results. Often there is a tendency to ignore the effects of specially selected subjects. In the following example, the authors appropriately point out limitations in the results because of sampling. It illustrates how one aspect of the methodology, subject selection, could influence the interpretation of the results.

EXAMPLE: INTERPRETATION BASED ON SUBJECT SELECTION

"The findings . . . confirmed empirically a commonly held belief in Israel about the relative quality of preschool teachers compared to elementary school teachers, but the small size of the sample and the fact that sample representativeness could not be ascertained limit the generalizability of these results." (Babad, Bernieri, and Rosenthal, 1987, p. 414)

In the next example, subject characteristics are mentioned as a possible reason for a failure to obtain expected results. Evidently some of the students who worked in cooperative teams lacked "competence".

EXAMPLE: INTERPRETATION BASED ON SUBJECT CHARACTERISTICS

". . . Student learning in groups may have been impeded by the lack of competent/confident students able to give direction to others. . . . It is likely that the most competent person in each group was at best an incompetent master, reluctant and unable to provide effective tutoring to others." (Ross, 1988, p. 587)

Differences in subjects are also examined to help explain findings, as illustrated in the following example of a study of students' locus of control.

EXAMPLE: INTERPRETATION BASED ON SUBJECT DIFFERENCES

"Advanced level students were more internally responsible for their intellectual-academic failures than general level students. Surprisingly, neither general nor advanced level students were more internally responsible for their intellectual-academic failures than the basic level students. . . . Students in a vocational school may have a culture and a set of beliefs about responsibility for academic failures slightly different than what they would have in an academic school." (Boss and Taylor, 1989, p. 320)

Interpretation Related to Measurement of Variables   A second type of interpretation is to examine how the measurement of variables may affect the results. Many of the points in Chapters 5 and 6 are relevant: (1) Instruments must show evidence of validity and reliability. (2) Procedures for administering an instrument can be important. (3) Possible effects of observers and interviewers need to be documented. (4) There is the possibility of response set and faking in noncognitive measurement. (5) Norms may not be appropriate. Sometimes results of two studies of the same thing will differ if different types of instruments are used in the studies. Discussion sections will most often refer to measurement of variables when the results do not meet expectations or when no significant differences are found.

EXAMPLE: INTERPRETATION BASED ON MEASUREMENT

"The low reliability of the instruments developed to measure these attitudes and the general nature of the questions may account for the failure to find differences in these variables." (McMillan, 1977, p. 327)

Interpretation Related to Experimental Treatments   A third category of factors in interpreting results concerns experimental treatments. The specific nature of some aspect of a treatment or the manner in which treatments are administered may influence the results. It is important, for instance, for each replication of a treatment to be the same.

EXAMPLE: INTERPRETATIONS BASED ON TREATMENT REPLICATIONS

"The results for academic achievement were not consistent with our hypothesis. This may be related, in part, to variations in implementation of the teaching practices across teachers." (Hawkins, Doueck, and Lishner, 1988, p. 45)

Interpretation is often based on differences that may be reflected in the treatments:

EXAMPLE: INTERPRETATIONS BASED ON TREATMENT DIFFERENCES

"The difference between the book and chapter results may be due to the amount of effort required for the assignments. The students indicated less effort was exerted in the chapter assignments than the book assignments; thus the effect of the effort variable was not as strong in the chapter as the book." (McMillan, 1977, p. 326)

Interpretation Based on Statistical Procedures

An important factor in a discussion is an analysis of the statistical procedures used in a study. Although a complete discussion of statistical problems is beyond the scope of this book, a few basic statistical principles need to be considered.

The first thing a reader should do is to check for any apparent errors in reporting statistical results. This is done by looking for consistency and agreement between numbers reported in tables and graphs and the statements written in narrative form in the article. Errors will inevitably appear despite proofreading because of the frequent transfer of data (from answer sheets to coding sheets to computers to manuscript to galley proofs).

A second concern is whether statistical procedures have violated important assumptions. A *t*-test or analysis of variance, for instance, assumes a population that has a normal distribution, about the same variance for each group, and interval-level measurement. In studies in which violation of the assumptions could have important implications, the researcher should indicate whether the assumptions have been met. In many educational studies there is a question about the appropriate unit of analysis. Because students influence each other in a class and treatments given to classes are not replicated for each individual student, most statisticians believe that the classroom, not the individual student, is the appropriate unit of analysis (the unit of analysis determines the level of significance of the statistical test). This point is emphasized in the discussion section of a recent article.

EXAMPLE: INTERPRETATION BASED ON UNIT OF ANALYSIS

"The data analyzed here demonstrated that a . . . group variable, such as classroom membership, can have significant effects on student performance. . . . When a . . . group effect is evident, students should not be used as observational units to test the effectiveness of a curriculum." (Brooks, 1988, p. 153)

It is also important not to make too much of the results of several statistical tests when a multivariate analysis is appropriate.

> ## EXAMPLE: INTERPRETATION BASED ON STATISTICAL PROCEDURES
>
> It should also be stressed that whenever dependent variables are themselves correlated, as were the four health belief constructs in this study, good practice requires a multivariate approach." (Brooks, 1988, p. 153)

Some researchers assume that the failure to find a statistically significant difference should be interpreted to mean that there is in reality no difference. As noted in Chapter 9, there are many reasons why researchers fail to find a significant difference or relationship, only one of which is that there really is no difference or relationship. Researchers also confuse statistical differences with practical or meaningful differences. That is, there is confusion between what is statistically significant and what is educationally significant. Meaningfulness should be judged by examining the difference between means, or the correlation coefficient, and by considering the specifics of the situation in which the results will be used. Often what are summarized as "significant differences" turn out to be very small actual differences with little practical value.

Interpretation Related to Previous Research

The purpose of a review of previous research is to place the study in the context of other investigations. Once the study is completed, the results should be discussed in light of the reviewed literature to help explain the reasons for the results and the meaningfulness of the study. Although the style of relating results to previous studies will vary, there is usually an indication of whether the current findings are consistent or inconsistent with previous research. When the results are inconsistent or contradictory, the authors should provide explanations, usually in terms of the research design. For example, suppose it is found, contrary to previous research, that principals with autocratic leadership styles communicate more effectively with teachers than do principals who use participatory leadership. An explanation might be found in different samples, different instruments of leadership style, or administration of instruments at different times of the year.

Interpretation as related to previous studies and other literature is the most common feature of discussion sections. Such an interpretation is very important because it places the results more directly and explicitly in the context of other research, thereby enhancing the contribution of the new research to a recognized body of knowledge. It also demonstrates that the authors have a good understanding of the literature, which increases their credibility.

The following are examples of how results are interpreted through referral to other studies or literature.

EXAMPLES: INTERPRETATION BASED ON PREVIOUS RESEARCH

"These modest but significant relationships between use of feedback practices and the importance assigned to external success attributions seem to clarify and extend previous findings, specifically that teachers' expectations about successful students may predispose them to give these students more interactive feedback than students perceived as being unsuccessful . . ." (Hall, Villeme, and Burley, 1989, p. 142)

"It should be no surprise, therefore, that previous studies have found teachers reporting interactive decisions only when the lesson seems to be going poorly. These findings do not necessarily mean that teachers are making decisions only when their mental scripts are violated. It is more likely that their decisionmaking is so automatic that they tend to report it only when the process is brought to awareness, either when a particular image is not being delivered or when a situation has no decision rule or routine developed." (Parker and Gehrke, 1986, p. 238)

"Instructional research in classrooms suggests that basic skills of reading and math are acquired most easily when most practice is at a high level of success and new material is introduced in small steps at a gradual rate, with enough time and practice to solidify new skills and concepts. . . . Yet in these six classrooms, the students who needed the most instruction in reading were the ones whose seatwork often had the opposite characteristics: the seatwork was difficult because the gaps between the students' knowledge and the knowledge required for the task were too great for them to bridge independently." (Anderson, Brubaker, Alleman-Brooks, and Duffy, 1985, p. 133)

CONCLUSIONS

One of the final parts of a research article is a statement of the conclusions. Conclusions are summary statements of the results as they pertain to the research problem, often stated as answers to the questions, hypotheses, or purposes of the research. Sometimes conclusions simply repeat a technical, statistical presentation of results in short, summary sentences in nontechnical language. In other studies the conclusions will be based on the interpretation of the results, reflecting the professional judgment of the investigators. Usually the major or most significant findings are summarized as conclusions.

Conclusions may be stated at the beginning or at the end of the discussion section and may precede or follow interpretations of the results. A common approach is to begin the discussion with the purpose or research problem, state the major findings, and then interpret the findings. If there are several major findings, one may be presented and discussed, followed by another that is summarized and discussed. The term *conclusion* may or may not be used. By beginning the discussion with conclusions, the author provides a succinct overview of the most important findings, which helps to orient the reader to the discussion that follows. Following are examples of conclusion statements that appear at the beginning of discussion sections.

EXAMPLES: CONCLUSION STATEMENTS

"The goal of the present project was to devise, implement, and assess the effectiveness of a comprehensive school-based program designed to enhance children's prosocial orientations. In this paper we have demonstrated . . . that the program was implemented by classroom teachers and that it had substantial positive effects on children's interpersonal behavior in the classroom (without impeding their achievement)." (Solomon, Watson, Delucchi, Schaps, and Battistich, 1988, p. 545)

"The results of this study offer strong support to the hypothesis that teachers' expectations of a child's ability will be higher after viewing that child during dynamic assessment than they will after viewing that child during static assessment." (Delclos, Burns, and Kulewicz, 1987, p. 332)

Researchers should indicate why the conclusions are supported, as illustrated in an article on effective school leadership.

EXAMPLE: SUPPORTING CONCLUSIONS

"The study data point to the conclusion that dramatic changes in the sociocultural context of schools can be expected as a result of changes in leadership. This conclusion is supported by two dimensions of the research data. First, as teachers described responses to various principals . . . they explained that their attitudes and behaviors tended to change significantly in response to changes in leadership. Second, examination of data . . . indicated important changes in culture. When teachers' perspectives were compared for each of the four principals at the school since 1974, significant shifts in the teachers' perspective, and thus school culture, were apparent." (Blase, 1986, p. 607)

Limitations

An important aspect of the discussion is to indicate any limitations to the conclusions, that is, factors or variables that need to be considered in their use. Authors will often point out that the results or conclusions are "limited" to subjects with certain characteristics, to features of the design, or to particular settings. This is essentially a way for the researcher to address the external validity, or generalizability, of the findings. Beyond the particulars of a research setting, you need to consider whether it is reasonable to expect the results to represent a general pattern that would occur again and again. This consideration can be directly addressed from the researcher's perspective in the article, but it is also necessary for you to judge the extent to which the conclusions are useful in your situation. For this reason it is helpful for you to think about several factors that limit the results.

Limitations Related to Subject Characteristics　　The subjects in a study have certain characteristics, such as age, race, ability, and socioeconomic status. Strictly speaking, results and conclusions are limited to other individuals who have the same, or at least very similar, characteristics. In research jargon, this factor is referred to as **population validity**.

Population validity: Generalizability to other individuals.

　　There are two ways in which limitations related to subject characteristics affect the use of the results. The first concerns generalizing from a sample, or the subjects used in a study, to a larger population or to other individuals. For example, if a study of fourth-grade students shows that cooperative learning strategies are better than individualized approaches, the results are limited to other fourth-graders with similar characteristics. Similarly, research conducted with high school students is limited to other high school students, research done with males should not be generalized to females, what may be true for one type of student may not be true for other types of students, and so forth.

One key to understanding the extent to which results should be limited to subject characteristics is to know the characteristics. That may seem rather obvious, but you will find in some studies that the subjects are not adequately described to be able to judge generalizability. Another important aspect of the study is whether there was probability sampling. If there was representative sampling, then the limitations apply to the population rather than to the sample. If available samples were used, you need to examine the procedures to see if limitations are suggested, for example, as with paid or volunteer samples. Results may be internally valid but limited to subjects who volunteer.

A second limitation is to be careful not to generalize what is true for a group of subjects to individuals or subgroups. For example, if you determine that teachers' expectations of students seem to be affected by reviewing test scores from the previous year, the overall finding is true for the group as a whole and may not be true for any individual teacher or for certain groups of teachers. In other words, expectations may be influenced in some types of teachers but not in other types of teachers, even though when all types of teachers are analyzed together there are significant results. It is similar to saying that although in the entire group of twelfth-grade students there is a positive relationship between attendance and achievement, the relationship may be less positive or more positive for particular groups of twelfth-graders.

The following example shows how results are limited because of how subjects were selected.

EXAMPLE: LIMITATION BASED ON SUBJECT SELECTION

"The major finding in this study . . . must be treated as suggestive at best . . . the small size of the sample and the fact that sample representativeness could not be ascertained limit the generalizability of these results." (Babad, Bernieri, and Rosenthal, 1987, p. 414)

Limitations Related to Situational Characteristics   Situational characteristics are specifics of the setting and context in which the study is conducted. They include the place of the study—whether in a classroom, laboratory, playground, home, and so on—and what is present in this setting—for example, the type of equipment in a playground or the objects in a classroom. If research on prosocial behavior is studied in a day-care center, for example, the results may not be generalizable to unstructured play in a neighborhood. What may occur in one school may not occur in another because of differences in their structure and specific features. Limitations because of settings are part of the conditions of conducting the research. (Other conditions are considered below.) Together they may be referred to as factors affecting the **ecological validity** of the research. Ecological validity is strong when the results can be generalized to many different settings. This is obviously a limitation in studies that occur in a single classroom or school. As with subject characteristics, your judgment of generalizability will depend on how well the setting is described. If your situation is in most respects similar, the findings may be useful. On the other hand, if your situation is quite different, for example, an inner-city school compared to a suburban school, the results may not be useful.

Ecological validity: Generalizability to other settings, times, treatments, and measures.

Limitations Related to When the Research Is Conducted   There are several ways in which time is related to limitations. The first is that treatments may be effective at one time but not at another. What may work in the morning may not work in the afternoon, and what may be effective in the fall may be ineffective in the winter. Responses of subjects to treatments and measures also vary according to time. Students' responses may be much more accurate in the morning than in late afternoon. Measures of self-concept will be affected by when the students respond, as will attitudinal measures. From a broader perspective, the sociohistorical context in which the research is carried out may limit the findings. That is, how students respond will be affected by the cultural values at the time the research is conducted.

Limitations Related to Treatments   In experimental research generalizability is limited by the nature of the treatment. It is necessary to know how a treatment is defined and carried out to know whether it will be useful to you in your situation. For example, there has been a great amount of research recently on what is termed "direct instruction," but its definition may vary from study to study. The same would be true for such practices as cooperative learning, homogeneous and heterogeneous grouping, individualization, praise, and reinforcement. You need to look at what is sometimes the fine print in the methodology section to know precisely how a treatment is defined and implemented. Results and conclusions are, of course, limited to this operational definition and the procedures for implementing the treatment.

One aspect of many treatments that limit generalizability is the individuals' knowledge that they are subjects in a study. In this case the treatment is confounded with the subjects' awareness of being studied. Because some people then act differently, the results are generalizable only to other people who know they are in a study. In other words, the treatment may work only when it is implemented as part of a "study." This is termed the **Hawthorne effect.** Also, if a new treatment disrupts a normal routine, the novelty or disruption is confounded with the treatment and limits the generalizability to other new or novel situations.

Hawthorne effect: From realization of individuals that they are subjects in a study.

Limitations Related to Measures   As in treatments, there are usually different ways to measure the same thing. Research is limited by the manner in which the variables, either independent or dependent, are measured. For example, an independent variable may be "on-task behavior" and the dependent variable "attitudes toward learning." Both of these variables can be measured in several different ways. That is, there are different approaches for measuring "on-task behavior" and "attitudes toward learning." Results of research are generalized to other situations in which the variables are measured, or at least conceptualized, in the same manner. Thus it is necessary to understand in some detail how the variables are defined and measured.

Reasonable Limitations   There is a tendency to be too strict in analyzing the limitations of research. If we are overly strict, the results of studies would be useful only in a few situations and to other individuals that are just like those in the study. It is better to use our best, reasonable, professional judgment. The situation may be somewhat different, as may be the measures or subjects, but the differences may not be great enough to affect the usefulness of the findings. For example, suppose you read a study that examines the effect of advance organizers on a lesson (advance organizers are broad conceptual frameworks to structure and organize the material). The study is conducted with a biology unit, using seventh-graders as subjects, and finds that students who use advance organizers show better learning and retention. Your class is sixth grade and you need to teach a social studies unit. Should you simply dismiss the implications of the study because your situation is not exactly the same? In a case like this the limitations of the study may suggest some caution in using advance organizers in your class, but overall there is sufficient overlap to conclude that what worked in the study would probably work for your social studies unit as well.

Recommendations and Implications

Toward the end of the discussion section you will usually find statements that suggest future research or practice as a result of the study. These statements are called recommendations and implications. In journals primarily intended for other researchers, the recommendations tend to be oriented toward changes in specific methods in the study, such as instruments, sampling, or procedures. Recommendations and implications in journals that practitioners are likely to read tend to be related to practice. It is important for researchers to be specific in their recommendations and implications. It is inadequate for researchers to say, simply, "Further research is needed in this area." What is needed is an indication of what types of research are necessary. The following example illustrates recommendations that are too general to be of much use.

EXAMPLE: INADEQUATE DETAIL IN RECOMMENDATIONS

"The sex differences found in this study are interesting; however, it is recommended that additional research be completed to explore these relationships." (Boss and Taylor, 1989, p. 321)

Following are examples of recommendations and implications that have adequate specificity.

EXAMPLE: RECOMMENDATIONS FOR FURTHER RESEARCH

"Finally, further research is needed: descriptive-correlational studies of teachers' management systems in different grade levels and content areas and with various types of students would enrich our current understanding of management practices and how they are influenced by context. In addition, experimental research would greatly aid in identifying the degree to which the various management characteristics are malleable and the effects on student behavior of variations in management behaviors. (Evertson and Emmer, 1982, p. 497)

EXAMPLES: IMPLICATIONS FOR PRACTICE

"This study of attributions may have important implications for preservice and inservice teacher education. It has been found that training in and different uses of teacher and student attribution statements have resulted in changes and differences in the attributions used by students ... what is being found ... may be important in understanding how students interpret and use feedback about their academic performance. ... For these reasons, attribution training may deserve a place in the future training and development of teachers." (Hall, Villeme, and Burley, 1989, p. 142)

"In closing, this article has a strong message for those who would reform our schools ... the findings in this article suggest that improving the design of teachers' jobs and the managerial structures of schools are also critical in enhancing teacher motivation and retention" (Conley, Bacharach, and Bauer, 1989, p. 76)

CONSUMER TIPS
Criteria for Evaluating Discussion Sections

1. **The results should be adequately interpreted.** It is important to do more than repeat the major findings of the study. The discussion should include interpretations of the research problem, methodology, and previous research. The interpretation should include a detailed analysis of how imperfections in the design and extraneous variables may have affected the results and how the results are integrated with other literature on the topic. All major findings should be addressed in the discussion, including those that are unexpected, surprising, and conflicting. There should not be an analysis of every specific result, but important findings should not be ignored or overlooked.

2. **Conclusions should answer research problems.** Each problem or research question should be clearly answered by the conclusions. The answers should accurately reflect the results and interpretations of the data. Conclusions that are not supported by the data should be avoided.

3. **Conclusions should be limited by subject characteristics and selection.** The discussion should include an analysis of how the characteristics of the subjects, such as age, gender, and socioeconomic status, limit the generalizability of the conclusions. Researchers should not overgeneralize either in terms of subject char-

acteristics or by suggesting that what may be true for the group of subjects as a whole is true for individuals or subgroups.

4. Conclusions should be limited by the nature of treatments and measures. Researchers should indicate how specific aspects of treatments and measures should be considered in interpreting conclusions. They should point out, when appropriate, how different operational definitions of treatments and measures might lead to different conclusions.

5. Statistical significance should not be confused with practical significance. Researchers should not interpret statistically significant results to mean that they have practical value or importance. Statistical significance does not necessarily mean that the results will have important practical implications.

6. Failure to show statistical significance does not necessarily mean that there is no relationship or difference. Researchers need to be careful in interpreting results that fail to show statistical significance. Most studies do not provide an adequate test of whether the statistical insignificance reflects no relationship nor whether weaknesses in the design account for the findings. Researchers should consider both possibilities in their interpretations and conclusions.

7. Limitations of findings should be reasonable. Researchers should find a middle ground between being overly strict or too confining and completely ignoring obviously important limitations. There are shortcomings to all research, but there is no need to dwell on every possible specific limitation. Important limitations should be mentioned even though the results support an hypothesis.

8. Recommendations and implications should be specific. Recommendations and implications for future research should be included in the discussion and should specifically describe the changes in methodology that would be desirable in subsequent studies. Recommendations and implications for practice should be made only when the data and design support such inferences.

OUTLINE SUMMARY

1. Discussion includes interpretations, conclusions, and recommendations.
2. Interpretation.
   A. Analysis of the results.
   B. Related to the research problem.
   C. Related to the methodology.
      (1) Selection and characteristics of subjects.

(2) Measurement of variables.

(3) The nature of treatments and procedures.

D. Related to statistical procedures.

(1) Violated assumptions.

(2) Interpretation of no statistically significant relationship.

E. Related to previous research.

(1) Explanations needed for findings that are inconsistent with previous research.

(2) Provides connection with other literature.

3. Conclusions.

A. Provide a summary of important findings.

B. Must be supported by data.

C. Limitations related to generalizability.

(1) Subject characteristics and selection.

(2) Timing of the research.

(3) Nature of treatment.

(4) Hawthorne effect.

(5) Nature of the measures.

D. Recommendations and implications.

(1) Indicate future studies.

(2) Point out practical applications.

(3) Specific, not general.

STUDY QUESTIONS

1. What is the purpose of a discussion section in an article?

2. What are the major components of a discussion section?

3. Why is it important to relate findings to previous research?

4. What aspects of the methodology of a study may have implications in interpreting the results?

5. Give an example of a specific feature of the design of a study that would be important in interpretation.

6. What is the purpose of the conclusions?

7. What is the difference between limitations based on generalizing to other people and generalizing to individual subjects?

8. In what ways should conclusions be limited to the timing of the research and to the nature of treatments and measures?

9. What is wrong with recommending that "further studies need to be done"?

10. Is it a mistake to conclude that no statistical significance means that there is no relationship? Why?

Chapter
12

The Intelligent Consumer: Putting It All Together

My aim in this book is to present and explain fundamental principles of educational research that you will be able to use in evaluating research. As a consumer of educational research, you need to be able to locate, read, critically analyze, and then use, when appropriate, the results of research to enhance teaching and learning. Throughout the book there has been an emphasis on how knowledge derived from research can enhance your role as a professional who will constantly make decisions and judgments about how to do things and what to think.

Research on educational problems can provide information that will improve your judgments, but there is a great amount of variability in the quality of published research. In fact there is evidence that a substantial percentage of published studies has serious flaws. It is essential that you have the knowledge and skills to evaluate critically the research you read. A consumer of educational research may use the information provided in studies, but you must be an *intelligent* consumer. Intelligent consumers can make their own judgments about the credibility and usefulness of research. By being able to understand the intent of the researcher, the type of design used, the deficiencies in sampling and measuring, the results, and the conclusions, the intelligent consumer can judge the quality and usefulness of the study.

Throughout the book key points for analyzing and evaluating different aspects of research reports have been summarized as Consumer Tips. In this chapter these tips are rephrased as questions that you will want to ask yourself when reading a study. The intent is to put in one place the most important questions that should guide your evaluation. If you remember that every study will contain some deficiencies, the answers to these questions, when considered as a whole, will provide an overall impression of the credibility and usefulness of the findings. You may also find what could be called "fatal flaws." These deficiencies are so serious that the results are useless.

Following the outlines of questions are three complete research studies. Each article is critically analyzed by answering the appropriate questions in these outlines.

QUESTIONS FOR QUANTITATIVE STUDIES

1.0 Research Problem
    1.1 What are the independent and dependent variables?
    1.2 Is the problem researchable?
    1.3 Is the problem significant? Will the results have practical or theoretical importance?
    1.4 Is the problem stated clearly and succinctly?
    1.5 Does the problem communicate whether the study is descriptive, experimental, or nonexperimental?
    1.6 Does the problem indicate the population studied?
    1.7 Does the problem indicate the variables in the study?

2.0 Review of Literature
    2.1 Does the review of literature seem comprehensive? Are all important previous studies included?
    2.2 Are primary sources emphasized?
    2.3 Is the review up to date?
    2.4 Have studies been critically reviewed, and flaws noted, and have the results been summarized?
    2.5 Does the review emphasize studies directly related to the problem?
    2.6 Does the review explicitly relate previous studies to the problem?
    2.7 If appropriate, does the review establish a basis for research hypotheses?
    2.8 Does the review establish a theoretical framework for the significance of the study?
    2.9 Is the review well organized?

3.0 Research Hypothesis
    3.1 Is the hypothesis stated in declarative form?

3.2 Does the hypothesis follow from the literature?

3.3 Does the hypothesis state expected relationships or differences?

3.4 Is the hypothesis testable?

3.5 Is the hypothesis clear and concise?

4.0 Selection of Subjects

4.1 Are the subjects clearly described?

4.2 Is the population clearly defined?

4.3 Is the method of sampling clearly described?

4.4 Is there probability sampling? If so, is it proportionate or disproportionate?

4.5 What is the return rate in a survey study?

4.6 Are volunteers used?

4.7 Is there an adequate number of subjects?

5.0 Instrumentation

5.1 Is evidence for validity and reliability clearly stated and adequate? Is the instrument appropriate for the subjects?

5.2 Are the instruments clearly described? If an instrument is designed for a study by the researchers, is there a description of its development?

5.3 Are the procedures for gathering data clearly described?

5.4 Are norms appropriate if norm-referenced tests are used?

5.5 Are standard-setting procedures appropriate if criterion-referenced tests are used?

5.6 Do the scores distort the reality of the findings?

5.7 Do response set or faking influence the results?

5.8 Are observers and interviewers adequately trained?

5.9 Are there observer or interviewer effects?

6.0 Design

6.1 Nonexperimental

6.11 If descriptive, are relationships inferred?

6.12 Do graphic presentations distort the findings?

6.13 Are causative conclusions reached from correlational findings?

6.14 Is the correlation affected by restriction in the range and reliability of the instruments?

6.15 If predictions are made, are they based on a different sample?

6.16 Is the size of the correlation large enough?

6.17 If causal-comparative, has the causal condition already occurred? How comparable are the subjects in the groups being compared?

6.2 Experimental

    6.21 Is there direct manipulation of an independent variable?

    6.22 Is the design clearly described?

    6.23 What extraneous variables are not controlled in the design?

    6.24 Are the treatments very different from one another?

    6.25 Is each replication of the treatment independent of other replications? Is the number of subjects equal to the number of treatment replications?

6.3 Single Subject

    6.31 Is the measurement of the target behavior reliable?

    6.32 Is the target behavior clearly defined?

    6.33 Are there enough measures of the behavior to establish stability?

    6.34 Are procedures, subjects, and settings described in detail?

    6.35 Is there a single treatment?

    6.36 Are there experimenter or observer effects?

7.0 Results

    7.1 Is there an appropriately descriptive statistical summary?

    7.2 Is statistical significance confused with practical significance?

    7.3 Is statistical significance confused with internal or external validity?

    7.4 Are appropriate statistical tests used?

    7.5 Are levels of significance interpreted correctly?

    7.6 How clearly are the results presented?

    7.7 Is there a sufficient number of subjects to give valid statistical results?

    7.8 Are data clearly and accurately presented in graphs and tables?

8.0 Discussion and Conclusions

    8.1 Is interpretation of the results separate from reporting of the results?

    8.2 Are the results discussed in relation to previous research, methodology, and research problem?

    8.3 Do the conclusions address the research problems?

    8.4 Do the conclusions follow from the interpretation of the results?

8.5 Are the conclusions appropriately limited by the nature of the subjects, treatments, and measures?

8.6 Is lack of statistical significance properly interpreted?

8.7 Are the limitations of the findings reasonable?

8.8 Are the recommendations and implications specific?

8.9 Are the conclusions consistent with what is known from previous research?

QUESTIONS FOR HISTORICAL STUDIES

1.0 Research Problem
    1.1 Is the problem clear and specific?
    1.2 Are sufficient data available to answer the questions?
    1.3 Are definitions of terms specific and consistent?
2.0 Methodology
    2.1 Are the sources of data primarily secondary or primary?
    2.2 Are the procedures for obtaining data clear?
3.0 Discussion and Conclusions
    3.1 Are the data adequately analyzed with respect to internal and external criticism?
    3.2 Is correlation confused with causation?
    3.3 Are facts confused with inferences?
    3.4 Are the findings overgeneralized?
    3.5 Are appropriate limitations indicated?

QUESTIONS FOR QUALITATIVE STUDIES

1.0 Introduction and Problem
    1.1 Are the researcher's background, interests, and potential biases clear from the outset?
    1.2 Does the researcher have the skill and training needed to conduct the study?
    1.3 Is the problem feasible?
    1.4 Is the problem significant?
    1.5 Is there a clear conceptual and theoretical framework for the problem?
    1.6 Does the introduction include an overview of the design of the study?
    1.7 Is the purpose of the study clearly stated?
2.0 Review of Literature
    2.1 Is the review preliminary? Does it indicate that the

       researcher is knowledgeable of previous work in the area?

  2.2 Is the review up to date?

  2.3 Does the review establish an adequate background and theoretical framework for the study?

  2.4 Is the review well organized?

  2.5 Is the literature analyzed as well as summarized?

3.0 Methodology

  3.1 Is the method of selecting participants clear?

  3.2 Is the selection of participants biased?

  3.3 Will the participants selected provide a credible answer to the research question?

  3.4 How involved is the researcher in the setting? Will the researcher's involvement affect the findings?

  3.5 How detailed are the field notes?

  3.6 Are data collectors properly trained?

  3.7 Are there multiple methods of data collection?

  3.8 Is the study long enough?

4.0 Discussion and Conclusions

  4.1 Are descriptions clearly separate from interpretations and researchers' opinions?

  4.2 Is the credibility of the findings addressed in terms of reliability and internal and external validity?

  4.3 Are the results discussed in relation to previous research?

  4.4 Do the conclusions follow from the interpretation of the results? Are the conclusions consistent with what is known from previous research?

  4.5 Are appropriate limitations indicated?

  4.6 Are appropriate recommendations and implications indicated?

EXAMPLES OF RESEARCH ARTICLES

Article 1

A Study of Academic Time-on-Task In the Elementary School

by H. Lyndall Rich and Mary J. McNelis ·

Memphis State University

This study of academic time-on-task was conducted to evaluate the current use of elementary school time. An observational method was used to measure allocated time for academic learning, students' time-on-task, and selected teacher traits related to task time. The sample included 489 elementary students and 132 teachers in six elementary schools. Students, on the average, were in the classroom four hours of the six-hour school day (66.5%) and they were allocated time for academic learning slightly less than three hours per day (49.07%). During the allocated academic time, they were on-task 69.65% of the time or 32.2% of the school day. Significant ANOVA differences for sex and race but not for level were in evidence.

Over the past decade considerable research attention has been centered on student academic time-on-task as a predictor of academic gains (Good & Brophy, 1986). Most of the research results have reported only a modest relationship between time and learning outcomes (Frederick & Walberg, 1980). Even so, students' time-on-task is consistently reported to be a necessary prerequisite to effective increases in school achievement (Good & Beckerman, 1978). This emphasis on academic task time appears to be such a critical learning variable that the National Committee on Excellence in Education (1983) included "time" as one of its five primary recommendations. "We recommend that significantly more time be devoted to learning. . . . This will require more effective use of the existing school day, a longer school day, or a lengthened school year" (p. 29). This recommendation was subsequently endorsed by the National Governors' Association who consider the effective use of school time to be a national priority (Alexander, 1986).

Before implementing dramatic changes in the school time structure, such as increasing the school day and/or school year, evaluation of the use of time in the existing school day could prove to be a profitable endeavor. Specifically, there is a need to measure the time devoted to learning or the use of academic time to partially explain learning outcomes (Rosenshine, 1979). While "time," per se, may be limited in explaining differential learning outcomes (Shulman, 1986), the importance of student academic time-on-task is potentially such a significant variable that it requires more systematic study (Hawley, Rosenholtz, Goodstein & Hasselbring, 1984).

The amount of time that students are allocated and are engaged in academic learning has been the subject of numerous research studies. For example, the Beginning Teacher Evaluation Study (BTES), reported that 58% of the school day was allocated to academic learning (Denham & Lieberman, 1980). The remaining 42% of the school day included scheduled breaks, a variety of interruptions, and other non-academic activities. Of the allocated time for academic learning, students were engaged 70 to 75% of the time— or 41 to 44% of the school day. The Effective School Research data (Mariotta & Boles, 1984) are consistent with the BTES results in that students were allocated approximately 60% of the school day for academic learning time.

The variance among students for time-on-task, or engaged time, has been attributed to a number of school related variables. Some of the school variables identified include: the type of academic activity (Rosenshine, 1979); teacher and student mobility (Berliner & Tikuoff, 1976); intrusive behavior management (Brophy & Good, 1986); rate of student success (Anderson, 1984); and, from the BTES data, the degree of teacher engagement, the subject matter, the grade level involved, the racial mixture, and the SES of the students (Berliner, Fisher, Filby, & Marliave, 1978).

It is suspected that the variance among schools and teachers in the provision of allocated time and among students for time-on-task is related to academic achievement. In particular, achievement and competency-based measures of student learning outcomes in the elementary school have shown a regression in grade level performance at the intermediate grades (4–6) when compared with primary grades (1–3) (Hawley et al., 1984). Analysis of a few selected schools additionally reveals that a disproportionate percentage of black students and male students substantially contribute to this comparative regression in academic outcome scores.

This research was designed to measure school time allocated to academics and student time-on-task in elementary school. Several questions regarding time were addressed:

1. What percentage of a six-hour school day (excluding lunch) are students in the classroom (school time)?

2. What percentage of time in the classroom (including the library) are students allocated time to be on academic tasks (class time)?

3. What percentage of time, when students have allocated time for academic tasks, are students attending to the academic tasks (individual time)?

4. To what extent are there differences between races (black and white), sexes (male and female), and levels (primary and intermediate)?

5. To what extent is the frequency of selected teacher behaviors (eye contact, mobility, and verbal management) correlated with student academic time-on-task?

METHOD

This research is an observational study using random five-minute time samples focusing on individual students in naturally occurring classroom environments (Good & Beckman, 1978). Students were coded as to the percentage of time attending to academic tasks for individual time, class time, and school time. Visual clues for "attention" (Rinne, 1984) were used to determine and code student attending behaviors. Attending behaviors included, for example, facing the speaker, asking or answering related questions, maintaining eye contact with curriculum materials or other academic sources, and writing from the text, worksheet, or chalkboard.

The sample consisted of 489 elementary students enrolled in 132 different classrooms (grades 1 through 6) in six elementary schools located in three school districts. All classrooms were observed in five schools and, in the sixth school, observation was administratively restricted to 12 classrooms, two at each grade level. When available, four students, representing both races and sexes, were observed in each classroom. Within each classroom, students were selected randomly within the limitations of their visibility to the observers and degrees of freedom for sex and race. The number of subjects by race, sex, and grade level was not significantly different. The represented schools were public and constituted a range from urban to rural, inner city to middle class, and 100% black enrollment to 95% white enrollment.

The selected teacher behaviors were coded as to whether or not they were evidenced one time during each five-minute observation of individual students. Eye contact was scored if the teacher looked at the student; mobility was scored if the teacher came within touching distance of the student; and verbal management was scored if a behavioral correction, warning, and/or action was audible. The authors collected all observational data and had an inter-rater reliability of .92 for student time-on-task and .97 for teacher behaviors. The unit of analysis for all statistical procedures was the students (N = 489) since all of the time conditions and behaviors were scored while observing individual students.

RESULTS

This study addresses several questions related to school, classroom, and individual academic time. The first three questions concerned the amount of time the students were in the classroom (including the library) within the six-hour school day, the amount of time allocated to academic tasks while in the classroom, and, for individual students, the amount of allocated time that was on task.

Actual Time on Task

The data revealed that during the six-hour school day, the students were actually in the classroom 66.5% of the time, or approximately four hours (school time). While in the classroom, students were allocated approximately three of the four hours or 49.07% of the school day, to be on academic tasks (classroom time). Of the three allocated hours, students were on-task 69.95% of the time or 32.27% of the school day (individual time).

The time spent in school but out of the classroom was devoted primarily to three scheduled activities: recess, restroom and extra-curricular activities. Recess or "rest time" was evident in all primary grades; however, at the intermediate level, schools varied in their use of recess. Those elementary schools that were departmentalized, particularly the fifth and/or sixth grades, tended not to have scheduled recess. However, the intermediate grades more frequently participated in physical education, special programs, assemblies, and other curricular activities outside the classroom. These three activities, on the average, accounted for over 1½ hours of the school day. Other miscellaneous activities, such as fire drill, counselor sessions, errands, going to the school office and late bus, accounted for the remaining time outside the classroom.

While in the classroom, the students were allocated the time to be on academic task less than three hours or 69.9% of the classroom time. This allocated time constituted about one-half, or three hours, of the school day.

The one hour of classroom time not allocated to academic learning was primarily used in four basic areas: procedures, transitions, waiting, and interruptions. Procedures relating to classroom and lesson organization including activities such as distributing worksheets, collecting homework, calling the roll, collecting money, making announcements, and clarifying or making classroom rules averaged 32 minutes per school day. Of these procedures, distributing and collecting materials was the most time-consuming and often appeared to be related to spontaneity, disorganization and/or the lack of systematic procedures on the part of the teacher. Student confusion, the unavailability of materials, and collecting and sorting student papers detracted from allocated academic time.

Transitions, that is, moving from one activity to another, were the single most frequent cause for reducing allocated academic time while in the classroom. Changing from one subject to another, from one class to another, from the class to recess, lunch, or restroom, typically required time to prepare for the change, then time to get ready to learn again. Transition time per classroom averaged almost 20 minutes per day and ranged from 15 to 40 minutes per classroom.

Waiting was a more subtle category of non-allocated academic classroom time. Students were coded as not having allocated academic time when they had no task involvement and they were waiting, for example, for the next spelling word to be announced, or for a turn to complete a problem at the chalkboard, or for other students to finish a test. The average waiting time was almost five minutes but the range was variable from zero to at least 20 minutes. It was apparent that many students spent a great deal of time waiting for other students to complete an academic task before they could continue.

Unscheduled interruptions in the classroom averaged less than five minutes per day. Interruptions from outside the classroom, particularly other teachers or students entering the class and intercom announcements, were the most frequent sources of interruptions. Interruptions from within the classroom, such as obvious student behavior problems and teacher management involving most of the classroom, were infrequently observed.

Sex, Race, Grade Level

The next research question concerned the percentage of time students were engaged in academic on task behavior by race (white, black), by sex (male, female), and by level (primary, intermediate). The frequency distributions showed that, on the average, students were engaged in academic time-on-task 69.65% of the allocated time with the following percentages by race and by sex: black males, 63.57%; white males, 67.28%; black females, 72.35%; and, white females, 75.86%.

These results seem to indicate that female students (white and black) spend more time engaged in academic on-task behavior than do male students (white and black). Also, white students (male and female) spend more time-on-task than do black students (male and female). In addition, the data revealed that, for individual time, students in the primary grades were on task 68.48% of the time, whereas students in the intermediate grades were on task 71.09% of the time.

To verify the significance of these differences and to determine what, if any, interactions exist among the variables, a three-factor analysis of variance was performed using time-on-task as the dependent variable and sex, race and grade level as the independent variables.

The ANOVA yielded significant main effects for sex ($p = <.001$) and race ($p = <.05$), but no significant main effects for grade level and no interaction effects (see Table 1). These results support the original conclusions drawn from the frequency distributions that females spend more time-on-task than males and that white students spend more time-on-task than black students. However, the results fail to support the conclusion that students in the intermediate grades spend less time-on-task than students in the primary grades. Analysis by individual grades was not performed because two of the schools used multigraded classes, that is, 2nd–3rd grade and 4th–5th grade combined assignments.

Differences in the types of on-task and off-task behaviors may influence the quantity and quality of student time-on-task. Primary students, at a ratio of nearly 2:1, more often engaged in solitary off-task behaviors (e.g., playing with an object, staring out of the window, and exploring the contents of their desks); intermediate students, by the same ratio, more often engaged in off-task behaviors that involved peers (e.g., moving to another student and talking to or showing something to another student). Comparatively, peer-oriented, off-task behaviors tended to be sustained for longer periods of time and appeared to have a contagious quality in that subsequent off-task behavior involved the same peers. This was

TABLE 1   ANOVA: TIME-ON-TASK BY SEX, RACE AND LEVEL ($N = 489$)

Source of variation	Degrees of freedom	Mean square	F	p
Main Effects				
Sex	1	18316.56	27.20	***
Race	1	3081.23	4.58	*
Level	1	780.82	1.16	.282
2-Way Interactions				
Sex by Race	1	820.43	1.22	.270
Sex by Level	1	5.93	.01	.925
Race by Level	1	176.50	.26	.609
3-Way Interaction				
Sex/Race/Level	1	19.47	.03	.865
Explained	7	3331.70		
Residual	481	673.40		

* $p = < .05$
*** $p = < .001$

especially true for male students and black students, perhaps contributing to the significant difference for time-on-task when compared with females and white students.

Teacher organizational methods for instruction at the primary level often differed from those at the intermediate level. Primary teachers more often instructed small groups, particularly in reading, while the remainder of the class was expected to perform an independent seatwork activity. Methods at the intermediate level, on the other hand, more often included total classroom group instruction with a commensurate reduction in individual seatwork activity. For the allocated academic time, small group instruction was associated with higher than average time-on-task (75.66%), followed by the total classroom group instruction that approximated the average (70.10%), then individual seatwork which was associated with less than average time-on-task (65.22%).

Student off-task time was more likely to occur when the task required a single, passive behavior, such as reading, watching, or listening. This single on-task behavior (62.0%) was less than tasks that required multiple behaviors, particularly when they involved a motor activity, such as writing, calculating, marking and drawing (78.75%).

Teacher Behaviors

The final question concerned the selected teacher behaviors that relate to student time-on-task. The first step in this analysis involved computing a correlation matrix for the student time-on-task variable (unit of analysis) and the three teacher variables (eye contact, mobility, and verbal management).

The results indicate that eye contact has a strong positive correlation with time-on-task ($r = .47$), meaning that an increase in eye contact by the teacher is accompanied by an increase in on-task behavior by the students. Teacher mobility has a weaker positive correlation with time-on-task ($r = .21$), but it also shares a correlation of similar direction and magnitude with eye contact. Verbal management has a weak negative correlation with time-on-task ($r = -.12$), possibly due to what appeared to be a dual function of verbal management. That is, while verbal management appeared to more often result in on-task behavior for students who were off-task, there tended to be the unintentional function of creating off-task behavior among students who were on task. Primary students, especially, tended to shift their attention from the task to the subject of the verbal management.

Next, a multiple regression was performed to determine which of the three teacher behaviors best predicted the amount of student time-on-task. The results showed that teacher eye contact is the strongest predictor of student time-on-task. Actually, both eye contact and verbal management entered the final regression equation, but clearly eye contact, with a beta weight of .46, was the stronger of the two. In fact, verbal management has a very weak beta weight ($-.08$), so there is some question as to its significance as a predictor.

Interestingly, mobility, which had a stronger correlation with time-on-task than did verbal management, did not enter the regression equation. Of course, the most likely explanation for this is that it shares common variance with eye contact and, thus, would add only redundant information to the model.

The final model (eye contact and verbal management) accounted for only 23% of the total variance in the dependent variable time-on-task. While this is a significant proportion, it is obvious that there are other factors influencing the dependent variable.

Finally, the standardized residual plot indicates that the model does a fairly accurate job in predicting time-on-task scores, especially in the case of high scores.

In summary, the results of this research reveal that students were in the classroom 66.5% of the six-hour school day; and, when in the classroom, they were allocated 69.9% of the time to be on academic tasks. Of this in-class, allocated academic time, students were individually on academic tasks 69.65% of the time or a total of 32.27% (2 hours) of the school day. Significant sex and race differences were found, with females and white students spending proportionately more time-on-task. No differences were found between primary and intermediate grade levels for time-on-task. There were significant correlational differences among the selected teacher behaviors, with teacher eye contact with the students being positively related to time-on-task, followed by teacher mobility, and a negative relationship with teacher verbal management.

CONCLUSIONS

The data suggest that academic "time" may be increased in the existing school day. Even though students appear to be on-task the majority of the time allocated for academic tasks, the frequency and duration of non-academic activities constitute more than one-half of the school day. Non-academic time, such as scheduled recess, going to the restroom, distributing materials, transitions between activities, classroom procedures, and extracurricular programs account for a disproportionate amount of the school day—three hours.

The percentage of allocated academic time and student time-on-task reported in this study is less than that reported in previous studies, including the BTES and Effective School Research. However, this difference may not be significant and may be a function, in part, of the classification of "waiting" time as non-allocated academic time.

While the data seem to shed some light on the differential results of competency and standardized test outcomes regarding sex and race, the reason for the regression in grade level performance from the primary to the intermediate level is not answered. Failure to show differences between students' time-on-task in the primary and intermediate grades may be attributable to several factors, including:

1. The small group instruction that is more prevalent at the primary level may be of greater qualitative intensity when compared with the total classroom group instruction that is more often evident at the intermediate level. The small group instruction appeared to be shorter but more intense and may be a better predictor of learning outcomes than large group instruction.

2. The competency and achievement tests tend to measure lower level or knowledge based objectives at the primary level while intermediate level tests tend to measure higher level objectives. This difference in testing items was found by Armbruster, Stevens and Rosenshine (1977) who reported a low correlation between classroom curricula, including textbooks, and standardized test items. While the curricula emphasized high level skills (e.g., inference, interpretation and synthesis), the standardized test items tended to measure lower level skills, particularly facts. It well may be that time-on-task, per se, does not predict success on higher level objectives.

3. Intermediate students may have learned better to "play the role" of a student in terms of teacher expectations. That is, they physically appear to be attending to task while engaging in intrapersonal thinking processes (e.g., daydreaming) about topics other than the task.

This research has limitations with regard to the observational methodology, descriptive data, and correlational analyses. Even so, it is apparent that a considerable amount of time in school (66.73%) involves off-task and non-academic activities. It seems that additional allocated time for students to be on academic tasks can be organized within the existing school day for all students—black and white, male and female, primary and intermediate. Further, student time on academic tasks may be increased by teachers who reduce the time devoted to transitions, waiting, and procedures, and who monitor on-task behavior through eye contact and mobility, rather than use verbal management.

REFERENCES

Alexander, L. (1986). Time for results: An overview. *Phi Delta Kappan, 68,* 202–204.

Anderson, L. W. (Ed.). (1984). *Time and school learning: Theory, research and practice.* London: Crone Helm.

Armbruster, B. B., Stevens, R. J., & Rosenshine, B. (1977). *Analyzing content coverage and emphasis: A study of three curricula and two tests* (Tech. Rep. No. 26). Urbana-Champaign: University of Illinois.

Berliner, D., Fisher, C., Filby, N., & Marliave, R. (1978). *Executive summary of the Beginning Teacher Evaluation Study.* San Francisco: Far West Laboratory.

Berliner, D. & Tikunoff, W. (1976). The California Beginning Teacher Evaluation Study: Overview of the ethnography study. *Journal of Teacher Education, 27,* 24–30.

Brophy, J. & Good, T. L. (1986). Teacher behaviors and student achievement. In M. C. Wittrock (Ed.), *Handbook of research on teaching* (3rd. ed.), (pp. 328–375). New York: Macmillan.

Denham, C. & Lieberman, A. (Eds.). (1980). *Time to learn.* Washington, DC: National Institute of Education.

Fredrick, W. C. & Walberg, H. J. (1980). Learning as a function of time. *Journal of Educational Research, 73,* 183–194.

Good, T. L. & Beckerman, T. M. (1978). Time on task: A naturalistic study in sixth-grade classrooms. *The Elementary School Journal, 78,* 193–201.

Good, T. L. & Brophy, J. E. (1986). School effects. In M. C. Wittrock (Ed.),

Handbook of research on teaching (3rd ed.), (pp. 570–602). New York: Macmillan.

Hawley, W. D., Rosenholtz, S. J., Goodstein, H. & Hasselbring (1984). Good schools: What research says about improving student achievement. *Peabody Journal of Education, 61,* (No. 4).

Mariottia, D. & Boles, P. (1984). Coaching your teachers in time on task. *The Effective School Report. 2,* 2–3.

National Committee on Excellence in Education. (1983). *A nation at risk: The imperative for educational reform.* Washington, DC: U.S. Government Printing Office.

Rinne, C. H. (1984). *Attention: The fundamentals of classroom control.* Columbus, OH: Charles E. Merrill.

Rosenshine, B. V. (1979). Content, time, and direct instruction. In P. L. Peterson & H. J. Walberg (Eds.), *Research on teaching: Concepts, findings, and implications* (pp. 28–56). Berkley, CA: McCutchan.

Shulman, L. S. (1986). Paradigms and research programs in the study of teaching: A contemporary perspective. In M. C. Wittrock (Ed.), *Handbook of research on teaching* (3rd ed.), (pp. 3–36). New York: Macmillan.

Evaluation of Article 1

This evaluation and the two that follow are organized according to the questions in the preceding outline. Article 1 is a quantitative study; hence, the following numbers correspond to the numbers and questions for quantitative studies.

1.1. There are three parts to this study. The first describes the amount of time students were on-task. There are no independent or dependent variables for this part of the study. The second part examines differences in time-on-task, depending on gender, race, and grade level. In this part there are three independent variables, gender with two levels (male and female), race with two levels (black and white), and grade level with two levels (primary and intermediate). There is one dependent variable, time-on-task. In the third part of the study, teacher behaviors (eye contact, mobility, and verbal management) are used to predict student time-on-task. Thus, teacher eye contact, mobility, and verbal management are independent variables, and time-on-task is the dependent variable.

1.2. The problem is clearly researchable. Data can be gathered to provide empirical answers to the questions.

1.3. A good case is made for the significance of studying time-on-task, but it is less clear how this research will contribute to our knowledge of how time-on-task can be improved. Saying simply that it "requires more systematic study" is not a good justification for the significance or potential importance of the results.

1.4. There is no general statement of the research problem. It would be easier to follow the study if a general statement of purpose or a general question was included at the beginning of the study. The research questions just before the methodology are clear and well written. They appropriately indicate each of the analyses that will be presented.

1.5. The research questions indicate methodology (questions 1, 2, and 3 are descriptive, 4 is relationship, and 5 is predictive relationship).

1.6. The sentence before the questions indicates, in a general manner, the population studied (elementary grades).

1.7. The questions do indicate the variables and levels of variables.

2.1. The review of literature includes some significant studies related to time-on-task, but it is not comprehensive. The review begins in the third paragraph, and only a few studies are cited in an area that has been heavily researched over the past ten years. I would characterize the review as being relatively short.

2.2. With the exception of the reference to findings from the Beginning Teacher Evaluation Study (BTES), most of the references appear to be secondary sources (look at their titles).

2.3. The secondary sources are up to date, but the primary sources appear to be somewhat dated. I would expect more current primary sources.

2.4. The studies and research that are reviewed are summarized but not criticized. There is no critical review, and no flaws are indicated. The research in general indicates a need to examine grade level and race.

2.5. The review does emphasize studies that are directly relevant to the questions.

2.6. The research reviewed is related to the questions in that studies of similar questions are summarized, but there is no indication of particular questions to be researched or implications for the methodology of the present study.

2.7. There are no research hypotheses.

2.8. The review does establish the significance of the study in a general way. There is little or no reference to a theoretical framework.

2.9. The review is well organized, beginning with more general research and then summarizing studies more specific to the variables that are investigated.

4.1. The students are fairly well described. The teachers are not described very well. There is no indication of their gender, race, age, years of teaching experience, or other characteristics that may be important.

4.2. The population of students was clearly defined, but not that of the teachers.

4.3. Most of the entire population was used as an available sample at the classroom level (the exception was the sixth school, and there is no indication of how or why the choice of classrooms was "administratively restricted"). Within classrooms students were evidently more or less randomly selected. Strictly speaking, since the observers' choices of students was influenced by "limitations of their visibility" and the need to obtain equal numbers of students in each category, the sample is not scientifically random. The sampling of four students in each class is stratified, although informally, by race and gender.

4.4. The probability sampling within classrooms was disproportionate since there was no difference in the number of students by race, gender, or grade level.

4.5. Not applicable.

4.6. While the three school districts probably volunteered to be in the study, it is unlikely that this would bias the results.

4.7. There is a large number of both students and teachers in this study, certainly an adequate number for the questions and statistical procedures.

5.1. There is no evidence of validity. There is an indication of high interrater reliability, although it is limited in the sense that the two researchers were also the observers.

5.2. There is only a general description of the observational procedure and recording criteria for both students and teachers. There should be a summary of the development of the instruments and observational procedures constructed by the researchers.

5.3. The procedures for gathering data are only briefly summarized. There should be more details of such procedures as how they gained entrance to the classrooms, when the observations were made, what the teachers were told about the research, and how two observers could survive 132 different observations. (For instance, how long were they in each classroom?)

5.4. Not applicable.

5.5. Not applicable.

5.6. The scores are in the form of percentages and frequencies of behaviors. They do not seem to distort reality.

5.7. Response set is not applicable with an observational system. Faking could occur to the extent that both students and teachers might provide socially desirable behavior (being on-task).

5.8. There is no indication of the training of the researchers (observers).

5.9. Since the observations are made by the researchers, there is a possibility of observer bias. There is also a possibility that the presence of observers could affect the students and teachers (more likely, the teachers).

6.11. Relationships are appropriately limited to the results concerning specific relationships. The descriptions are, with one or two exceptions, limited to the first part of the study.

6.12. Not applicable.

6.13. Yes, the last sentence is a causal conclusion from data that are correlational.

6.14. There are insufficient data to know if restriction in range was a factor in the correlations. It would be helpful if the authors had included a table of means and standard deviations (they might have, and the editor may have cut it for space). The high interrater reliabilities suggest that the correlations are not adversely affected.

6.15. Predictions are based only on the subjects used in this study.

6.16. The correlations reported are large enough for the interpretations that are made. Appropriate language is used in describing some correlations as "weak" or "very weak."

6.17. Not applicable.

7.1. The summary of descriptive statistical data is not sufficient. It would be much easier to interpret the results if the descriptive data were summarized in a table. Also, there is a need to indicate the variability of the percentages of time-on-task for students, the means and variabilities of the teacher behaviors, and the intercorrelations of teacher behaviors used in the multiple regression.

7.2. Statistical significance did not seem to be confused with practical significance, but the lack of descriptive data makes it difficult to know for sure. For instance, there is a reported statistically significant difference between the percentage of time blacks and whites were on-task but no clear indication of what those percentages are.

7.3. Statistical significance is not confused with internal or external validity.

7.4. The statistical tests are appropriate, although the unit of analysis for the multiple regression should be the number of teachers, 132 if a different teacher was in each classroom, not 489.

7.5. Levels of significance are interpreted correctly.

7.6. The results are well organized by research question but would be easier to understand if tables or graphs were used. The narrative summaries of the results are clear.

7.7. Yes, this study has a relatively high number of subjects.

7.8. The only table is clear and accurate, although the details of the ANOVA are really not necessary. As indicated earlier, it would be better to summarize the descriptive data.

8.1. The authors do a good job of keeping the presentation of results separate from interpretations, although some of the interpretations are at the end of each section in which results are reported.

8.2. The results are related to the research questions very clearly. The results are also discussed in relation to instructional differences between primary and intermediate elementary grades. Some of the discussion focuses on findings not included in the research questions (e.g., what was done in class when students were not on-task; differences in time-on-task between small group, large group, and individual seatwork instruction). There is a good discussion in the second paragraph of the conclusions section of how the results may relate to previous research. It would be helpful if other results were similarly discussed.

8.3. If the paragraph before the conclusions section is included, the conclusions address each of the research questions.

8.4. For the most part the conclusions follow from the interpretations of the results.

8.5. The conclusions are not limited by the characteristics of the subjects, and there is only a general statement of limitations caused by the methodology, descriptive nature of the data, and correlational analyses. All of the limitations should be specified in greater detail.

8.6. There is a good discussion of why there were no statistically significant differences for some of the variables.

8.7. The limitations are too vague to be adequate.

8.8. There are no methodological recommendations for future research. The implications are not well supported by the findings (e.g., "that academic 'time' may be increased in the existing school day" and the last sentence of the article).

8.9. There is some discussion of whether some of the findings are consistent with previous research, with some reasons why there is not greater consistency. It would be helpful if all the results were analyzed with respect to consistency with other literature.

Article 2

Reducing Teacher Stress

Michael R. Bertoch
Elwin C. Nielsen
Jeffrey R. Curley
Walter R. Borg

Utah State University

Abstract. A prototype treatment developed to significantly reduce symptoms of stress among inservice teachers was tested in this experiment. Thirty participants selected for high stress levels were randomly assigned to treatment and control groups. They were assessed on environmental, personality, and emotional variables, using self-report and expert-judge measures, at both pre- and posttreatment. The experimental treatment was holistic, incorporating all processes previously found to be related to reducing teacher stress. At posttreatment, the treatment group averaged 1.02 standard deviations lower on the stress measures than the control group. Significant differences in the posttest means, favoring the experimental group, were found for 23 of the 39 variables measured on the three self-report instruments. As a group, the participants demonstrated substantially lower stress levels than the control group after the treatment, with a substantial decrease from their pretreatment stress levels. Since the control group received no treatment, some of the difference may be due to Hawthorne effect.

The present study reflects the authors' concern with the serious threat to teacher mental health caused by occupational stress. Teacher stress is recognized as serious by virtually everyone who has studied the problem (Phillips & Matthew, 1980). A recent search of the ERIC database revealed a substantial amount of descriptive and correlational research regarding teacher stress. However, an extensive literature review failed to produce any reports of projects that used experimental design to evaluate the validity of stress reduction treatments by demonstrating reductions in stress symptomatology. Descriptive and correlational studies have provided important information on possible causal factors. However, these studies are frequently restricted because of research design characteristics and theoretical limitations. The authors' interest was to develop and evaluate a prototype treatment focused on the apparent causal factors of stress, utilizing the most promising treatment strategies that have emerged from previous research.

Selye's (1956) establishment of a final common pathway of physiological responses evoked by stressful events has provided an anchor for a body of theory and research directed toward identifying unique "evocative agents" that result in stress. This work has prompted research along many lines of inquiry. However, a critical mass of knowledge seems to have been achieved in recent years. This knowledge has allowed several integrative paradigms to emerge (Derogatis, 1987; Lazarus, 1966, 1981; Osipow & Spokane, 1983; Pettegrew & Wolf, 1982). These paradigms related many of the variables identified by previous research that have stress-inducing potential.

One's current stress level may be determined by an interaction among the stress events taking place in the environment, the nature and intensity of resulting emotional responses, and personality characteristics of the individual. The exact nature of the relationships among these three areas is incompletely known. Substantial evidence exists, however, to suggest that stressors from these three sources may potentiate one another, and they are at least additive (Derogatis, 1987). It follows that assessment and treatment of persons experiencing high levels of stress may benefit from consideration of these three sources and their possible interactions.

A survey of recent studies of teacher stress shows that many identified stressors appear consistently and may be subsumed under the general domains of environmental and personality-based stressors. Environmental stressors include student discipline and attitude problems, teacher competence, and teacher-administrator relations. Additional stressors include accountability laws, large classes, low salaries, intense pupil dependence, and declining community support. Sources of personality-induced stressors relate to one's self-perception. Negative self-perception, negative life experiences, low morale, and a struggle to maintain personal values and standards in the classroom all take their toll (Goodman, 1980; Schnacke, 1982; Schwanke, 1981).

Emotional response sets that may contribute to high stress levels have been reported rarely. This may be due to an unrecognized need to identify this class of stressor separately from environmental and personality variables. Negative emotions, however, have been reported as effects of stress. Correlations have been noted between high stress levels and anger, self-doubt, lack of confidence, exhaustion, hypertension, absenteeism, and early retirement.

In summary, the emerging views of the concept of stress and the identification of stressors from many aspects of the teaching profession suggest the futility of trying to remediate teacher stress with a univariate intervention. Stress operates in many dimensions, and it is not always predictable. The authors believe, therefore, that stress management must be conceived and implemented from a holistic perspective with consideration of many research- and theory-based sources of stressors. Similarly, the authors believe that interventions would be enhanced by incorporation of all processes previously found to be effective in reducing teacher stress.

This article represents the development and validation of a treatment program designed to significantly reduce symptoms of stress among inservice teachers whose pretreatment assessment indicated high levels of stress. A prototype treatment was administered to a sample of teachers screened for high stress levels. An experimental design was developed to test the null hypotheses: (a) there will be no difference between the stress level of teachers who complete the experimental treatment and comparable control group teachers, and (b) there will be no difference between the pre- and posttreatment stress level of teachers who complete the experimental treatment. Hypothesis b is secondary and is concerned with experimental group gains rather than experimental-control differences. We believe that testing this hypothesis adds to the reader's insight into treatment effects.

METHOD

Participants

The accessible population was public school teachers in northern Utah. Teachers from middle and high schools gained admission to the program through a three-stage process: (a) submitting an application after a presentation about the program at school faculty meetings, (b) scoring in the top 30 on a screening measure indicating stress level (TSM, see Measures section), and (c) being randomly assigned to treatment ($n = 15$) or control ($n = 15$) conditions. Experimental group members completing the treatment received four units of graduate credit in education, and those in the control group were given priority for the treatment during replication. Demographic information is summarized in Table 1.

Table 1   SUMMARY OF DEMOGRAPHIC INFORMATION

	Treatment (n = 15)	Control (n = 15)
Male/female	6/9	6/9
Average age (years)	38.1, SD = 8.28	38.1, SD = 6.99
Married/divorced	15/0	13/2
Average number of children	2.5	3.1
Average years teaching experience	9.5	9.1
Number of schools of employment	2.1	2.2
Percentage of spouses employed	60%	73%
Average years spouses employed	9.2	9.5
Previous mental health care	27%	20%
Alcohol use (moderate)	27%	40%
Nonprescription drug use	0%	0%
Percentage Caucasian	100%	100%

Treatment

Various processes were used in the 12 2-hour treatment sessions, including lecture-discussion, small-group sharing of progress and problems, audiovisual presentations, written test evaluations, and homework. Two experienced clinical psychologists conducted the treatment sessions. Activities from the past week(s) were reviewed at the beginning of each session. Session content was as follows[1]:

Session 1, Introduction   Administrative details, program content, and processes were covered. The clinicians managed the group-forming process while establishing norms of participation, respect, and openness, and modeled the relaxation response.

Session 2, Concept of Stress   Stress, distress, eustress, Type A and B personality characteristics, and other manifestations of stress were covered. Stages, common causes, consequences, and symptoms of stress were presented.

Session 3, Task-Based and Role-Conflict Stress   Task-based and role-related stress were compared. Participants' unique stressors were identified with force-field analysis planning sheets and stress logs. Group members shared individual analyses in small groups.

Session 4, Assertiveness Life Style   The importance of assertiveness was discussed, along with confusions, myths, differentiation from aggression, and the relationship of assertiveness to self-confidence.

Session 5, Relaxation and Breathing   Experiential breathing and relaxation processes were introduced. A process of systematic relaxation of all muscle groups was then practiced. Members were encouraged to practice regularly until a "relaxation response" became automatic.

Session 6, Meditation   Meditation was described as an alternative to achieve a deeper level of relaxation and of contact with the self. All subsequent sessions were initiated with a short session of guided relaxation or meditation.

Session 7, Nutrition   A nutritional evaluation inventory was discussed relative to the participants' current diets. A lecture-discussion of nutritional habits important in stress management followed, with individual commitment to make changes.

Session 8, Exercise, Mini-Relaxation, and Stretching   A physical exercise evaluation provided individual assessment of needs in this area. Group discussion furthered insight into personal needs for more exercise and methods that could be used. Mini-relaxation and stretching exercises were taught.

Session 9, Holistic Living, Mind and Body   The concept of mindfulness, defined as awareness of self and environment, and awareness of choice and personal creativity were discussed. The importance of making a balance in one's life was emphasized.

Session 10, Coping with Disappointment, and Chemical Stressors
The place of disappointment in the development of stress was discussed. Participants discussed customary ways of coping with disappointment and explored less stressful alternatives.

The endocrine system was described briefly to show how sympathomimetic agents such as caffeine and nicotine trigger an elevated baseline of activity. Agents that reduce this baseline of stress, such as alcohol, minor tranquilizers, barbiturates, and narcotics, were discussed.

Session 11, Support Systems, Life Stressors, and Teacher Stress
The importance of having an adequate social support system, both at work and in one's personal life, was discussed.

It was emphasized that to maintain balances, information about stress, and the various coping ideas and techniques need to be utilized from day to day.

Session 12, Understanding Situations, Letting Go of Resentments, and Where to from Here   A review of the experiences and learning from the previous sessions was held, with planning to maintain gains made during the workshop.

Measures

Multiple measures of stress were used, as recommended by Bergin and Lambert's (1978) review of therapeutic outcome research. Ratings were completed by participants, clinicians, and an independent rater. Participants completed a pre- and posttreatment test battery and videotaped clinical interviews. Follow-up data will be collected upon commencement of the replication phase.

Structured Clinical Stress Interview   Recent meta-analytic studies (Edwards, Lambert, Moran, McCulley, Smith, & Ellingson, 1984; Lambert, Hatch, Kingston, & Edwards, 1986) support the authors' view that interviews by experienced clinicians may assess stressors not probed by self-report measures, thus providing a more complete picture of the subjects' stress levels. The Structured Clinical Stress Interview (SCSI) was developed to provide a uniform format covering participants' current or recent stressors, environmental context and possible precipitants, behavioral and physical symptoms, and self-rating of stress level. Interviews were conducted during the week before and after the treatment. The interviewers were blind to group assignment at the pretest but not at the posttest, since the clinicians were involved in the treatment (fiscal restraints prohibited independent interviewers). A third clinician with more than 35 years of experience, blind to groups and sequence, rated a random sample of pre- and posttest interview tapes ($n = 16$) on the SCSI to provide a reliability check. Videotapes of four pre- and four posttreatment interviews (SCSI) with the two clinicians were collapsed into a single group to provide an adequate number of cases. Correlations with the independent clinician's ratings yielded an $r = .66$. This correlation represents a minimum estimate of interrater reliability because the sample of interviews was divided between the two clinicians.

Self-Report Measures   In addition, stress level was assessed across 39 variables using three self-report measures that completed the assessment battery: the Derogatis Stress Profile (DSP; Derogatis, 1987), the Occupational Stress Inventory (OSI; Osipow & Spokane, 1983), and the Teacher Stress Measure (TSM; Pettegrew & Wolf, 1982).

The DSP consists of 77 items that assess stress levels in environmental, personality, and emotional domains. The developers reported alpha reliabilities on 11 subscales ranging from .79 to .99. Test-retest coefficients ranged from .79 to .93 on the subjects and was .90 for total scores (see Table 4). Some evidence of construct validity and predictive validity was also reported.

The OSI consists of 140 items that assess stress levels in three dimensions of occupational adjustment: occupational stress, psychological strain, and coping resources. The developers reported alpha reliabilities on the three dimensions of .89, .94, and .99, respectively, and on the 14 subscales from .71 to .94. Two-week test-retest coefficients from .88 to .94 were reported on the three dimensions, and from .56 to .94 on the individual scales. Some evidence of construct and concurrent validity was also reported.

The TSM consists of 70 items that assess stress levels on 14 variables. The author reported alpha reliability coefficients ranging from .57 to .91. Median reliability was .82 with only two scales below .75. Some evidence of concurrent validity was also reported.

The above measures represent the most promising measures identified in an extensive review of contemporary instruments. Each self-report measure and the SCSI yielded total scores based on a 5-point (SCSI, DSP, OSI) or 6-point (TSM) scale. These provided the main indices of change in teacher stress. To estimate the concurrent validity for the self-report measures using the clinical interview as a criterion, and to provide a rationale for including all measures in an assessment battery, correlations were computed between pretest scores across groups ($N = 30$). Ninety-five percent confidence intervals (95% CI) were determined based on Fisher's Z transformations used to provide a normal distribution. The results presented in Table 2 show correlations ranging from .56 to .72, suggesting that the measures are moderately correlated but do not all measure the same construct. Correlations between the SCSI and the DSP, OSI, and TSM were moderate and consistent at .58, .56, and .57, respectively.

Table 2   PEARSON CORRELATIONS BETWEEN MEASURES ON PRETESTS ($N = 30$)

Measure	SCSI			DSP			OSI		
	r	p	95% CI	r	p	95% CI	r	p	95% CI
DSP	.58	<.001	.280–.884						
OSI	.56	<.001	.245–.762	.56	<.001	.255–.767			
TSM	.57	<.001	.260–.770	.58	<.001	.273–.775	.72	<.001	.490–.859

Data Analysis

The first hypothesis, which predicted no differences between the stress levels of participants who completed the treatment and a comparable control group, was examined using analyses of covariance (ANCOVA) between-group posttest scores from the DSP, OSI, TSM, and SCSI, with the pretest scores entered as covariates. This analysis allowed the slope relating the pretest and posttest to be estimated rather than forced to be 1, as when gain scores alone are used as the dependent variable, thus providing a more sensitive test due to reduced error variance (Hendrix, Carter, & Hintze, 1978; Linn & Slinde, 1977).

The second hypothesis, which predicted no difference between the pre- and posttest stress level of participants who received the

Table 3   SUMMARY OF t TESTS, ANCOVAs, AND EFFECT SIZES

Measure	DSP	OSI	TSM	SCSI
	t Tests: Control group pre-post			
$t(14)$	2.21	−0.25	1.39	−2.27
p	.04	.80	.19	.04
M_{pre}, SD	142.40, 24.01	360.53, 38.66	232.40, 34.98	42.20, 6.98
M_{post}, SD	132.87, 25.26	362.07, 36.31	224.90, 43.60	48.47, 9.56
	t Tests: Treatment group pre-post			
$t(14)$	3.98	4.20	5.56	3.89
p	.001	.001	.001	.001
M_{pre}, SD	152.60, 24.08	377.47, 26.68	260.53, 29.18	50.60, 11.16
M_{post}, SD	117.30, 43.00	348.20, 29.37	208.70, 40.80	40.00, 10.38
	ANCOVAs between treatment and control posttests			
$F(1, 27)$	6.02	8.35	12.68	10.22
p	.021	.008	.001	.004
$M_{c,adj}$[a],	137.68	368.05	238.18	50.25
$M_{t,adj}$[a]	112.44	342.22	195.49	38.22
SD_{pool}[a]	25.24	34.37	38.79	9.86
	Effect sizes			
ES	1.00	0.75	1.10	1.22

[a] $M_{c, adj}$ and $M_{t, adj}$ = posttest means adjusted for the pretest means (i.e., the covariate), SD_{pool} = pooled SDs from control pre- and posttests and treatment pretests. On all measures higher scores indicate higher stress. All t tests were two-tailed.

treatment, was examined using correlated means *t* tests. Since the 12 treatment sessions concluded near the end of the school year— a period described by teachers as highly stressful—this analysis provided information on the direction of change (i.e., whether the treatment group improved or the control group deteriorated; see Table 3).

To determine whether the measures employed provided comparable data for assessing treatment effects, an effect size (*ES*) was computed for each measure. Findings were thus transformed into

Table 4   VARIABLES AND SIGNIFICANCE OF CHANGES BETWEEN PRE- AND POSTTREATMENT FOR TREATMENT VS. CONTROL GROUP

Subscale	Alpha[a]	Treatment mean		Control mean		F
		Pre	Post	Pre	Post	
DSP						
Time Pressure	.93	18.2	15.8	17.1	15.5	0.447
Driven Behavior	.88	12.9	10.3	12.2	11.7	2.975*
Attitude Posture	.86	16.1	13.5	15.5	14.5	2.977*
Relaxation Potential	.91	15.5	10.6	13.2	12.2	3.061*
Role Definition	.90	12.5	8.7	11.7	10.6	4.956**
Vocational Satisfaction	.79	13.3	11.7	12.5	11.7	0.293
Domestic Satisfaction	.86	12.5	8.8	11.1	10.4	3.570*
Health Posture	.85	11.7	9.1	11.3	10.2	0.139
Hostility	.81	10.6	8.7	10.7	10.9	4.596**
Anxiety	.84	18.3	12.6	16.3	14.8	3.667**
Depression	.85	11.1	7.6	10.9	10.4	5.237**
OSI						
Role Overload	.83	32.3	29.5	30.3	29.1	0.748
Role Insufficiency	.90	28.7	23.9	28.3	28.3	5.123**
Role Ambiguity	.78	26.5	22.3	23.3	23.5	0.107
Role Boundary	.82	26.3	20.1	25.7	23.0	6.666**
Responsibility	.71	29.4	24.1	28.3	26.9	1.981
Physical Environment	.85	15.7	14.5	14.5	14.9	1.666
Vocational Strain	.71	24.5	18.4	21.9	22.1	17.532***
Psychological Strain	.89	30.2	21.3	24.7	23.3	4.910**
Interpersonal Strain	.81	27.8	21.2	26.5	22.9	4.124*
Physical Strain	.87	28.0	21.9	22.6	22.9	6.159**
Recreation	.71	22.0	25.0	24.5	26.3	−0.392
Self-Care	.73	22.5	31.3	23.7	27.4	−4.807**
Social Support	.83	24.7	39.7	36.7	40.1	−0.582
Rational/Cog. Coping	.78	28.8	35.2	29.4	31.2	−7.410**

Table 4   (continued)

Subscale	Alpha[a]	Treatment mean		Control mean		F
		Pre	Post	Pre	Post	
TSM						
Role Ambiguity	.79	15.3	12.1	12.8	11.6	0.199
Role Overload	.76	21.0	16.9	18.0	17.9	4.312**
Role Conflict	.82	20.7	17.3	18.5	17.7	4.253*
Nonparticipation	.76	19.1	13.5	17.1	16.3	4.767**
Role Preparedness	.57	15.1	12.9	15.0	14.6	7.173**
School Stress	.89	18.5	16.5	15.8	16.5	6.175**
Job Satisfaction	.86	18.1	15.1	16.5	15.1	0.300
Management Style	.74	16.7	12.5	15.7	15.1	13.040***
Life Satisfaction	.91	16.3	11.9	13.3	12.9	5.652**
Task Stress	.84	40.5	34.9	35.9	38.2	9.462***
Supervisory Support	.89	12.1	9.7	9.7	8.7	0.593
Peer Support	.84	9.1	6.5	7.8	7.9	4.703**
Untitled	NA	21.9	17.2	20.8	19.8	3.893*
Illness Symptoms	.82	16.2	11.8	15.5	12.7	0.451

[a] Alpha reliability coefficients as reported in the test manuals.
* $p < .01$. ** $p < .05$. *** $p < .01$.

a common metric (standard deviation units), rendering an index of the magnitude of effect or change.

To provide information concerning differences between the experimental and control groups on the subscores obtained from the self-report measures, ANCOVAs were computed between groups on posttreatment means scores with pretreatment scores entered as covariates. This analysis, which indicated variables showing significant change at the posttest, will be used, along with data from participant feedback forms completed after each session, to suggest possible refinements in the treatment program and the instrumentation (see Table 4). However, because of the small number of cases and the low reliability of some of the subscores, data in Table 4 should be regarded as tentative.

RESULTS

After the treatment, the experimental group demonstrated substantially lower stress levels than control group members. Significant differences between experimental and control groups in adjusted means were found on the OSI, DSP, TSM, and SCSI (see Table 3). Computation of effect sizes for the above measures indicates how many standard deviations the treatment group differed from the control group at posttreatment. A substantially lower stress level, averaging 1.02 *SD*, was found to be associated with participation in the treatment.

The experimental group demonstrated a substantial decrease in their stress level after the treatment. Table 3 shows that DSP means decreased from 152.60 pretreatment to 117.30 posttreatment. Similar decreases in means were observed on the OSI, TSM, and SCSI, with all four *p*s significant at the .001 level.

Control group means on the DSP decreased from 142.40 to 132.87 pre- to posttreatment, an improvement significant at the .05 level. On the SCSI, however, a significantly higher stress level was indicated at posttreatment (.05 level). The OSI and TSM showed very small changes that were not statistically significant.

Although the experimental group indicated higher stress levels than the control group on all pretreatment measures ($p = .16, .17, .024,$ and $.021$ on the DSP, OSI, TSM, and SCSI, respectively), they were significantly lower on all posttreatment means adjusted for pretreatment scores. A concern regarding internal validity in studies using samples selected for extreme scores is that statistical regression to the mean may account for treatment gains (Borg, 1987; Borg & Gall, 1983; Kazdin, 1980). Since the subjects with the highest scores were randomly assigned to treatment or control, both groups should have regressed a like amount. Had regression accounted for a significant increment of stress reduction in the treatment group, a similar change in the control group would be expected. However, although the treatment group's average means across measures dropped from 210.30 pretreatment to 178.55 posttreatment, corresponding control group means dropped only 1.3 points, from 193.38 to 192.08 during the same period. The relative stability of the control group average scores suggests that regression to the mean may have occurred in the context of a more stressful posttreatment environment, thus not detectable in score changes. However, large differences in experimental group scores also suggests that gain associated with the treatment was not confounded with regression effects.

DISCUSSION

The present study clearly demonstrates a reduction in teacher stress by subjects in the experimental treatment. Table 4 shows that significant experimental vs. control differences were found on 23 of the 39 variables measured by the self-report instruments, many of which may be related to specific treatment content. Interestingly, treated participants scored significantly higher (i.e., less favorably) on the self-care and rational/cognitive coping subscales of the OSI after the treatment. This finding correlates with comments from participants on feedback forms from later sessions such as, "It all seems so helpful, but I need more practice on the things learned," "We covered it all—very quickly," or even "A little bit of ignorance is bliss." Taken together, these may suggest that a sense of overload and need for integration may have been caused by the numerous methods employed to reduce stress, paradoxically introducing a new source of stress. In response to a question on the feedback questionnaires asking which areas had been most beneficial, individual participants stressed different areas. This further suggests that increased reduction of stress in individual cases may be enhanced through idiographic pretreatment assessment and a more focused treatment based on individual needs. An understanding of the process variables imbedded in the treatment package will require further research to determine whether specific factors emerge, thus allowing a better match to individual needs.

The present study addressed a need for remediation of teacher stress with a complex, multifaceted treatment package. As many strategies as practicable were included; some, perhaps, were unnecessary or differentially effective in individual cases. With the main questions resolved—validation that the treatment package alters stress levels overall in the desired direction—interest shifts toward more specific concerns. Which of the variables covered in the treatment contribute most to stress reduction? Will a dismantling of components of the treatment package into multiple treatments aid in understanding the sufficient and necessary conditions of stress reduction? Ultimately, further research is needed to develop a treatment strategy that will vary specific aspects of the treatment with respect to subject variables to determine how to maximize stress reduction within teacher populations (Kazdin, 1980). More immediately, several analyses pertinent to the present study await additional funding and time to complete. Follow-up assessment to determine the durability of the reductions in stress over time are anticipated at approximately 6 months and 1 year, contingent upon grant funding for two replication phases allowing further investigation of this important area.

NOTE

1. Persons wanting a detailed set of lesson plans for the 12 sessions should contact Professor Michael Bertoch, Department of Psychology, Utah State University, Logan, UT 84322-2810.

REFERENCES

Bergin, A. E., & Lambert, M. J. (1978). The evaluation of therapeutic out-comes. In A. E. Bergin & S. L. Garfield (Eds.), *Handbook of psycho-therapy and behavior changes: An empirical analysis.* New York: Wiley.

Borg, W. R. (1987). *Applying educational research: A practical guide for teachers.* New York: Longman.

Borg, W. R., & Gall, M. D. (1983). *Educational research: An introduction.* New York: Longman.

Derogatis, L. R. (1987). The Derogatis Stress Profile (DSP): Quantification of psychological stress. *Advances in Psychosomatic Medicine, 17,* 30–54.

Edwards, B. C., Lambert, M. J., Moran, P. W., McCully, T., Smith, K. C., & Ellingson, A. G. (1984). A meta-analytic comparison of the Beck Depression Inventory and the Hamilton Rating Scale for Depression as measures of treatment outcome. *British Journal of Clinical Psychology, 23,* 93–99.

Goodman, V. B. (1980). *Urban teacher stress: A critical literature review.* ERIC Document Reproduction Service No. ED 221 611.

Hendrix, J. L., Carter, M. W., & Hintze, L. J. (1978). A comparison of five statistical methods for analyzing pretest-posttest designs. *Journal of Experimental Education, 47,* 96–102.

Kazdin, A. E. (1980). *Research design in clinical psychology.* New York: Harper & Row.

Lambert, M. J., Hatch, D. R., Kingston, M. D., & Edwards, B. C. (1986). Zung, Beck, and Hamilton rating scales as measures of treatment out-come: A meta-analytic comparison. *Journal of Consulting and Clinical Psychology, 54,* 54–59.

Lazarus, R. W. (1966). *Psychological stress and the coping process.* New York: McGraw-Hill.

Lazarus, R. W. (1981). The stress and coping paradigm. In C. Eisdorfer, D. Cohen, A. Kleinman, & P. Maxim (Eds.), *Models for clinical psycho-therapy.* New York: Spectrum.

Linn, R. L., & Slinde, J. A. (1977). The determination of the significance of change between pre- and posttesting periods. *Review of Educa-tional Research, 47*(1), 121–150.

Osipow, S. H., & Spokane, A. R. (1983). *Manual for measures of occupa-tional stress, strain and coping (Form E-2).* Columbus, OH: Marathon Consulting and Press.

Pettegrew, L. S., & Wolf, G. E. (1982). Validating measures of teacher stress. *American Educational Research Journal, 19*(3), 373–396.

Phillips, B. N., & Matthew, L. (1980). The changing role of the American teacher: Current and future sources of stress. In C. L. Cooper & J. Marshal (Eds.), *White collar and professional stress* (pp. 93–111). New York: Wiley.

Schnacke, S. B. (1982). *Burnout: Coping with predictable professional life crises.* Paper presented at the annual meeting of the American Association of Colleges for Teacher Education, Houston, TX. (ERIC Document Reproduction Service No. ED 257 836)

Schwanke, D. C. (1981). *Teacher stress: Selected ERIC resources.* Washington, DC: ERIC Clearinghouse on Teacher Education. (ERIC Document Reproduction Service No. ED 204 258)

Selye, H. (1956). *The stress of life.* New York: McGraw-Hill.

Evaluation of Article 2

1.1. The independent variable is the program to relieve stress, with two levels (treatment and control). There are many dependent variables, SCSI, DSP, OSI, TSM scores, and 39 subscale scores from the self-report measures.

1.2. Yes, the problem is clearly researchable.

1.3. The problem is significant, as developed in the first paragraph, and the results would appear to have practical importance.

1.4. A clear, general problem is stated at the end of the first paragraph. The problem is repeated in the first sentence of the last paragraph before the method section. This problem statement is also clear and is more specific.

1.5. Both problem statements clearly communicate that the study is an experiment.

1.6. Neither problem indicates the population studied, other than that it is apparent in-service teachers will be involved.

1.7. There is an indication in each problem statement that the independent variable will be some type of treatment to reduce stress. Although it is clear that the dependent variable is stress, it is unclear that there will be so many different measures of stress.

2.1. The review appears to be fairly comprehensive, although more references could be expected since the authors indicate that there is a "substantial amount of descriptive and correlational research regarding teacher stress." We cannot be sure that all important previous studies are included in the review.

2.2. Most of the references are secondary sources.

2.3. The review seems to be a few years out of date. We could suspect that more recent studies of stress are not cited.

2.4. The research is summarized very well but not criticized.

2.5. Most of the cited literature relates to stress generally and not to stress in teachers. One paragraph in the review summarizes factors related to teacher stress, and none of those studies evidently looked at ways to reduce stress. More detail could be provided from the studies in this paragraph.

2.6. Previous studies are related in a general way to the problem.

2.7. The review does not establish a basis for a hypothesis because little in the review suggests that a particular treatment will reduce stress.

2.8. The review does establish a theoretical framework for understanding stress and the program used to reduce stress.

2.9. The review is well organized, moving from the literature on stress in general to studies of teacher stress and then to implications for the study.

3.1. This article is unusual in stating the null rather than research hypotheses. The null hypotheses are stated as declarative sentences.

3.2. The implied research hypotheses do follow from the literature.

3.3. The null hypotheses do not state expected differences, but these expected differences are implied.

3.4. The hypotheses are clearly testable.

3.5. The hypotheses are clear and concise.

4.1. The summary of demographic information on the teachers provides a very complete, detailed description of the subjects.

4.2. The population is described very generally (middle and high school teachers in northern Utah).

4.3. The method of sampling is clearly indicated in the "participants" paragraph.

4.4. There is no probability sampling. Subjects are selected on the basis of their scores on the instrument measuring teacher stress.

4.5. Not applicable.

4.6. Volunteers are used. This is not a major limitation to the study since the primary purpose is to investigate the effectiveness of the program to reduce stress. Generalizability to other teachers, even those in northern Utah, is not a concern. One possible effect of using volunteers is that teachers in the control group may want to reduce stress on their own, or they may feel more stress because they are not in a program they volunteered for. This potential problem is lessened by assuring the control group teachers that they will participate in the program at a later time.

4.7. The number of subjects is marginal but adequate. If the results are not statistically significant, one reason could be the small number of subjects.

5.1. The evidence for validity is mentioned but little detail is provided. Validity is strengthened by the use of multiple measures of stress. Reliability information is complete and well detailed. Some concern should be noted for the .66 reliability of the interviews and the low reliabilities of some of the subscales. The instruments are appropriate for the subjects.

5.2. The instruments are fairly well described. It would be helpful if examples of the items were included. More detail could be provided on the development of the interview (SCSI).

5.3. The procedures for collecting the information could be more specific. There is no indication when (except "near the end of the school year") or in what circumstances the instruments were administered. There should be an indication of whether the instruments were counterbalanced.

5.4. Not applicable (there is no interest in how teacher stress compares to the stress levels of others).

5.5. Not applicable.

5.6. The scores of the self-report instruments changed many "points," which could be misleading. The authors calculate an "effect size," based on variability, which is an appropriate and very helpful index of whether the point change was important. Generally, effect-size changes of one or more standard deviations are considered important changes for practical purposes. It would help further if normative data could be provided to show a range of changes in the scores that would be expected without a treatment.

5.7. Response set or faking could influence the results. It is possible that treatment-group subjects faked responses somewhat to please the researchers or provide socially desirable answers.

5.8. There is no indication of training for the interviewers. Since they are clinical psychologists, they would have had extensive training in interviewing in general.

5.9. Since the interviewers were the researchers and knew which subjects were in the control group and which subjects were in the treatment group for the posttest, it is likely that there is interviewer/researcher bias.

6.21. There is direct manipulation in the form of the program for subjects assigned to the treatment group.

6.22. The design is clear, although more details could be given about the setting in which the programs were taught. The detail of the contents of the sessions is very good.

6.23. Selection, maturation, pretesting, and subject attrition are controlled in the design. History is possible but unlikely. Statistical regression is possible and addressed very well by the authors. Diffusion of treatment is possible. It would have been good to check with control subjects to determine if diffusion had occurred. Experimenter effects are possible, especially since the experimenters did the interviews and administered the instruments. Subject effects are also possible; the subjects may present themselves as less stressful because they received "a treatment," even though there may have been little actual change. This threat is reduced by the use of multiple instruments. The most serious threat is from treatment replications. Presumably the treatment sessions were presented to all 15 subjects at the same time, which would mean that there is only one replication of the treatment. Effects associated with the group being together, quite separate from the treatments per se, may have ameliorated stress.

6.24. Yes, there is a clear difference between treatment and control conditions.

6.25. See the explanation in 6.23. The number of treatment replications (1) does not equal the number of subjects.

7.1. Table 3 provides a summary of the descriptive statistics, although it is somewhat difficult to understand because inferential statistical information is included in the same table. Table 4 also contains both descriptive and inferential results but is easier to understand.

7.2. Statistical significance is not confused with practical significance. The use of effect size provides a good indication of practical importance, and the discussion of results suggests the need to examine specific aspects of the treatment that may be most helpful in reducing stress.

7.3. Statistical significance is not confused with internal or external validity. The discussion of regression in relation to the results suggests that there is no confusion.

7.4. The appropriate statistical tests are used. If there had been more subjects, it would have been better to use multivariate tests. Cautions are appropriately made concerning the subscore results.

7.5. Levels of significance are interpreted correctly.

7.6. The results are very clearly presented, with narrative that summarizes the direction of the statistical findings.

7.7. Since the differences between the groups are consistent and fairly large, there is a sufficient number of subjects.

7.8. The data are presented clearly and accurately in the tables, with the possible exception of tables 2 and 3, which are somewhat difficult to understand because the descriptive results are combined with inferential test results.

8.1. The reporting of results is completed in the first three paragraphs in the results section. The last paragraph of this section is a discussion of the results, which is continued after the discussion heading.

8.2. The discussion relates the results to one previous study of teacher stress. More studies could be integrated into the discussion. Some aspects of the methodology are related to the results, specifically the discussion of statistical regression and the finding that some of the dependent variables actually showed greater stress. The quite different pretest scores on the SCSI could be given some attention. With random assignment it is expected that these pretest scores would be about the same. The discussion is clearly related to the research problem.

8.3. The conclusions clearly address the problem.

8.4. The conclusions follow from the interpretations of the results, as illustrated in the last paragraph of the study.

8.5. Appropriate limitations due to the nature of the treatment are indicated, particularly in the last paragraph. More discussion would be appropriate of limitations due to the subjects, especially since there were only 30 subjects, and due to the measures, some of which had questionable reliability.

8.6. The lack of statistical significance for some of the subscales of the dependent measures is properly interpreted and discussed.

8.7. Limitations are reasonable, suggesting a clear effect with variations depending on specific aspects of the overall treatment package.

8.8. Both recommendations and limitations are specific and appropriate.

8.9. The conclusions are generally supportive of previous literature.

Article 3

Kindergarten Readiness and Retention: A Qualitative Study of Teachers' Beliefs and Practices

Mary Lee Smith

Arizona State University

Lorrie A. Shepard

University of Colorado-Boulder

The issues concerning teachers' beliefs about and use of retention were explored in a qualitative study. Clinical interviews with teachers, participant observation in kindergarten classes, analysis of documents, and interviews with parents revealed that teachers' beliefs about the development of school readiness could be described and ordered along a dimension of nativism, that these beliefs relate to their use of retention as a solution to unreadiness or incompetence, and that elements of the organization of the schools in which they teach may also account for beliefs and practices. Teachers' endorsement of retention diverges both from extant propositional knowledge and from the perceptions of other interested groups.

The authors wish to acknowledge the thoughtful contributions of the teachers, administrators, and parents involved with the study. We also note with thanks the good work of our graduate assistants: Evelyn Belton-Kocher, Nancy Cummins, Marla Diaz, and Mary Catherine Ellwein. Among those who read and commented thoughtfully on various drafts of the paper, we would especially like to thank Nick Appleton, Gene Glass, and Alan Peshkin.

The educational reforms of the 1980s call for promotion from grade to grade on the basis of the mastery of grade-level curriculum or objectives. Another school of thought (e.g., Ilg, Ames, Haines, & Gillespie, 1978) suggests that individual differences in maturational readiness be the basis for progress through grades; children, regardless of age, should be protected from curriculum that is too advanced for their individual levels of readiness. Although these two positions have different philosophical roots, they are alike in advocating variations on the traditional pupil career that typically begins at age 5 with kindergarten and continues uniformly with correspondence between age and grade until age 18 or so. Such diversions take the form of retention in grade (until the pupil attains mastery of grade level curriculum or, alternatively, grade-appropriate readiness), transition classes between kindergarten and grade 1, or placement of 5-year-olds into developmental kindergartens. Both schools of thought challenge prevalent practice in American schools, often pejoratively labeled "social promotion." The latter might be defended as keeping age cohorts together to promote individual self-esteem or group cohesiveness. Labaree (1984) found a different rationale for such a practice: Large-scale, bureaucratic school organizations require batch instruction and batch promotion for efficient management.

Should the pupil career be driven by competence, by readiness, or by age and grade cohort uniformity? Although the clash of ideas presented here can readily be found in the popular and professional literature, one cannot be sure if they occur in similar forms in the thoughts of teachers or are reflected in the actions they take in the classroom. This study is an attempt to address this issue in such a way that understanding of beliefs and practices is carefully grounded in the social and educational contexts within which teachers work. The questions addressed initially were these: What do kindergarten teachers regard as the proper basis for promotion through early grades? What are the beliefs of teachers about the mechanisms of development and early learning? Is there any pattern that relates teachers' beliefs to retention practices? Are there patterns that relate retention practices and beliefs to what is taught, how it is taught, and to classroom organization? What in the context of the school helps account for teachers' beliefs and practices?

The topic of belief is widely encountered in psychology and philosophy and, more recently, in educational research as well. In this work, we follow the analysis of beliefs by H. H. Price (1969). A belief is that which an individual holds to be true. Following Price, a belief is a disposition of a person with respect to the truth of a proposition.

When we say of someone "he believes the proposition p" it is held that we are making a dispositional statement about him, and that this is equivalent to a series of conditional statements describing what he *would* be likely to say or do or feel if such and such circumstances were to arise. For example, he would assert the proposition (aloud, or privately to himself) if he heard someone else denying it or expressing doubt of it. He would use it, when relevant, as a premise in his inferences. If circumstances were to arise in which it made a practical difference whether P was true or false, he would act as if it were true. If P were falsified he would feel surprised, and would feel no surprise if it were verified. (p. 20)

Beliefs are like emotional attitudes in that one can believe a proposition without realizing it, and there are unconscious or repressed beliefs. Beliefs have degrees, ranging from a vague suspicion to complete conviction. Beliefs are distinct from knowledge, in that knowledge is based on conclusive facts and truths. According to Price, "believing that" is inferior to "knowing that," but because knowledge is in short supply, belief is better than nothing. "We need beliefs for the guidance of our actions and our practical decisions . . . [and] use them (when relevant) as premises in our practical reasoning" (p. 98). Beliefs may be reasonable or unreasonable, depending on what evidence is available to the person believing and the weight of the evidence for and against the proposition. Evidence can be of several kinds: direct experience, testimony, and inference.

Applied to the present study, we use the concept of a teacher's beliefs to refer to those propositions about development and early learning that a teacher holds to be true, with what degree of credulity, with what kind and quality of evidence, in relation to what other beliefs, values, and emotional attitudes, and in light of what consequences such beliefs have in actions she[1] takes.

Practices refer to actions taken, in this case, recommendations and decisions to retain or promote pupils, which may reflect beliefs of teachers as well as other facets of the situation such as school and district policies.

BACKGROUND OF THE STUDY

The study reported here was embedded in a policy study commissioned by a school district. With no central district policy on processes and criteria for grade promotion, individual schools had devised their own, with the result that wide variation existed in the extent to which they retained children for a second year in kindergarten or provided transition or developmental kindergarten programs. In some schools, a fourth of the kindergartners spent 2 years in public school before first grade. In other schools, no children, or as few as 1% or 2% were retained for a second year. The district wanted to know the efficacy of these varying practices. Preliminary analysis showed that high-retaining and low-retaining schools could not be distinguished by variables such as average socioeconomic status, average levels of tested academic abilities, or ethnic or linguistic composition of the pupils.

Although schools within this district exhibited some variation on such characteristics as socioeconomic status and tested academic abilities of pupils, the district as a whole can be described as predominantly middle class, with no schools of more than 20% ethnic or linguistic minority composition. The average tested cognitive abilities and achievement of the schools were consistently above national averages. There were both rural and suburban schools, but none that could be described as urban. The population of the district was generally well educated and actively involved in educational and social issues. The district was organized so as to give individual schools autonomy in such matters as textbook selection. Although curriculum guides were provided, adherence to common curricula was not strictly enforced. Nor were there accountability demands placed on schools by means of district competency examinations.

In agreeing to do the policy study, we requested and received permission to conduct a qualitative study, for two reasons. First, we believe that outcome studies such as the one we designed[2] cannot be interpreted adequately without thorough understanding of the social context within which the practices occur. Second, we wanted to pursue our program of research on school policies that result in diversions in pupil careers.[3]

METHODS OF THE STUDY

This is a qualitative study honoring the assumptions and canons of evidence suggested by Erickson (1986). Collection of data over one year's time comprised an interweaving of clinical interviews with teachers, participant observation of kindergarten classes and decisionmaking events, analysis of documents, and semistructured interviews with parents. Each of these methods is described separately.

Teacher Interviews

Forty of the 44 kindergarten teachers in the district were interviewed, using a semistructured, clinical interview format. In developing the interview protocol, we adopted the working assumption that teachers' beliefs are best known by inference from their
case knowledge, or that which people know how to do "without
being able to state what they know" (Feiman-Nemser & Floden,
1986, p. 506). Unlike formal or scientific knowledge, a teacher's
case knowledge cannot be stated in the form of generalized propositions; rather, it is tied to specific events and persons within the
teacher's immediate experience. Case knowledge helps the teacher
decide what to do in a given circumstance, such as whether to request a tutor for a child she perceives as ill-prepared for first grade,
or assign the child to a group that progresses slowly and is destined
for retention. The teacher bases her decision on previous encounters with similar children in her kindergarten or in those of her
mentors, as well as on the feedback she has received from parents
and teachers on the results of similar interventions in the past. Thus
she knows *what* to do without necessarily being able to state directly her underlying belief in propositional form, for example,
"Children who are ill-prepared for first grade may make up for their
lack of preparation if given intensive, individual academic assistance." Thus, case knowledge is equivalent to "knowing how"
rather than "knowing that" (Price, 1969). Furthermore, case knowledge is revealed in the form of stories that are told in interviews
(Mishler, 1986).

   Thus, for the purpose of the interviews, rather than asking directly for each teacher to state her philosophy about the nature of
child development, we framed a series of indirect questions that
would tap case knowledge. For example, we asked the teachers to
recall specific children they had taught and to describe in concrete
terms their characteristics, such as the inability to follow a series
of directions. We asked them to think of particular children who,
in their opinion, had not been ready for school, to tell as much about
their characteristics and circumstances as they could, and to speculate on the reasons for their lack of preparation. The interview
agenda progressed from indirect to direct questions, under the assumption that the most valid and least reactive data are those related
to the purpose of the study but expressed in the teacher's own
words, prompted by neutral, fact-oriented questions and nondirec-
tive probes. Teachers were assured that their responses would not
be associated with their names or the names of their schools. Even
though the interviews were understood to be a part of the policy

study, good rapport was attained. The teachers were forthright and productive, and they seemed to welcome the chance to describe their practices and provide rationales for their beliefs and programs.

The interviews averaged 1 hour in length. They were tape recorded, and the tapes were transcribed. A list of 47 categories was developed from our initial research questions, issues raised in the policy study, and categories that emerged from the participant observations, parent interviews, and initial reading of the transcripts. Transcripts were coded accordingly. From the coded transcripts, categorization schemes of teachers' beliefs about readiness and retention were constructed.

Participant Observations

Six schools were selected from the 26 in the district. Selection was governed by the need to capture the variability of retention practices within the district. For example, two schools with high-retaining and three with low-retaining kindergartens were selected, along with one school that had a developmental kindergarten and a transition (between kindergarten and first grade) class. Four advanced graduate students conducted the participant observations and wrote case studies. At least 30 hours of data collection were spent in each class. Although this amount of time would usually be insufficient for case studies, these had narrowly bounded goals: to characterize the curriculum, the teaching methods, and the organization of the classes; to describe any differences between the classes observed; to reflect on retention criteria and processes in the schools; and to discover any contextual features of the schools that might help us interpret other data. The authors closely supervised the students' observation, data record keeping, methods of interviewing, and the like. In addition, the observers served as informants as we began to formulate working hypotheses and initial propositions in analysis.

Document Collection

Many materials were made available to us, including school policies on retention, pamphlets for parents on the topic of school readiness, district curriculum and objectives for kindergarten and first grade, existing studies of the effects of extended day kindergartens in the district, test results, pupil records, and the like. These documents extended our knowledge of the social and educational context and suggested working hypotheses for analysis.

Parent Interviews

Samples of parents of children with known characteristics were selected for interviews. The children consisted of groups who were matched at the time they first came to kindergarten on age, sex, and measured readiness, but who were either retained or not retained in kindergarten, depending on whether they attended schools with high retention practices. At the time of the interviews, the children were finishing first grade. The purpose of the interview was to ascertain the parents' assessments of their children's progress through kindergarten and first grade and readiness for second grade. In addition, we wanted to chronicle, from the parents' point of view, the decisionmaking process that resulted in the retention of some and the promotion of other, seemingly equivalent, children. We telephoned the parents selected in the sample and asked them to think back to the time the child first entered kindergarten. What was the initial encounter like? What screening was done, and what were the results? Then, how did the child progress during kindergarten? When was the possibility raised that the child should spend an extra year in school before first grade? What evidence was presented, and how was the decision made? What were the various issues raised by each party? What feelings and meanings were held and expressed?

With the parents' permission, the interviews were tape recorded. Qualitative analysis procedures were used to make sense of their responses. After multiple readings of the data, we found that responses could be categorized in three ways: (a) by time— that is, by sequence of episodes in the pupil's early career; (b) by outcome classification, of children who were retained (or otherwise spent an extra year in school before first grade), who were not retained, but promoted directly to first grade, who were recommended by the kindergarten teacher for retention but whose recommendation was refused, and who were promoted to first grade but who were going to be retained in first grade; and (c) by attitude valence (positive, negative, or neutral feelings about the process and outcome). Excerpts of data were selected to illustrate the resulting typology.

Analysis of Data

According to Erickson (1986, p. 146), to analyze data from qualitative studies is to "generate empirical assertions, largely through induction" and to "establish an evidentiary warrant" for these assertions by systematically searching for disconfirming as well as confirming data and analyzing negative cases. Following this advice, we repeatedly and thoroughly read the entire data record accumulated from the four sources of data described above. From this reading and the questions with which the study began, we derived four empirical assertions that survived the subsequent analysis of negative cases and search for disconfirming evidence.

For example, when categories or typologies were constructed, they were verified by a second analysis from blinded data. To the extent possible, data from self-report were cross-checked with data from observation and documents. No assertion was constructed from data generated by one single research method.

Last, as a means of establishing for the reader the validity of the assertions, excerpts from the data record itself are presented so that the reader may follow the logic of the analysis. This took three forms: quotations from teachers in different categories of analysis, descriptions of retention practices and effects excerpted from interviews with parents and teachers, and descriptions of classroom and school structure. All are actual data, reorganized and presented in such a way that, according to Erickson (1986), they illustrate the interpretations we made and show the reader that the events described actually happened.

RESULTS OF THE STUDY

The four empirical assertions are stated as follows:

Assertion 1. Teachers' beliefs about developing readiness fall along a dimension of nativism.

Assertion 2. Teachers' beliefs about developing readiness are related to retention practices.

Assertion 3. Teachers' beliefs about retention diverge from beliefs of parents and from propositional knowledge.

Assertion 4. Teachers' beliefs about developing readiness and retention practices are related to school structures.

Assertion 1: Teachers' Beliefs About Readiness Fall Along a Dimension of Nativism

Throughout the history of ideas there has existed a dimension of beliefs about human development that runs from nativism to environmentalism.[4] We adopted as a working assumption, both in the design of the interview agenda and in preliminary analysis, that such a dimension might exist in the beliefs of teachers. We took care, however, to avoid taking such a dimension for granted. Furthermore, reevaluation of the complete transcripts revealed that our working hypotheses could not have been detected by the teachers based on the wording of the questions. Thus, we sought information that would allow us to classify teacher beliefs along such a dimension should it exist, and to provide opportunities for teachers to express contrary or alternative beliefs.

It was clear from reading the transcripts that teachers differed among themselves in the extent to which they construed the development of school readiness as an internal, organismic process unrelated to environmental intervention (i.e., nativism), or, in contrast, as a process amenable to influence by parents, teachers, and other forces in the child's environment. As a first approximation, we ordered teachers along a dimension of nativism and environmentalism, based on a holistic interpretation of the transcripts. Then, proceeding more systematically, we identified seven categories related to beliefs about school readiness and the nature of child development: (a) constructions of child development, (b) beliefs about the rate of development of school readiness (c) sources of evidence that the teacher draws upon to conclude inadequate school readiness, (d) beliefs about whether a child not ready for school can catch up to his classmates, (e) beliefs about whether inadequate school readiness can be remedied, (f) what the best method of remediation (if any) might be, and (g) beliefs about the causes of unreadiness for first grade. Taken together, these seven categories constituted the components of the belief systems of the teacher about the nature of the development of school readiness. Each transcript was scored according to our understanding of the extent of nativism, and the teachers were ordered along the dimension. Only 2 of the 40 teachers for whom we had interview transcripts could not be classified because they expressed internally inconsistent beliefs about the categories we considered components of the belief system. For example, although they believed that the cause of unreadiness was low developmental maturation and that it could be detected on the Gesell School Readiness Test before kindergarten (two beliefs characteristic of Nativists), they also believed that teachers could intensify instruction and remedy the unreadiness (a nonnativist view).

In spite of these two negative cases, the analysis that separated Nativists from other types of belief was robust. The transcripts were blinded, and a second analyst who understood the construct of nativism read and classified a sample of the transcripts with no misclassifications. Thus the categorization scheme was confirmed. In addition, the observers were asked to characterize the teachers they observed, and there were no disconfirmations across these two methods.

The 19 teachers labeled Nativists believe that, within some normal range of environments, children become prepared for school according to an evolutionary, physiologically based unfolding of abilities. This process, which unfolds in stages, is largely or completely outside the influence of parents and teachers. The only thing teachers can do to help a child who is in a developmental stage that is not appropriate for kindergarten curriculum is to provide more time for that child to develop.

The remainder of the teachers, all of whom believed that school readiness can be influenced, fell into three types according to the sort of intervention they believed could influence the child's readiness. Those labeled Remediationists believed that children of legal age for kindergarten are ready for school and can be taught and that what the teacher does can influence the pupil's readiness and ability to learn. These teachers believe that instruction can be managed by breaking the curriculum into segments and providing pupils with ample opportunities to learn. Children who learn this material more slowly than their peers are given remediation with the help of volunteers, parents, cross-age tutors, academic assistance programs, and the like. In general, teachers in this group believe that additional instruction can correct the deficits in readiness that may exist in some children.

Teachers of the second type were labeled Diagnostic-Prescriptive teachers because they have adopted the philosophy, prevalent in special education, that any inadequacies in school readiness in a child of legal school age occur because one of several separate traits necessary for learning and attention (e.g., auditory memory, visual-motor integration) is not intact. A deficit in any of these traits can be diagnosed and corrected by concentrated training tailored to the defect. In other words, if a diagnostician identifies a deficit in visual memory, she can prescribe a specific training program to correct the deficit. After treatment, the child will be able to function more or less normally, like his or her peers in kindergarten.

"Interactionist" is the label applied to the third type. These teachers subscribe to a stage theory of development, thus placing them closer philosophically to the Nativists. They believe, however, that readiness develops according to a complex pattern of interactions between the psychological nature of the child and the environments provided by caregivers. Followers of Dewey or the British infant school philosophy, they believe that the environment and materials should be arranged by the teacher based on an ongoing study of each child and on what interests the child has that might awaken the process of learning. These teachers believe that the social configuration of the classroom makes a difference in how children develop and learn. Children also learn from and provide environments for each other and respond to the expectations that teachers and parents have of them.

Table 1 contains the results of data reduction from the hundreds of pages of interview transcripts to a comprehensible and meaningful subset. The columns of the table represent the four types of teacher. The rows represent the seven categories of data that constitute the teachers' belief systems. Within the cells of the table are paraphrases that were constructed to represent beliefs of teachers. This display is meant to illustrate the diversity of beliefs. So that the reader can follow the logic of our method of constructing typical paraphrases, we present in the Appendix actual quotations from selected parts of the analysis.

For example, the "beliefs about development" held by Nativists (see the upper left-hand cell of Table 1) was paraphrased this way: "Development is a physiological process such that the time when a child is ready to learn is governed by the same mechanisms that govern the time when he begins to walk. The child passes through fixed developmental stages at variable rates. Not all 5-year-olds are ready for kindergarten." A teacher classified as nativist said this:

> Some children when they come to school are ready for the school situation so that they can be able to meet the school and with not a lot of stress. . . . Other children are just not ready developmentally. And by that I mean they are not ready to let go of Mom, they're not ready to take directions from another person, and I just feel like this is a developmental stage. And that every child will eventually go through the stages. But right now in kindergarten the first part of school is just really hard on a lot of little children. . . . Some children crawl, walk, or talk early, or they have their teeth early or they cut their teeth late and there are early talkers and walkers and late talkers, and I think a lot of that tells us about developmental stages. . . . All children develop at different—at their own rate of speed. And we cannot push that development. There is no way we can say, "I want him to cut his teeth at a year old. I want him to walk." Because you cannot make a child walk, because they're not ready. You cannot make a child talk. But in our school system right now, because a child is 5 years old, everybody assumes that that 5-year-old is ready developmentally to come and meet a school situation and what it has to offer. And I really feel like that each child is an individual about how he is developing.

Assertion 2: Teachers' Beliefs About Readiness Relate to Retention Practices

One expects on logical grounds that teachers who believe that time alone is the remedy for children with inadequate readiness would more likely recommend an extra year of school than compensatory

Table 1 PARAPHRASES OF BELIEFS ABOUT MAJOR ISSUES FOR DISTINCT SUBGROUPS OF TEACHERS

Category of beliefs	Nativists	Diagnostic-prescriptives	Interactionists	Remediationists
Beliefs about nature of development	"Development is a physiological process such that the time when a child is ready to learn is governed by the same mechanisms that govern the time when he begins to walk. The child goes through fixed developmental stages at variable rates. Not all 5-year-olds are ready for kindergarten."	'Specific abilities either develop normally or dysfunctions develop. Kindergarten-aged children can learn provided one or more of these abilities is not disordered."	"Children go through natural stages, but progression is influenced by parents and teachers. Teachers can influence the child's ability to focus, internalize controls, and gain interest in others."	"Within broad limits of chronological age, children's readiness is a function of their experience, learning program, and environment."
Beliefs about rates of development	"Because development constitutes physiological unfolding, rates of development are smooth, continuous, with no spurts or discontinuities. The child who is 6 months behind in September will be 6 months behind in June."	"Rates of development are uneven and unpredictable; spurts, discontinuities and regressions are to be expected if there is an underlying dysfunction in some specific abilities."	"Within broad limits of chronological age, rates are not predictable, and discontinuities can occur as a result of quality learning experiences tailored to a child's interests."	"Because learning and development are poorly understood, the teacher should expect spurts, discontinuities, and regressions related to opportunities to learn."
Beliefs about evidence for lack of preparation	"In many cases, you can tell the first time you see them that they are not ready; Gesell provides supporting evidence for teacher observation; tests permit an early and accurate diagnosis of readiness."	"The best evidence is multifactor diagnosis of specific traits and abilities, tests by clinical specialists, similar to special education staffing."	"The teacher can observe children's use of environment, materials, and relationships; assessment of readiness must be context-dependent; tests provide only partial indication."	"Teachers rely on observation throughout the year, to reveal lack of academic preparation and social immaturity; formal tests are viewed with caution."

Table 1 (*continued*)

Category of beliefs	Nativists	Diagnostic-prescriptives	Interactionists	Remediationists
Beliefs about the possibility of catching up	"There is little likelihood that a child who is developmentally behind his agemates would close the gap that separates them."	"If deficits in abilities can be corrected, child can progress."	"You cannot predict when and under what circumstances a child will progress."	"A child who is less prepared than his peers can close the gap given the right educational circumstances; academic assistance is required."
Beliefs about possibilities of influencing a child's preparation for school	"Because learning is governed primarily by internal mechanisms, intervention is futile with a developmentally unready child. Extra help or remediation causes pressure, frustration and compensation. Teacher cannot influence psychomotor abilities, ability to attend, social maturity, and so forth."	"Deficits can be remedied by direct intervention in the disorability."	"The teacher can make a difference, though it is more difficult with less mature child; learning is a complex interaction between child's abilities and opportunities provided. The teacher can influence psychomotor development, attention, and emotional maturity."	"The teacher can make a difference as can the parent and other aspects of environment; within a broad range of pupil abilities, what the pupil learns is largely a function of opportunities and experiences."
Beliefs about causes of lack of preparation	"Children are not ready because of low developmental age, chronological age, sex, *not* IQ, small emphasis on preschool or environment."	"Children are not ready because of lack of background experiences, family stability, family inheritance of special abilities, within normal range of development."	"Children are not ready because of cognitive or emotional immaturity, stress, lack of availability of parents, limited preschool or prior academic experience, instructional failure, low expectations."	"Children are not ready because of poor intellectual ability, inattentive or unskilled parents, prior educational and enrichment experiences, the teacher or educational program."

Table 1 (*continued*)

Category of beliefs	Nativists	Diagnostic-prescriptives	Interactionists	Remediationists
Beliefs about what the teacher can do	"Teachers can provide child with more time to mature; place child in developmental kindergarten, preschool, send him home another year; place in slow group in class; reduce instruction below frustration level, lower expectations, boost self-concept, use manipulatives; retain in kindergarten or transition; providing academic assistance is irrelevant and harmful."	"The teacher can identify problem area, refer for professional evaluation, build up or work around problem area; adapt instruction; provide academic assistance aimed at correcting the disordered ability."	"The teacher can arrange the environment so every child can be successful; study the child to see what interests him; set up cooperative, peer teaching, individualize instruction; retain only if first-grade teachers are not likely to accommodate individual differences."	"The teacher can provide additional academic help; accommodate differences in achievement; hold high expectations, reinforce and train; work hard and encourage the pupil to work hard."
Beliefs about endpoints of kindergarten	"By the end of kindergarten, almost all children should meet a common standard."	"Most readiness skills should be mastered so that first-grade phonics can commence; differences in preparation are expected to be accommodated by first-grade teachers or special education."	"There are multiple standards and multiple ways of achieving them; children come into kindergarten variable and they leave variable; variability does not mean failure."	"Not all children will be at the same level; though mastery of skills is a goal, first-grade teachers should be able to accommodate diversity."

tutoring. Therefore, we looked for evidence to indicate a relationship between what teachers believed and their retention practices. The most reliable evidence was the rate of retention of kindergartners in the schools where each teacher taught. When this documentary evidence was not available (such as when a teacher was new to a school), we asked the teacher to report the percentage of kindergartners that were retained in her most recent class.

Figure 1 is a display constructed to illustrate this assertion. Each circle represents one teacher. The teachers are ordered from right to left according to their extent of nativism (the highest degree of nativism is farthest to the right). The vertical line represents the demarcation discovered between Nativists and non-Nativists. The four types are labeled (e.g., Remediationist). The number within each circle is the retention rate for that teacher. Those with asterisks indicate teacher-reported rates rather than official school rates. Daggers indicate negative cases. A pattern is apparent in the display, with a greater rate of retention for Nativists than for other belief types. A test of the difference in retention rates corresponding to the belief system dichotomy (Nativist vs. non-Nativist) was statistically significant ($t = 6.15$, $p < .01$), verifying what can be seen in the display. Reclassification of the data from the two teachers whose beliefs could not be classified failed to disconfirm this assertion. The data record was examined to shed light on the negative cases. The Nativists with low retention rates had recommended about a third of the kindergartners for retention, but the parents had refused. The schools in question were in lower socioeconomic neighborhoods where parents could not bear the expense of private childcare during the half days the child would not be taken care of

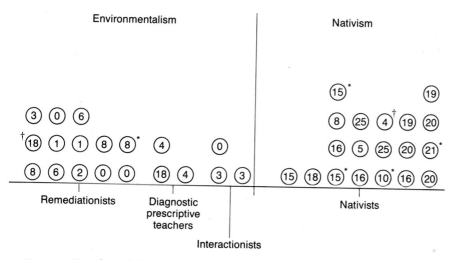

Figure 1. Display of the relationship of retention practices (percentage of kindergarten retentions), degree of nativism, and belief type.
Note. Degree of nativism increases from left to right. The vertical line is the demarcation between Nativists and non-Nativists. A circled number represents teacher's retention rate. * = teacher = reported rate. † = negative case.

in the kindergarten. Nonnativist teachers with high retention rates used retention in kindergarten as a way of coping with the limited English proficiency of immigrant children in a school without satisfactory language programs. The analysis of these negative cases shows that beliefs and practices are not always congruent, but are mediated by the educational and social context.

Assertion 3: Teachers' Beliefs About Retention Diverge from Parents' Beliefs and from Propositional Knowledge

Considering the rich diversity in teachers' beliefs about readiness and their retention practices, there is remarkable unanimity of sentiment, even among those who rarely retain, in favor of adding a year to the pupil's career, when the pupil lacks either the competence or the maturity for the next grade. Of course, the teachers differed with respect to the criteria they would apply to standards of maturity or competence. Among the benefits mentioned by teachers in the interviews or heard in the course of participant observation were these: An extra year provides time for the child to mature, moves a child from the bottom of his age-appropriate class to the top of the class into which he is retained, makes the child a leader, prevents a later and more painful retention, and prevents deviant behavior later in life.

Here are some characteristic statements by teachers:

> Those kids who repeat tend to become the leaders. One little boy that repeated this year, last year maybe said three words and was very self-conscious. And this year he is just bubbling, and I mean he is just thrilled with himself, he has such a good, positive self-concept.

> If we teach them here, and they don't make it, and we pass them on to first grade, they would not be ready. So they would in essence have had a year in kindergarten where they didn't do well, and in first they don't do well. So they're just passed on. And then after a while those children have just gotten very tired of not doing well, so either they drop out or they start ganging around with their other buddies who haven't done well. So then they get into the drug act or whatever makes us feel a little bit better about ourselves. I think we need to start right down at the very bottom, catch those babes before they start having self-image problems.

Some teachers qualified their endorsement of retention by stating that it is beneficial only for children who are immature. For children with low academic ability, low motivation, or handicaps, retention will not solve the problem. Other teachers preferred a transition program or developmental, 2-year kindergarten program to retention, still endorsing the addition of a year to the pupil career. A few others felt that retention in first grade was more effective than retention in kindergarten.

Not one teacher subscribed to the opinion that social promotion is a desirable policy for governing transitions from grade to grade. The Japanese view that agemates should be kept together to promote group cohesiveness and mutual responsibility (O'Hanion, 1987) was not expressed, nor was the notion that, to preserve children's self-esteem, one ought to promote them with their classmates.

Probed for their views on any risks or costs that might be associated with retention, the teachers felt that few exist, and that these are minor and temporary. As one teacher said:

> One little girl had problems with it. I think the first few days she wanted to be in the first grade with her friends. But she is fine now. I feel the social-emotional peer stuff is not so present as it might be in a higher grade.

Asked whether the children ever became bored during the second year of kindergarten, one teacher expressed the typical view that the children do not remember from year to year what they did, and therefore boredom is unlikely.

The only qualification to this belief in the benefits and lack of problems teachers mentioned in connection with retention was the parents' cooperation with the decision. "There is no stigma to retention as long as the parents are supportive of it. I've had great success once I've convinced the parents that they haven't failed in any way." The teachers were careful to present the picture that the decision to retain or promote was ultimately the parents'. Evidence from the participant observation and parent interviews verified this picture in certain schools but contradicted it in others. For example, several parents reported being intimidated by teachers' having stated that the school would not be held responsible for the subsequent success or failure of the pupils if the parents insisted on promotion, or when the teachers called in "experts" to give tests to verify inadequate developmental readiness, or quoted "statistics" that show that most 5-year-old boys need to be retained. Fearing retaliation, parents capitulated. Said one, "We learned to live with it. But I never, ever want to go through anything like that again."

Teachers underestimated the degree of conflict with parents over the decision and the extent of frustration, shame, and confusion the children felt (as reported by parents). Unlike the teachers, parents were readily able to name the problems that their children experienced. For example, they mentioned physical size in relation to their grademates, derogatory comments on the part of family and neighbors, missing agemates who had been promoted, feelings of failure in spite of the parents' presenting the retention in a positive light, teasing by peers, boredom at having to repeat the same material, and being overconfident and careless about repeated material.

Asked to name the advantages their children received because of retention, parents repeated those indicated by the teachers, such as improved self-confidence, prevention of failure, and that "going over the same stuff gives her an advantage over the other kids."

Not having access to the children in this district, we relied on the work of Byrnes and Yamamoto (1984) for the perspective of the child who directly experiences retention. They found that stigma, stress, and shame formed part of the meanings of retention held by these children.

Other studies confirm the results of Byrnes and Yamamoto. The meta-analysis of results of studies on the effects of retention (Holmes & Matthews, 1984) showed that these effects are negative on both achievement and adjustment. Thus the beliefs of teachers about retention diverged from available evidence as well as from the beliefs of at least a substantial number of parents and pupils.

Assertion 4: Teachers' Beliefs About Readiness and Retention Practices Relate to School Structure

To a remarkable extent, teachers' beliefs were shared within a school. In only one out of the 26 schools in the district did teachers fall on two sides of the line we constructed to separate Nativists from non-Nativists. Nor did variables such as training or experience account for beliefs. Thus, we looked for patterns at other system levels to try to describe and account for teachers' beliefs and practices.

At the school district level, there were formal rules for the kindergarten curriculum that determined that the nature of kindergarten would be academics rather than socialization. According to guidelines from the district, the teachers must spend a certain number of minutes each day teaching reading readiness, math readiness, and language. Furthermore, the guidelines required that children at the end of kindergarten should know their letters, numbers, shapes, colors, and so on. In addition, the amount of time allocated for kindergarten is determined by the district. Except for a few extended-day programs of about 4 hours' duration, kindergartens lasted for 2½ hours. Portions of this time were allocated, according to district rules, to "specials," that is, to art, music, and physical education, for which children left the regular classroom and were taught by a specialist. This structuring of kindergarten by the district placed constraints on what teachers can do and perhaps on what they believe. When the "specials" were over and the requisite minutes had been spent on readiness skills, there was little time left for the teachers to follow the pace of little children. The reverse is true; these constraints required that teachers organize the kindergarten in such a way that academic demands are satisfied and children conform to the pace of the school.

Aside from the formal rules, informal pressures at the school level also influenced the structure of kindergarten. In some instances, parents demanded that the curriculum consist of a heavier dose (compared to that specified in the district guidelines) of reading, writing, and math and that pupils be pushed farther along a direct path toward literacy. For example, one father insisted that, because his child already knew her letters, the kindergarten as a whole should be moved into the first-grade basal reader, or his daughter's year "would be a waste of time." In this respect, the parental demands echo the reform rhetoric that calls for literacy-focused curriculum and early acquisition of skills.[5] This form of pressure occurred to some extent in all schools but was more deeply experienced in the half-dozen schools in more prosperous neighborhoods. In low-retaining schools, teachers had tactics for resisting it. Some teachers accepted the value of this downward push of academic curriculum into kindergarten, some worrying, for example, when children could not count to 100 or execute consonant blends.

Further informal constraints on school structure came from teachers in grades 1 and above. Data from interviews revealed some kindergarten teachers' perception that first-grade teachers expected to begin their reading programs during the first week of school, an expectation that required all incoming pupils to have mastered reading readiness skills such as letter-sound associations, beginning and ending sounds, and knowledge of some sight-words. Because these programs require a considerable degree of independent seatwork, pupils must also be ready to work independently and complete worksheets on their own. First-grade teachers in some schools, therefore, made clear their expectations to kindergarten teachers, either by direct statements or, indirectly, by sending already-promoted children back to kindergarten. At these schools, the first grade was viewed by kindergarten teachers as a harsh place from which a marginally prepared child should be protected and for which most children had to be forearmed. As a result, where the formal guidelines called for "introduction to" such things as letter-sound associations, kindergarten teachers reinterpreted requirements to mean "mastery of." Clearly, teachers went beyond the district policy to provide a fast-paced, rigorous academic experience. This general description, however, fails to explain why some schools retain fewer pupils and teachers in them hold alternative beliefs.

We used all the sources of data to categorize the schools by the ways learning opportunities were structured. For example, we characterized content of curricula and teaching methods, we coded instances of grade segregation, kindergarten teachers' perceptions of first-grade teachers' expectations, use of rigid ability groupings as the sole method of dealing with heterogeneity, availability of pullout programs for academic assistance, between-class movements, and the like. A rough categorization scheme was constructed and confirmed. From this scheme we have selected illustrations from four schools of which the pseudonyms are Fillmore, Madison, Lincoln, and Mountain Shadows.

With a few exceptions, the content of what the children throughout the district were presented was fairly uniform and failed to distinguish schools and teachers with different retention practices. Neither did the teaching methods employed, although there was more diversity among schools in the latter. Emphasis was usually placed on phonics instruction, with a sprinkling of language experience methods in some schools.

A great deal of attention was devoted to behavioral methods for fitting the children to the structure of the school (the "hidden curriculum"). The developmental kindergarten at Fillmore is illustrative, differing in degree but not in kind from the programming of others. Of the 2½-hour day, 30 minutes is spent getting settled in for the "opening," listening to a 10-minute story, taking a 15-minute recess, and, for 4 days per week, going to another classroom for a 30-minute special. On the day when there is no special class, the children have free time, which is the only time that is not programmed by the teacher and that is devoted to pupil-generated interests. Activities designed to promote readiness for the reading and math curriculum are worksheets (e.g., "circle all the numbers on the page," "circle all the things that begin with 's,' " "trace all the pictures that are squares") and manipulatives ("count all the beans in the dish"). Whereas the children may have studied three or four letters or words, they will have heard more than 60 statements of rules—some repeated many times—as well as reprimands for breaking rules. Rules are instituted for the level of noise that can be tolerated in different activities. Rules determine how children must turn in papers, line up for drinks, use scissors, select books, listen to tapes, and clean up. Children are expected to know the rules for the maximum number that can play a particular game.

There are rules that require children to raise their hands before speaking and lower their heads to their desks to signal completion of a task. In addition, perhaps as much as 10% of the content of what was taught had to do with explicit training in following directions and filling out worksheets.

Even in the nativist intellectual environment of Fillmore, there was remarkably little emphasis on designing instruction based on the needs, interests, or "developmental readiness level" of the children. The needs of the school for order and efficiency seemed to predominate. Children who dawdle at the drinking fountain, hold their crayons awkwardly, fall asleep during the story, or pester their neighbors steal time from the harried teacher who needs to drill the ABCs.

Although the curriculum and methods of kindergarten did not form any consistent patterns with retention, we found differences in the ways schools allocated learning opportunities to children and to their organizational structures as a whole. High-retaining schools were characterized as more bureaucratic and as having a greater degree of grade segregation. (See Labaree, 1984, and Wise, 1979, for analyses of bureaucratic school organization.)

Fillmore, once again, is illustrative of the group of bureaucratic schools. At the kindergarten "roundup" the previous March, parents of children of legal school age (4 years, 11 months by September 1) are informed of Fillmore's organization. In March, before they intend to enter, all children must be tested on the Gesell. Those who score below the developmental age of 4½ (or 5 by September 1) are offered (though this verb suggests a stronger sense of choice than is actually conveyed) the chance to enroll in Developmental Kindergarten. After completing Developmental Kindergarten (which no one repeats), the child progresses to Regular Kindergarten. Children with higher scores, as well as those whose parents decline the chance for Developmental Kindergarten, enroll in Regular Kindergarten. Of these, some will be asked to repeat Regular Kindergarten for a second year or enter a transition, or "prefirst grade," based on teacher judgment or another administration of the Gesell. Others are promoted directly to first grade. There is no repeating of prefirst grade, nor is there a second retention in kindergarten. Although in theory the possibility exists, there is no progressing upward; if a child placed in Developmental Kindergarten were to show a surge of progress in November, the child would not be advanced into Regular Kindergarten but would complete the year where he or she is. Early admissions, such as that of a 4-year-old who tests out above 4.5, are almost nonexistent. Nor would a 5-year-old who was developmentally 7 be allowed to enter first grade. Backward transitions do exist, however. For example, a child placed by virtue of the Gesell score into Regular Kindergarten may be judged by his teacher to be unready and sent back to Developmental Kindergarten (or from first grade to Regular Kindergarten or prefirst). Children who are promoted from kindergarten to first in another school and move into Fillmore's attendance area over the summer may be judged unready by the first-grade teacher, who then sends them back to kindergarten for the rest of the year. We found from observations and interviews that children were slotted into this structure in regimented fashion. The fate of their learning opportunities and pupil careers was decided early and rarely reconsidered. The positive effect of the system, according to the teachers, is that it allows all children to enter first grade "on an equal footing." First-grade teachers, as a result, can commence their basal reading program without the need for individualizing instruction for children who still cannot discriminate beginning sounds.

At more bureaucratic and grade-segregated schools such as Fillmore and Madison, teachers had more rigid ideas about what the correct content of a grade should be, standards of proficiency, and the like. It was common practice for teachers to send back a grade children whom they perceived not to have "the background for this class" or to vilify teachers of earlier grades who do not retain children who are short of mastery of grade-level standards. A kindergarten teacher described first grade at Madison in this way:

> [The first grade teachers] would not be able to teach the reading from the curriculum if our children didn't learn the alphabet and the sounds and didn't learn the numbers and didn't learn how to approach sitting down and writing and holding the pencil and doing these kinds of things; they would not be able to go on with their curriculum because they would have to teach the readiness first and then teach first-grade curriculum.

From the low-retaining schools like Lincoln, we found in the participant observation data that teachers in different grades worked cooperatively. For example, a second-grade teacher of a child reading at the first-grade level consults with the first-grade teacher on appropriate materials, or perhaps that child spends 1 hour a day in the first-grade classroom for extra reading instruction, but the rest of the day is spent in second grade. Accelerated students likewise pass back and forth between classes of different grades, without the need to move permanently. Teachers at Lincoln seem willing to go slower or faster with certain children and feel more flexible about what constitutes grade level instruction.

A kindergarten teacher at Lincoln had this to say:

We would like them to know all their letters and sounds when they go out of here. But there is generally a group that goes out of here who needs further help with those, and the first-grade teachers are very comfortable with that. Our school's philosophy is that you take the child where you find them and move them to the extent of their abilities.

Our observations confirmed that teachers at Lincoln acted upon these beliefs.

In schools with few retentions, teachers dealt with individual differences in more fluid and less permanent ways than teachers did in high-retaining schools. In schools like Lincoln (as we learned from participant observation), teachers had aggressively recruited parents, neighbors, and university students to tutor children on specific areas of difficulty. Children from higher grades were also brought in as tutors. Teachers felt that these short-term solutions are effective and kept children with their peers in some tasks while difficulties in the other tasks were being corrected. In these schools, ability groups, if they were used at all, were reassessed on a regular basis so that expectations would not be crystallized into unequal learning opportunities. At Madison, a boy having similar difficulty was sent home for a year or assigned to a color-coded group and likely to remain in that group for the year. It is typical for the child to spend most of his time in nonacademic activities, for example, in unsupervised time at the water table. Thus the teacher had organized his learning opportunities in such a way that he would be free from the stress of academic learning, would also be free of the competition (or viewed alternatively from the opportunity for peer learning) of more advanced classmates, and the teacher's expectations for him would be negatively structured. Retention is almost as sure as it would have been had he enrolled at Fillmore and been tested into the Developmental Kindergarten sequence.

Mountain Shadows Elementary School is the official alternative school in the district, comprised of carefully selected teachers who variously claimed allegiance to the labels "experiential education" or "whole language education." Curriculum in this school is pupil directed rather than teacher or program directed. Two of the teachers categorized as Interactionists taught there. What stands out clearly in the studies of Mountain Shadows is, first, its nonbureaucratic organization and, second, the prevailing view of curriculum. There were no standards that determined where children in a particular grade should be performing. One teacher said, "Yes, we would like them to know their letters by the end of kindergarten, but if they don't, the first-grade teacher can accommodate. If the child is not reading until the end of second grade, we don't get disturbed, as long as he is working and interested and growing."

Neither is there a climate among the teachers that conveys the feeling, "this child does not belong in this grade" or "is not capable of third-grade work." Ideas about curriculum contradict the philosophy that there is a natural (as opposed to a socially constructed) standard content for each grade level—that it can be broken down into small learning activities, sequenced, drilled until mastery, tested in standardized way, and so on. Instead, teachers accepted the possibility of spiraling, sudden reorganizations, intuitive leaps to understanding, false starts, regressions, and other unpredictable paths to learning, all of which must be facilitated by flexible teachers in flexible school organizations. As a consequence, retention was not a common practice at Mountain Shadows.

This analysis demonstrated that retention practices are related to, and form an integral part of, school structure—how teaching and learning opportunities are organized, both formally and informally. The official district curriculum sets a formal organizational context for teachers' beliefs and practices. Associated with reform rhetoric, the souped-up expectations for kindergarten performance as well as parental pressure for academics set a social context that affected teachers' beliefs. The resulting curriculum, teaching methods, and organization of kindergartens may be too severe for some children. To protect them from inappropriately difficult schooling, teachers may have used practices such as retention and couched them in the nativist theory of child development. In other words, teachers' use of retention and beliefs in the nativist theory of development may have been a response to inappropriately difficult and standardized curriculum and to rigid school organization and severe standards for academic performance and behavior. In schools with low retention rates, teachers may have resisted informal pressures more successfully and may have been better able to individualize instruction or provide alternative methods for dealing with unequal readiness and competence. Alternatively, teachers with strong beliefs may have been instrumental in creating the school structures that were found to relate to retention practices.

DISCUSSION

In this study we found that teachers believe sets of propositions about how children develop readiness for school and how this development can best be dealt with. The sets of propositions believed by individual teachers are, for the most part, coherent and internally consistent. Among teachers, however, interesting variation exists in what teachers believe and how they act on these beliefs. The dimension that cuts most clearly across this variation is that of nativism. In this regard, beliefs relate to practice in patterned ways. Moreover, the beliefs held by individuals are related to beliefs held by others in the same environment, though it is quite unclear about the cause of the similarities. Beliefs appear to be interwoven with school structure and social climate. Despite the variations in beliefs, we found that overt confrontations between belief types are rare. Nor is the available evidence against one's beliefs given much attention or credence. The question about whether teacher beliefs such as these are justified awaits further research, probably using a critical paradigm. Particularly, this research should address whether closely held and unquestioned beliefs constitute an ideology that protects some interests and hurts others. The present study showed how beliefs could be revealed in context and typified in understandable ways. We found that teachers believe that the pupil career should be driven by competence or readiness rather than by social promotion and that for the most part, they act according to these beliefs.

APPENDIX

Quotations Illustrating Construction of Paraphrases in Teacher Belief Systems

We paraphrased "Beliefs about Rate of Development" held by Nativists in this way: "Because development constitutes physiological unfolding, rates of development are smooth, continuous, with no spurts or discontinuities. The child who is 6 months behind peers in September will be 6 months behind in May." A typical quotation that led to this paraphrase follows:

> You do see improvement [in the unready child over the course of the school year], but there's also improvement in other children, and they are showing us that they are really ready to go on. They want to do first-grade work. But this child is still playing. And you see the young that comes through. . . . But you see a lot of times at the end of the school year the child who is not quite ready for a school situation at the first of the year. By the end of the year, he is functioning about like the other children were when school began.

In contrast, "Beliefs about Rate of Development" held by Remediationists were paraphrased, "Because learning and development are poorly understood, the teacher should expect spurts, discontinuities, and regressions in relation to opportunities to learn." As one Remediationist said:

Some children have parents who don't help them, don't play with them, all of the educational things that children generally learn at home. Some parents are not able to give the children some of those 3-, 4-, and five-year-old skills because they just don't have those skills themselves. So those children come in, and if they're able to learn, they learn very rapidly. But you have that first month where you can't tell whether they are children who can learn or can't learn or are slow learners or what. You have to give them time to adjust to the kind of atmosphere that we have here at school. And sometimes they just amaze you. That's why you have to keep your expectations up and say, "Hey, forget that first impression you had," and do it as near for the individual as you can.

Finally, the words of teachers provide the best evidence for the diversity of beliefs when they answer the question, "Is there anything the teacher can do about [a particular] kindergartner who is not prepared for first grade?"

A Nativist:

He's young. He's a boy and very low in a lot of those areas like following directions, attending, and things like that. I just feel he needs another year to get him ready for first grade. Just to give him a big start. If he doesn't, school's going to be a struggle for him. If he's struggling now in kindergarten what will it ever be like in first and second grade? When I present that to parents, I just say they need another year just to grow, a catch-up time. Then if the parents agree, we take the pressure off, probably by giving him different expectations than I will give the other kids. I'm worried about parents thinking they can push them ahead by working with them. If they're not getting it from what we're teaching, it's probably because they're not ready to do it; and all this work is going to frustrate parents terribly and it's not going to really help the child a lot and it may frustrate her terribly.

A Remediationist:

I think we as educators have to give them the most benefit of the doubt or do something different and help that child. And maybe the way we taught it is not correct. Maybe we ought to change our style or drill or do something different and help that child. And I think if you marked them and said, "If he doesn't get it now, he'll never get it. We'll try for another year of maturity, maybe he'll get it next year," I think you give up.

A Diagnostic-Prescriptive Teacher:

You always have children who can handle everything else but have problems with visual motor coordination, and those children probably are going to have those problems so that that wouldn't be any reason for retention. We have our academic assistance program, and children that are showing these problems work there. If a child absolutely couldn't listen, I'd certainly try very hard to find out what the problem is before wanting to keep him in kindergarten another year. The reason he can't attend may be because he has an auditory problem. If he has this block or a problem, then he's got to learn to work around that to compensate for it, and that's what we'll try to give him are ways to compensate.

An Interactionist:

> With the variety of materials we have in experiential education, the child will plug in right where he is comfortable. And you can see right away by the way the child works with materials the kinds of experiences he is going to need that year. Every child can be successful in this classroom, and I'm not sure that's true of a very paper-oriented, teacher-directed kindergarten where each child is making the same clown face or cat. When there is a wide range of kids, you've got to offer a wide range of experiences.

NOTES

1. All teachers interviewed for this study were women.
2. The results of the quantitative study are available in Shepard and Smith (1987). The full report (Shepard & Smith, 1985) can be obtained from the district; for price information, write to Dr. George Kretke, Boulder Valley Public Schools, 6500 E. Arapahoe Ave., Boulder, CO 80301.
3. We believe that it is important for the reader to be able to evaluate research studies in the light of the human and institutional purposes that motivated them. In our conduct of policy research, we are committed to the notion that the results should serve educational and democratic functions so that all stakeholders can participate in policy formation in more enlightened ways. Still, some teachers may have reacted to our presence and our questions as if we were hired to serve the interests of the administrators who commissioned the study or as if their programs were threatened by the results. We tried to build in as many checks as possible, but the reader must judge.
4. The dimension of nativism and environmentalism recurs in the history of philosophy and psychology (Smith, 1983) and in the ideas embedded in early childhood education (Weber, 1986). Nativism as a philosophy holds that nearly all functions of the organism, including the mental ones such as perception, are innate rather than acquired through the senses. Constitutional structures are inherited and predetermined. Weber stated that Gesell's theoretical and practical ideas fall into this intellectual camp. That is, the belief that the deterministic principles of developing school readiness fall primarily in innate and developing physiological and constitutional structures out of which the psychological structures underlying learning unfold. In contrast, from the empiricist philosophical traditions, the deterministic principles of development occur in the social environment. The individual can be quite totally structured by events and conditions in his or her social and cultural milieu. Weber names associationism, additive learning, behavioral engineering, connectionism, reinforcement principles with this camp. We should note that the extremes of environmentalism were not expressed by teachers in this study. Nor do we claim that the nativist views, many of which were extreme, are exact interpretations of the work of the Gesell Institute. We operated inductively to discover what the beliefs of the teachers actually were.

5. Refer to Weber (1986) for alternative ideas about the nature of kindergarten.

REFERENCES

Byrnes, D., & Yamamoto, K. (1984). *Academic retention: An inside look.* Unpublished paper, Utah State University, Logan.

Erickson, F. (1986). Qualitative methods in research on teaching. In M. C. Wittrock (Ed.), *Handbook of research on teaching* (3rd ed., pp. 119–161). New York: Macmillan.

Feiman-Nemser, S., & Floden, R. E. (1986). The cultures of teaching. In M. C. Wittrock (Ed.), *Handbook of research on teaching* (3rd ed., pp. 505–526). New York: Macmillan.

Holmes, T. M., & Matthews, K. M. (1984). The effects of nonpromotion on elementary and junior high school pupils. *Review of Educational Research, 54,* 225–236.

Ilg, F. L., Ames, L. B., Haines, J., & Gillespie, C. (1978). *School readiness: Behavior tests used at the Gesell Institute.* New Haven, CT: Gesell Institute of Human Development.

Labaree, D. F. (1984). Setting the standard: Alternative patterns for student promotion. *Harvard Educational Review, 54,* 67–87.

Mishler, E. G. (1986). *Research interviewing.* Cambridge, MA: Harvard University Press.

O'Hanion, S. (1987). Notes on Japan from an American schoolteacher. *Phi Delta Kappan, 68,* 360–367.

Price, H. H. (1969). *Beliefs.* London: Allen and Unwin.

Shepard, L. A., & Smith, M. L. (1985) *Boulder Valley kindergarten study: Retention practices and retention effects.* Boulder, CO: Boulder Valley Public Schools.

Shepard, L. A., & Smith, M. L. (1987). Effects of kindergarten retention at the end of first grade. *Psychology in the Schools, 24,* 346–357.

Smith, S. (1983). *Ideas of the great psychologists.* New York: Harper & Row.

Weber, E. (1986). *Ideas influencing early childhood education.* New York: Teachers College Press.

Wise, A. E. (1979). *Legislated learning: The bureaucratization of the American classroom.* Berkeley: University of California Press.

AUTHORS

MARY LEE SMITH, Professor, College of Education, Arizona State University, Tempe, AZ 85287-0611. *Specializations:* qualitative research methodology, policy studies.

LORRIE A. SHEPARD, Professor, School of Education, Campus Box 249, University of Colorado-Boulder, Boulder, CO 80309. *Specializations:* psychometrics and educational policy.

Evaluation of Article 3

1.1. The authors do not indicate their potential biases at the outset of the study, nor is there any indication of their background. From the references we can conclude that the researchers have conducted previous research in the area. Note 3 gives some indication of the researchers' orientation to the study, placing it in the context of beliefs about a larger program of research on school policies. Working assumptions are revealed in the results section.

1.2. It appears evident from the methodology employed that the researchers are well qualified to conduct the study.

1.3. The problem is feasible. It is well focused.

1.4. The problem is clearly significant, related to an important contemporary issue.

1.5. A theoretical framework is provided by the discussion of the nature of beliefs, by the section summarizing the background of the study, and by note 3.

1.6. An overview of the design is included in the abstract.

1.7. The purpose of the study is clearly stated in the second paragraph.

2.1. There is a very limited initial review of the literature. The literature used throughout the study shows that the researchers are knowledgeable of previous work in the area.

2.2. The review is up to date.

2.3. There is an adequate background and theoretical framework for the study, although more references would be desirable.

2.4. The review is well organized in the introduction and the literature is well integrated into the discussion of results.

2.5. The literature is for the most part a summary of previous findings.

3.1. The methods for selecting teachers and schools are clear. Almost all kindergarten teachers were interviewed, and six schools were purposefully sampled to "capture the variability of retention practices." It is less clear how the parents were selected and how many parents were interviewed.

3.2. The selection of subjects does not appear to be biased.

3.3. The subjects were carefully selected and should provide credible answers to the problem.

3.4. The researchers conducted interviews with teachers and parents, and graduate students conducted the observations. The nature of the observations was such that the involvement of the graduate students would be unlikely to affect the setting in ways that would alter the findings for the study. Note 3 at the end of the article demonstrates sensitivity to possible effects due to perceptions of teachers about the nature of the study.

3.5. From the excerpts provided and the transcript analyses there is very good detail in the findings.

3.6. Although there is no direct evidence of appropriate training for the interviewers and observers, there are several methodological procedures that suggest that the data gathering was reliable and unbiased. For example, the authors "closely supervised" the graduate students, and the interviews with teachers proceeded carefully over an hour and were tape-recorded for analysis.

3.7. This study is an excellent example of the use of multiple methods of data collection (as summarized in the analysis of data section).

3.8. The teacher interviews were long enough (one hour) and the observations, although not as long as in most qualitative studies (30 hours), were of sufficient duration for the purposes of this study.

4.1. The summaries of results are separate from the researchers' interpretations and opinions. The results are clearly described after each assertion; at the end of each "assertion" section the authors interpret the results.

4.2. The credibility of the findings is high in this study. Although the authors do not directly address credibility by saying something such as "the credibility of this study is supported by . . ." the many examples of methodological procedures assure high credibility (e.g., examining the data for disconfirming evidence, using a statistical test where appropriate, analyzing negative cases, and extensive use of subject excerpts).

4.3. Some of the results are discussed in relation to previous research, although much of this discussion occurs without citations. More discussion of the relationship of the findings to the literature would be helpful.

4.4. The conclusions (as stated in the discussion section) follow from the interpretations of the results. There is little mention of how the conclusions relate to previously conducted studies.

4.5. Limitations are appropriately noted throughout the study (e.g., all female teachers, conducting the study in the context of a larger effort to examine policy, relatively short duration of the observations, and what is not answered by the findings in the last paragraph of the article).

4.6. Recommendations and implications are appropriately summarized in each of the sections of the results part of the study and in the last paragraph.

References

Abramson, M., Cooney, J., and Vincent, L. (1980). Induction, emergence, and generalization of logical operations in retarded children: A training-to-criterion procedure. *Journal of Special Education, 14,* 190–198.

Anderson, L. M., Brubaker, N. L., Alleman-Brooks, J., and Duffy, G. G. (1985). A qualitative study of seatwork in first-grade classrooms. *The Elementary School Journal, 86,* 123–140.

Babad, E., Bernieri, F., and Rosenthal, R. (1987). Nonverbal and verbal behavior of preschool, remedial, and elementary school teachers. *American Educational Research Journal, 24,* 405–416.

Baker, D. P., and Stevenson, D. L. (1986). Mothers' strategies for children's school achievement: Managing the transition to high school. *Sociology of Education, 59,* 156–166.

Ben-Chaim, D., Lappan, G., and Houang, R. T. (1988). The effect of instruction on spatial visualization skills of middle school boys and girls. *American Educational Research Journal, 25,* 51–71.

Blase, J. J. (1986). A qualitative analysis of sources of teacher stress: Consequences for performance. *American Educational Research Journal, 23,* 13–40.

Blase, J. J. (1987). Dimensions of effective school leadership: The teacher's perspective. *American Educational Research Journal, 24,* 589–610, 1987.

Bogdan, R. C., and Biklen, S. K. (1982). *Qualitative research for education: An introduction to theory and methods.* Boston: Allyn & Bacon.

Borg, W. R., and Gall, M. D. (1989). *Educational research: An introduction,* 5th ed. White Plains, NY: Longman.

Borich, G. D., and Madden, S. K. (1977). *Evaluating classroom instruction: A sourcebook of instruments.* Reading, MA: Addison-Wesley.

Boss, M. W., and Taylor, M. C. (1989). The relationship between locus of control and academic level and sex of secondary school students. *Contemporary Educational Psychology, 14*, 315–322.

Brooks, C. H. (1988). A hierarchical analysis of the effects of an activity-centered health curriculum on general health beliefs and self-reported behavior. *Journal of Educational Research, 81*, 149–154.

Burns, R. B., and Lash, A. A. (1986). A comparison of activity structures during basic skills and problem-solving instruction in seventh-grade mathematics. *American Educational Research Journal, 23*, 393–414.

Butchart, R. E. (1988). Outthinking and outflanking the owners of the world: A historiography of the African American struggle for education. *History of Education Quarterly, 28*, 333–366.

Byrnes, D., and Yamamoto, K. (1986). Views on grade repetition. *Journal of Research and Development in Education, 20*, 14–20.

Carrier, C. A., and Williams, M. D. (1988). A test of one learner-control strategy with students of differing levels of task persistence. *American Educational Research Journal, 25*, 285–306.

Cauley, K. M., and Murray, F. B. (1982). Structure of children's reasoning about attributes of school success and failure. *American Educational Research Journal, 19*, 473–480.

Chun, K. T., Cobb, S., and French, J. R. P., Jr. (1974). *Measures for psychological assessment: A guide to 3,000 original sources and their application.* Ann Arbor: Institute for Social Research, University of Michigan.

Clements, D. H., and Nastasi, B. K. (1988). Social and cognitive interactions in educational computer environments. *American Educational Research Journal, 25*, 87–106.

Cole, D. A. (1986). Facilitating play in children's peer relationships: Are we having fun yet? *American Educational Research Journal, 23*, 201–216.

Collins, M. E. (1988). *Education journals and serials: An analytical guide.* New York: Greenwood Press.

Comrey, A. L., Backer, T. E., and Glaser, E. M. (1973). *A sourcebook for mental health measures.* Los Angeles: Human Interaction Research Institute.

Conley, S. C., Bacharach, S. B., and Bauer, S. (1989). The school work environment and teacher career dissatisfaction. *Educational Administration Quarterly, 25*, 58–81.

Conoley, J. C., and Kramer, J. J. (Eds.). (1989). *The tenth mental measurements yearbook.* Lincoln: University of Nebraska Press.

Delclos, V. R., Burns, M. S., and Kulewicz, S. J. (1987). Effects of dynamic asessment on teachers' expectations of handicapped children. *American Educational Research Journal, 24*, 325–336.

Dillon, D. R. (1989). Showing them that I want them to learn and that I care about who they are: A microethnography of the social organization of a secondary low-track English reading-classroom. *American Educational Research Journal, 26,* 227–259.

Elam, S. M., and Gallup, A. M. (1989). The 21st annual Gallup poll of the public's attitudes toward the public schools. *Phi Delta Kappan, 71,* 41–54.

Eldredge, J. L., and Quinn, D. W. (1988). Increasing reading performance of low-achieving second graders with dyad reading groups. *The Journal of Educational Research, 82,* 40–46.

The ETS test collection. Volume 1: Achievement tests and measurement devices. (1986). Phoenix, AZ: Oryx Press.

The ETS test collection. Volume 2: Vocational tests and measurement devices. (1988). Phoenix, AZ: Oryx Press.

The ETS test collection. Volume 3: Tests for special populations. (1989). Phoenix, AZ: Oryx Press.

The ETS test collection. Volume 4: Cognitive aptitude and intelligence tests. (1990). Phoenix, AZ: Oryx Press.

Evertson, C. M., and Emmer, E. T. (1982). Effective management at the beginning of the school year in junior high classes. *Journal of Educational Psychology, 74,* 485–498.

Fabiano, E. (1989). *Index to tests used in educational dissertations.* Phoenix, AZ: Oryx Press.

Freed, M. W., Hess, R. K., and Ryan, J. M. (1989). *The educator's desk reference: A sourcebook of educational information and research.* New York: Macmillan.

Frieze, I. H., and Snyder, H. M. (1980). Children's beliefs about the causes of success and failure in school settings. *Journal of Educational Psychology, 72,* 186–196.

Goodwin, W. L., and Driscoll, L. (1980). *Handbook for measurement and evaluation in early childhood education: Issues, measures, and methods.* San Francisco: Jossey-Bass.

Guttman, L., Levin, J. R., and Pressley, M. (1977). Pictures, partial pictures, and young children's oral prose learning. *Journal of Educational Psychology, 69,* 473–480.

Hall, B. W., Villeme, M. G., and Burley, W. W. (1989). Teachers' attributions for students' academic success and failure and the relationship to teaching level and teacher feedback practices. *Contemporary Educational Psychology, 14,* 133–144.

Haskins, R., Walden, T., and Ramey, C. T. (1983). Teacher and student behavior in high- and low-ability groups. *Journal of Educational Psychology, 75,* 865–876.

Hawkins, J. D., Doueck, H. J., and Lishner, D. M. (1988). Changing teaching practices in mainstream classrooms to improve bonding and behavior of low achievers. *American Educational Research Journal, 25,* 31–50.

Hoover-Dempsey, K. V., Bassler, O. C., and Brissie, J. S. (1987). Parent involvement: Contributions of teacher efficacy, school socioeconomic status, and other school characteristics. *American Educational Research Journal, 24,* 417–435.

Hudgins, B. B., and Edelman, S. (1988). Children's self-directed critical thinking. *The Journal of Educational Research, 81,* 262–273.

Johnson, O. G. (1976). *Tests and measurement in child development: Handbook I and II.* San Francisco: Jossey-Bass.

Kahoe, R. D., and McFarland, R. E. (1975). Interactions of task challenge and intrinsic and extrinsic motivations in college achievement. *Journal of Educational Psychology, 67,* 432–438.

Keyser, D. J., and Sweetland, R. C. (Eds.). (1984, 1987). *Test critiques,* Vols. 1–7. Kansas City, MO: Test Corporation of America.

Lagemann, E. C. (1989). The plural worlds of educational research. *History of Education Quarterly, 29,* 183–214.

Lambiotte, J. G., Dansereau, D. F., Rocklin, T. R., Fletcher, B., Hythecker, V. I., Larson, C. O., and O'Donnell, A. M. (1987). Cooperative learning and test taking: Transfer of skills. *Contemporary Educational Psychology, 12,* 52–61.

Lustberg, R. S., Motta, R., and Naccari, N. (1990). A model using the WISC-R to predict success in programs for gifted children. *Psychology in the Schools, 21,* 126–131.

McMillan, J. H. (1977). The effect of effort and praise in determining student attitudes. *American Educational Research Journal, 14,* 317–330.

McMillan, J. H., and Schumacher, S. (1989). *Research in education: A conceptual introduction,* 2nd ed. Glenview, IL: Scott, Foresman.

Marsh, H. W., Smith, I. D., Marsh, M., and Owens, L. (1988). The transition from single-sex to coeducational high schools: Effect on multiple dimensions of self-concept and on academic achievement. *American Educational Research Journal, 25,* 237–269.

Mastropieri, M. A., Scruggs, T. E., and Levin, J. R. (1987). Learning-disabled students' memory for expository prose: Mnemonic versus nonmnemonic pictures. *American Educational Research Journal, 24,* 505–519.

Miller, S. E., Leinhardt, G., and Zigmond, N. (1988). Influencing engagement through accommodation: An ethnographic study of at-risk students. *American Educational Research Journal, 25,* 465–487.

Mitman, A. L. (1985). Teachers' differential behavior toward higher and lower achieving students and its relation to selected teacher characteristics. *Journal of Educational Psychology, 77,* 149–161.

Mounts, N. S., and Roopnarine, J. L. (1987). Social-cognitive plan patterns in same-age and mixed-age preschool classrooms. *American Educational Research Journal, 24,* 463–476.

Murphy, J., and Decker, K. (1988/89). Teachers' use of homework in high schools. *Journal of Educational Psychology, 82,* 261–269.

Pajak, E., and Blase, J. J. (1989). The impact of teachers' personal lives on professional role enactment: A qualitative analysis. *American Educational Research Journal, 26,* 283–310.

Parker, W. C., and Gehrke, N. J. (1986). Learning activities and teachers' decision making: Some grounded hypotheses. *American Educational Research Journal, 23,* 227–242.

Parkway, F. W., Greenwood, G., Olejnik, S., and Proller, N. (1988). A study of the relationships among teacher efficacy, locus of control, and stress. *Journal of Research and Development in Education, 21,* 13–22.

Putnam, R. T. (1987). Structuring and adjusting content for students: A study of live and simulated tutoring of addition. *American Educational Research Journal, 24,* 13–48.

Rickards, J. P., and Slife, B. D. (1987). Interaction of dogmatism and rhetorical structure in text recall. *American Educational Research Journal, 24,* 635–641.

Robinson, J. P., and Shaver, P. R. (1973). *Measures of social psychological attitudes.* Ann Arbor: University of Michigan, Institute for Social Research.

Ross, J. A. (1988). Improving social-environmental studies problem solving through cooperative learning. *American Educational Research Journal, 25,* 573–591.

Simon, A., and Boyer, E. G. (1974). *Mirrors for behavior III: An anthology of observation instruments.* Wyncote, PA: Communications Materials Center.

Smith, H. W. (1987). Comparative evaluation of three teaching methods of quantitative techniques: Traditional lecture, Socratic dialogue, and PSI format. *Journal of Experimental Education, 55,* 149–154.

Smith, M. L. (1980). Teacher expectations. *Evaluation in Education, 4,* 53–56.

Smith, M. L., and Shepard, L. A. (1988). Kindergarten readiness and retention: A qualitative study of teachers' beliefs and practices. *American Educational Research Journal, 25,* no. 3, 307–333.

Solomon, D., Watson, M. S., Delucchi, K. L., Schaps, E., and Battistich, V. (1988). Enhancing children's prosocial behavior in the classroom. *American Educational Research Journal, 25,* 527–554.

Standards for educational and psychological testing (1985). Washington, DC: American Psychological Association.

Sweetland, R. C., and Keyser, D. J. (Eds.). (1986). *Tests: A comprehensive reference for assessments in psychology, education, and business,* 2nd ed. Kansas City, MO: Test Corporation of America.

Tiene, D., and Buck, S. (1987). Student teachers and classroom authority. *Journal of Educational Research, 80,* 261–265.

Van Houton, R., Nau, P. A., Mackenzie, S. E., Sameoto, D., and Colavecchia, B. (1982). An analysis of some variables influencing the effectiveness of reprimands. *Journal of Applied Behavior Analysis, 15,* 65–83.

Walker, D. K. (1973). *Socioemotional measures for pre-school and kindergarten children: A handbook.* San Francisco: Jossey-Bass.

Woodward, J., Carnine, D., and Gersten, R. (1988). Teaching problem solving through computer simulations. *American Educational Research Journal, 25,* 72–86.

Wrigley, J. (1989). Do young children need intellectual stimulation? Experts' advice to parents, 1900–1985. *History of Education Quarterly, 29,* 41–76.

Ysseldyke, J. E., Thurlow, M. L., Christenson, S. L., and Weiss, J. (1987). Time allocated to instruction of mentally retarded, learning disabled, emotionally disturbed, and nonhandicapped elementary students. *The Journal of Special Education, 21,* 43–55.

Acknowledgments

Walter R. Borg and Meredith Damien-Gall, *Educational Research: An Introduction.* Copyright © 1989 by Longman Publishing Group. Reprinted by permission of Longman Publishing Group.

Kenneth T. Henson, "Writing for education journals" (table is abridged), from *Phi Delta Kappan*, June 1988. Copyright © 1989 by Phi Delta Kappan. Reprinted by permission of the author and Phi Delta Kappan.

Donelson R. Forsyth and James H. McMillan, "Attributions, affect, and expectations: A test of Weiner's three-dimensional model," from *The Journal of Educational Psychology*, Vol. 73, No. 3. Copyright © 1981 by the American Psychological Association. Reprinted by permission of the publisher.

Robert B. Burns and Andrea A. Lash, "A comparison of activity structures during basic skills and problem-solving instruction in seventh-grade mathematics," from *American Educational Research Journal*, 1986.

Ralph T. Putnam, "Structuring and adjusting content for students: A study of live and simulated tutoring of addition," from *American Educational Research Journal*, 1987.

Harold G. Seashore, "Normal probability curve," from *Test Service Notebook* 148, 1980. Reprinted by permission of The Psychological Corporation.

James H. McMillan and Sally Schumacher, *Research in Education: A Conceptual Introduction.* Copyright © 1989 HarperCollins Publishers.

William A. Mehrens and Irvin J. Lehmann, *Using Standardized Tests in Education.* Copyright © 1987 by Longman Publishing Group. Reprinted by permission of Longman Publishing Group.

Norman E. Gronlund and Robert L. Linn, *Measurement and Evaluation in Teaching*, 6th ed., p. 26. Copyright © 1990 by Macmillan Publishing Company. Reprinted by permission of Macmillan Publishing Company.

J. D. Hawkins, H. J. Doueck, and D. M. Lishner, "Changing teaching practices in mainstream classrooms to improve bonding and behavior of low achievers," from *American Educational Research Journal*, 1988.

S. E. Miller, G. Leinhardt and N. Zigmond, "Influencing engagement through accommodation: An ethnographic study of at-risk students," from *American Educational Research Journal*, 1988.

Deborah R. Dillon, "Showing them that I want them to learn and that I care about who they are: A microethnography of the social organization of a secondary low-track English-reading classroom," from *American Educational Research Journal*, 1989.

R. C. Bogdan and S. K. Biklen, *Qualitative Research for Education: An Introduction to Theory and Methods*, 1982, pp. 45–48, 76–77 (figure is abridged). Reprinted by permission of Allyn & Bacon, Inc.

H. Lyndall Rich and Mary J. McNelis, "A study of academic time-on-task in the elementary school," from *Educational Research Quarterly*, Vol. 12, No. 1, 1987–1988, pp. 37–46. Reprinted by permission of the author.

Michael R. Bertoch, et al., "Reducing teacher stress," from *The Journal of Experimental Education*, Vol. 57, No. 2, Winter 1989. Reprinted by permission of the Helen Dwight Reid Educational Foundation. Published by Heldref Publications, 4000 Albemarle St., N.W., Washington, D.C. 20016. Copyright © 1989.

Mary Lee Smith and Lorrie A. Shepard, "Kindergarten readiness and retention: A qualitative study of teachers' beliefs and practices," from *American Educational Research Journal*, Fall 1988, Vol. 25, No. 3, pp. 307–333. Copyright © 1988 by the American Educational Research Association. Reprinted by permission of the publisher.

Index

Action research, 12
Analysis of covariance, 201
Analysis of variance, 198–202
    factorial, 200–202
    simple, 198–199
Applied research, 11–12
Assessment, 87
Attenuation, 154
Attitudes
    measurement of, 122–126
    reliability of, 126
    validity of, 126

Baseline, 186
Basic research, 11

Causal-comparative research, 13, 159–162
    correlational, 161
    criteria for evaluating, 161–162
Central tendency, 92–94
    mean, 94
    median, 94
    mode, 93
Chi-square, 202–203
CIJE. *See* ERIC
Coefficient of determination, 156
Complete observer, 218–219
Conclusions, 236–238
Confounding variable. *See* Variables
Contingency coefficient, 203
Correlation, 97–99
    correlation coefficient, 97–98
    definition, 97
    negative, 97–99
    positive, 97–99
Credibility
    of scientific inquiry, 7
Criterion-referenced. *See* Tests
Cross-sectional. *See* Surveys

Data base, 38
Degrees of freedom, 198
Dependent variable. *See* Variables
Description, 4
Descriptive studies, 144–147
    criteria for evaluating, 146–147
Discussion, 229–244
    criteria for evaluating, 243–244
Documents, 210–211

Ecological validity, 240
Education Index, 53
Educational research
    definition of, 9
    types of, 9
ERIC, 51
    CIJE, 52, 56–57
    RIE, 52
Evaluation, 86–87
Evaluation research, 12
Experimental research, 13–14
    characteristics of, 165–166
    criteria for evaluating, 183–185
    types of, 173–183
Explanation, 4
Ex post facto research, 13, 159–161
    characteristics, 160
    procedures, 160
External criticism, 211
External validity, 167
    qualitative, 224
Extraneous variable. *See* Variables

Factorial designs, 180–183
Field notes, 219–220
Foreshadowed problems, 215–216
Frequency distribution, 90–93
    frequency polygon, 91